Total Quality Management of Distance Education

Edited by

Nayantara Padhi

ATLANTIC

PUBLISHERS & DISTRIBUTORS (P) LTD

Published by
ATLANTIC
PUBLISHERS & DISTRIBUTORS (P) LTD
7/22, Ansari Road, Darya Ganj,
New Delhi-110002
Phones : +91-11-40775252, 23273880, 23275880, 23280451
Fax : +91-11-23285873
Web : www.atlanticbooks.com
E-mail : orders@atlanticbooks.com

Branch Office
5, Nallathambi Street, Wallajah Road,
Chennai-600002
Phones : +91-44-64611085, 32413319
E-mail : chennai@atlanticbooks.com

ISBN 978-81-269-1387-9

Printed in India at Nice Printing Press, A-33/3A, Site-IV,
Industrial Area, Sahibabad, Ghaziabad, U.P.

To

My Daughter Jhumpa

Acknowledgements

I would like to thank each and everyone who has encouraged and supported me in writing this book. My heartfelt thanks are due to all the case study contributors for their endeavours. Every effort has been made to trace and acknowledge the sources and copyright holders. However, if any has been left out, it is because of oversight, not intention. Thanks are also due to my colleagues and friends for their valuable suggestions and comments. I also thank everyone at Atlantic Publishers and Distributors (P) Ltd. for bringing out this book. Finally, I am grateful to my family members for their encouragement and support throughout the project.

Nayantara Padhi

Preface

Distance learning is growing at an exceedingly fast pace as an international enterprise. Whilst the most dramatic growth is in South East Asia, it is significant in North America, Europe and Australasia. This growth creates opportunities for people in many countries to have their first access to higher education. Ensuring the integrity and value of the distance learning curriculum is a core challenge for policy leaders, funders, academic executives, and faculty supporting and/or engaged in this expansion. Furthermore, conventional teaching institutions are increasingly adopting distance learning and e-learning techniques in the courses that they offer. Indeed, it is unlikely that any institution of higher education in the world does not have some distance learning or e-learning component in its offerings. As such, the quality of the learning provided is critical to its acceptance and continued development. Thus, "quality", a central issue for practitioners, academics and researchers in the field of education for many years, is gaining even greater attention.

Government and academic leaders also recognize that improving the quality of distance learning on a continuous basis is crucial. Consequently, educational institutions throughout the world are being influenced by Total Quality Management (TQM). This process was developed by business houses and industries to establish standards and techniques that ensure quality of products or services through continuous improvement rather than through final inspection. Athabasca University, the Open University of Malaysia, the University of Southern Queensland and the UK Open University—all apply TQM to their operation. In the US, the exploration of TQM has been pursued as "continuous quality improvement" (CQI) since the early 1990s. While still controversial, its implementation has been closely connected to the assessment of learning movement that began in the late 1980s.

This book brings together the knowledge, perspective, and practical experience of educators from across the globe to explore diverse approaches to quality in distance learning. It provides an up-to-date, international exploration of quality in distance learning by assembling new knowledge and framing key issues for policymakers and practitioners in both developed and developing nations. This books dwells upon the following aspects:

(1) Provide an overview of the scope of quality issues vis-à-vis distance learning.

(2) Address learning as the core process of Distance Education Institutions (DEIs) and the essential elements of assessing to improve the quality of learning.

(3) Describe the core challenges and issues of quality assurance for DEIs.

(4) Propose policy and practice responses for quality assurance for DEIs.

(5) Introduce the concepts and processes of TQM, review the adoption and use of TQM in Higher Education Institutions (HEIs), and provide an overview of the most useful elements, tools, and techniques of TQM.

(6) Provide a flexible strategic framework of Total Quality Management for DEIs.

(7) Describe how Quality Assurance and TQM inter-relate.

(8) Illustrate the existing practices of Quality Assurance and TQM in DEIs worldwide in the form of case studies.

(9) Provide a thought-provoking vision of the future for addressing issues of quality in DEIs and the key questions about the roles of accountability and productivity in the future.

The book is structured into two parts. Part A entitled "Total Quality Management: Concept and Applications" contains eight chapters, written by me. Part B entitled "Global Practices and Experiences" contains eight chapters—each representing a case study of quality practice in different DEIs across the globe—contributed by eminent researchers in this field.

Educators and support staff in developed and developing countries who are engaged in distance learning partnerships or competition will find the applied focus useful. Traditional institutions expanding into distance learning as well as those created solely as distance learning institutions will recognize the relevance of the issues addressed. The inclusion of both Quality Assurance issues and the introduction of Total Quality Management practices increases the book's appeal to both traditional leaders, regulators and leaders of innovation. Organized with an embedded conversation guide, this approach supports faculty and staff of distance learning institutions coming together in face-to-face or online communication to explore issues, practices, and case studies of Quality Assurance and Advancement as they relate to their institution. As a text in the preparation of administrators for all of higher education, the book addresses issues of quality in the expansion of online, virtual, and e-learning environments. Finally, selected chapters provide perspective and guidance for policymakers and leaders who face the accelerated movement of distance learning. I sincerely welcome any comments/suggestions about this book.

Nayantara Padhi
E-Mail: ntp210@hotmail.com

Contents

Contents

PART A

TOTAL QUALITY MANAGEMENT: CONCEPT AND APPLICATIONS

PART A

The Quality Movement

1

Chapter Outline

- Concept of Quality
- Approaches to Quality
- Quality in Retrospect
- Legacies of Quality Gurus
- Importance of Quality in Different Sectors
- Misconceptions about Quality
- Chapter Overview
- Discussion Questions
- Appendix 1: Approaches to Define Quality

Chapter Objectives

After completion of this chapter, the reader will be able to:

- Explain the concept of quality
- Discuss different approaches to quality
- Describe the legacies of quality gurus
- Appreciate the importance of quality in different sectors

Concept of Quality

The term 'quality' basically refers to an attribute or a characteristic, disposition or standard or simply a measure of a thing or a trait or ability or value. Given such a range of meaning and moreover a varied range of its application, logically there cannot be a single definition of it. Further as there is a utility/useful dimension to all objects/commodities, so there is an inescapable relativity or individual subjectivity to the fundamental aspect called 'quality'. For example, a thing which may be of use to one individual may not be so for another or a thing having superior quality for one may turn out to be inferior or of no relevance to another. So, one more essential aspect of 'quality' is relativism.

In management studies, the concept of quality, keeping in view its multifarious range of applications, has been described as 'slippery concept' (Pfeiffer and Coote, 1991). Some of the widely accepted definitions given by quality gurus are as follows.

- "Quality is a customer determination which is based on the customer's actual experience with the product or service, measured against his or her requirements—stated or unstated, conscious or merely sensed, technically operational or entirely subjective and always representing a moving target in a competitive market."—Feigenbaum, 1961.
- "Conformance to requirements"—Crosby, 1979.
- "Degree of uniformity and dependability at a low cost with quality suited to the market."—Deming, 1986.
- "Fitness for use"—Juran, 1988.

There is also an 'institutional' dimension to define quality. For example, the British Standards Institution (BSI, 1991) defines quality "as the totality of characteristics of an entity that bear on its ability to satisfy stated and implied needs." The international definition of quality is "degree to which a set of inherent characteristics fulfill requirements" (BS EN ISO 9000 (2000)).

The above cited are few definitions but, there are so many definitions that, authors have classified, and given different approaches to define quality. Garvin (1984) has examined various quality definitions, and classified them into five principal categories:

- Transcendental: achieving excellence and the highest standard.
- Product-based: dependent on the attributes.
- User-based: satisfying the need of a customer.
- Manufacturing-based: conformance to requirements.
- Value-based: value for money.

Details of these five categories are given in Appendix 1. Of these five; the value-based view is becoming more popular day by day. While, ingredients and materials are the key quality indicators in such categories as food, clothing, personal care, and beauty products, reflecting a product-based approach to quality, however, quality is increasingly apt to be discussed and perceived in relation to price.[1]

Green and Harvey (1993) have identified five different approaches to define quality:

- in terms of *exceptional* (exceeding high standards and passing a required standard);
- in terms of *consistency* (exhibited through "zero defects" and "getting right the first time", making quality a culture);
- as *fitness for purpose* (meaning the product or service meets the stated purpose, customer specifications and satisfaction);
- as *value for money* (through efficiency and effectiveness); and
- as *transformative* (in term of qualitative change).

Garvin (1987) has also listed eight important quality dimensions which influence customers in determining quality levels: performance, features, reliability, conformance, durability, serviceability, aesthetics, and perceived quality.

Kelda (1996) conducted an informal in-house survey on how the managers of different departments in various companies define quality. The following summarises the findings of the survey.

- For the marketing managers, the quality of the product is what makes it sell.
- For the finance department, a quality product is one that is profitable for the company.
- For the production personnel, quality means conformance to specifications, standards, drawings, blueprints or other technical documents.
- For the workers quality gets defined when their line supervisors do not complain about their work/product.
- For the purchasing personnel, quality is perceived as a lower limit.
- For the research and development personnel, quality is defined as the state of art which is instrumental to develop the best possible products.
- For the representatives of certain government organisations, a quality product is one that presents no threat to public safety and security.
- For the top managers, a quality product is one that enables them to satisfy the needs of the stockholders and the owners of the company.
- For the customers, the product quality represents the product's ability to satisfy their specific needs.

In today's business world, there is not a single accepted definition of quality. There are a number of ways or senses in which quality may be defined, but they all can be boiled down to either meeting requirements and specifications or satisfying and delighting the customer. But the examination of the above definitions and survey findings on quality reveal that a *quality product/service is one, which has fewer variations, value for cost, more satisfied customers, and which enjoys more competitive advantage in the market.*

Approaches to Quality

The term qualitative is usually used when quality is described in a non-technical situation. BS ISO 9000 (2000) says that the term 'quality' can be used with adjectives such as poor, good or excellent. The following are some examples of this.

- In advertising slogans building image and persuading buyers that its products and services are the best, e.g. Esso—Quality at work; Hayfield—Committed to quality; Kenu—Superior quality; Philips Whirlpool—Brings quality to life.
- By TV and Radio commentators: A quality player, a quality goal, etc.
- By directors and managers: Quality performance, quality of communication, etc.
- By people in general: Quality product, top quality, high quality, 100 per cent quality, etc.

Quality in Retrospect

Quality has emerged as a formal management tool. In its original form, quality was reactive and inspection oriented, but today, quality-related activities have become broad and are treated as *sine qua non* for strategic success. Quality is no more an exclusive province of manufacturing and operational departments. It embraces functions as diverse as purchasing, engineering, marketing research and even service sector including the education linked to it.

With the passage of time, many modern approaches to quality have emerged through series of discoveries stretching back over a century.

Such discoveries can be organized into seven distinct phases of quality movement:[2] Artisan, Mass Production, Inspection, Quality Control (QC), Statistical Quality Control (SQC), Statistical Process Control (SPC) and Total Quality Management (TQM). The entire journey of the quality concept from Artisan to TQM is shown in Fig. 1.1.

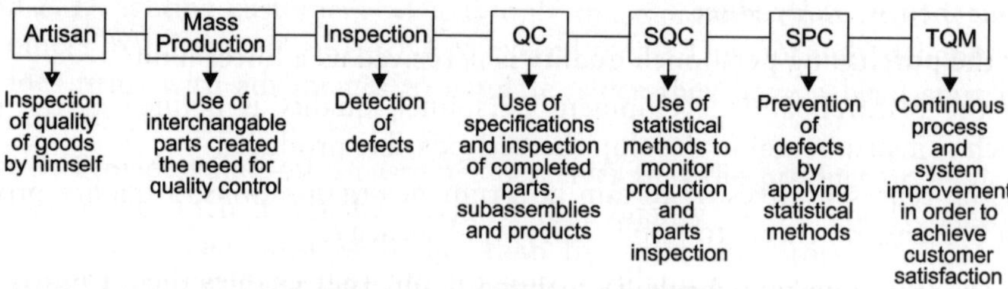

Fig. 1.1: Journey of Quality Concept

Stage I: Artisans

In the initial phase, quality control as we understand it today did not exist. Most manufacturing work was performed by artisans and skilled craftsmen or by journeyman and apprentices who were supervised by masters at the trade (Chandler, 1977). They used to produce the goods, inspect their quality as well as monitor their supplies through apprentices to the customer. The customers' complaint/dissatisfaction with the product were used to be directly dealt with by the artisan. A well-performing product was viewed as certificate of reliance or skilled tradesmanship with regard to design, manufacturing and service (Juran, 1976).

Stage II: Mass Production System

With the onset of mass production arrived the need for the use of interchangeable parts. In 1798, Eli Whitney started designing and manufacturing muskets with interchangeable parts.[3] Prior to that, firearms were made individually. The stock, barrel, firing mechanism, and other parts were fabricated for a specific musket. If part of the musket broke, a new product was painstakingly prepared for that particular firearm or else that piece was discarded. However, with the manufacturing of interchangeable parts by Whitney, firing mechanisms, barrels, or other parts could be used on any musket of the same design. Thus, by making parts interchangeable, Whitney created the need for Quality Control (Summers, 1997).

In a mass production setting, tasks necessary to create a finished product were divided among many individuals and each individual was performing a specific task. Proper assembling of parts required two important conditions: first, in order to be interchangeable, the parts must be identical. This allows the assembler to randomly select a part from a group and assemble it with a second randomly selected part. For this to occur without any problem, the machines must be capable of producing parts with minimal variation and within the specifications set by the designer. Thus, the second condition is producing 'with minimal variation and within specifications'. If a part is not in conformity with a randomly selected part, it may or may not fit together easily with its matching part during assembling process. This situation defeated the idea of interchangeable parts and in order to meet these two preconditions, Quality Principles evolved.

Stage III: Inspection

Inspection refers to specific activities designed to detect or find non-conformances existing in already completed products/services (Summers, 1997). The need for formal inspection arose only with the rise of mass production and the need for interchangeable parts. As volumes increased, parts could no longer be fitted to one another by hand. The process required a large pool of skilled labour and was both costly and time-consuming. This pressure gave rise to what has been called the American system of manufacturing, which means "the use of special-purpose machinery to produce interchangeable parts by following a pre-established sequence of operations" (Abernathy and Corcoram, 1983; Hounshell, 1984; and Smith, 1977).

In the beginning phase of quality control through inspection efforts were primarily confined to the military demand for armaments. However, the major breakthrough was made with the development of rational jig, fixture, and gauging system in the early 1800s (Hounshell, 1984). Inspection acquired a new respectability when activities that were previously conducted by eye were replaced by a more objective and verifiable process (Hounshell, 1984).

Inspection became even more important in course of time, and in the early 1900s, F.W. Taylor, Father of 'Scientific Management' added philosophical lip to it. In 1922, it was linked more formally to quality control, with the publication of G.S. Radford's *The Control of Quality Manufacturing*. For the first time quality was viewed as a distinct management responsibility and as an independent function.

For several years, quality control remained confined to inspection and to such narrow activities as counting, grading, and repair. Troubleshooting was considered beyond the reach of available inspection department (Bicking, 1958).

Stage IV: Quality Control

In the fourth phase, Quality Control (QC) acquired the dimension to the use of specifications and inspection of completed parts, sub-assemblies, and products to design, produce, review, sustain, and improve the quality of a product or service. QC in this phase went beyond inspection by:

(i) Establishing standards for the product or service, based on the customer needs, requirements and expectations;

(ii) Ensuring conformance to these standards. Poor quality is evaluated to determine the reasons why the parts or services provided are incorrect;

(iii) Taking action in case there is a lack of conformance to the standards. These actions may include sorting the product to find the defects. In service industries, action may involve contacting the customer and correcting the situation; and

(iv) Implementing plans to prevent future non-conformance. These plans may include design or manufacturing changes and in a service industry, they may include procedural changes.

These four activities work together to improve the basic device of the production/service. QC efforts were enhanced by the use of statistics.

Stage V: Statistical Quality Control

Building on these four tenets of QC, statistics were added to map the results of inspection of parts. In the 1920s, statistical charts to monitor and control product variables were developed by Walter A. Shewhart of Bell Telephone Laboratories. At the same time, Harold Dodge and Harry G. Romig of Bell Telephone Laboratories developed the area of sampling as a substitute for 100 per cent inspection. The use of statistical methods of production monitoring and parts inspection was known as Statistical Quality Control (SQC), wherein statistical data were collected, analysed, and interpreted to solve quality problems.

Stage VI: Statistical Process Control

With the development of quality area, the need to become more proactive while dealing with quality problems was seriously felt. Thus, the emphasis was shifted from utilising SQC methods for the inspection or detection of poor quality to their use in the prevention of poor quality. Prevention of defects by applying statistical methods to control the process is known as Statistical Process Control (SPC). Here, prevention refers to those activities designed to prevent defects, and non-conformance in products/services. Four separate elements were involved in defect prevention: quantifying the costs of quality, total quality control, reliability engineering and zero defects.

Stage VII: Total Quality Management

As the use of SPC got intensified in the 1980s, industry began to see the need to monitor and improve the entire system of providing a quality product and service. Sensing that meeting customer needs, requirements, and expectations involve more than providing a product or service, industry began to integrate quality into all areas of operations from the receptionist to the sales and billing departments and to the manufacturing to shipping and even to the service departments.

Accordingly, methods of quality management were developed and utilised to encourage the design, production, marketing, sales and service of quality products/services. This integrated approach took into account involvement of all departments in a company in providing a quality product/service and is known as Total Quality Management (TQM). Thus, TQM is a management approach that places emphasis on system improvement as a means of achieving customer satisfaction to ensure long-term success of a company (Summers, 1997).

However, Garvin organised the quality movement into four distinct 'Quality Eras': Inspection, Statistical Quality Control (SQC), Quality Assurance (QA) and Strategic Quality Management. According to him, the evolution pattern was strategic in nature with continuous improvement as the driving force in quality planning and employee involvement as the key objectives. The evolutionary pattern is given in Table 1.1.

Table 1.1: Evolution Pattern of Quality Management

Phases of Quality Movement / Identifying characteristics	Inspection	SQC	QA	Strategic Quality Management
Primary concern	Detection	Control	Coordination	Strategic view
Emphasis	Product uniformity	Product uniformity with reduced inspection	Entire production chain	Market and consumer needs
Methods	Gauging and measurement	Statistical tools and techniques	Programmes and systems	Strategic planning and setting
Role of quality professionals	Inspection, acceptance, sampling	Troubleshooting and the application of statistical methods	Quality measurement, planning, programme design	Goal setting, education, training and consultation
Who has responsibility for quality	Inspection department	Manufacturing, engineering departments	All departments	Everyone in the organisation
Orientation and approach	Inspects in quality	Controls in quality	Builds in quality	Manages in quality

Source: Garvin (1987)

Dale and Plunkett (1980) have developed a hierarchy of quality movement (Table 1.2).

Table 1.2: Hierarchy of Quality Management

Total Quality Management	Involves supplier and customers Aims for continuous improvements Concerns products and processes Responsibility of all workers Delivered through team work
Quality Assurance	Use of statistical process control Emphasis on prevention External accreditation Delegated involvement Audit of quality systems Cause and effect analysis
Quality Control	Concerned with product testing Responsibility of supervisors Limited quality criteria Some self-inspection Paper-based system
Inspection	Post production review Re-working Rejection Control of workforce Limited to physical products

Source: Dale and Plunkett (1980)

Similarly, Sallis (1996) has put the chronology of quality movement as shown in Table 1.3.

Table 1.3: The Chronology of Quality Movement

Pre-1900	Quality as an integral element of craftsmanship
1900-20	Quality control by foreman
1920-40	Inspection-based quality control
1940-60	Statistical process control
1960-80	Quality assurance/total quality control (the quality department)
1980-90	Total quality management
1990-Present	TQM, the culture of continuous improvement, organization-wide quality management

Source: Sallis (1996)

Legacies of Quality Gurus

Many researchers have made substantial contribution in the field of evolution of quality. Notable among them are: W. Edwards Deming, Joseph M. Juran, and Philip B. Crosby. Of course, the names of Ishikawa and Feigenbaum are also worth mentioning.

Deming's Legacy

Quality is firmly established today, thanks in large part to the pioneering work of W. Edwards Deming. Ironically, the mathematician credited with Japan's post-World War II quality revolution rarely talked in terms of quality. He instead preferred to discuss "good management" during the hard-hitting seminars he delivered till his death at the age 93 in 1993 (Trumbull, 1993; and Hillkirk, 1993). Deming's passion was the statistical measurement and reduction of variations in industrial processes.

Deming suggested the following four components making a system popularly known as the *System of Profound Knowledge.*

1. **Appreciation for a system:** The need for managers to understand the relationships between functions and activities, and that the long-term aim is for everyone to win—employees, shareholders, customers, suppliers and the environment.
2. **Knowledge of statistical theory**: Knowledge and understanding of variation, process capability, control charts, interactions and loss function.
3. **Theory of knowledge**: As all plans require prediction based on historical information, the theory must be understood before it can successfully be copied.
4. **Knowledge of psychology**: The understanding of human interactions, how people are motivated and what disillusions them.

This famous management philosophy given by Deming (1993) has been synthesized in 14 points (Table 1.4).

Table 1.4: Deming's 14 Points

1. Create and publicise to all employees a statement of the aims and purposes of the company or organisation. The management must demonstrate constantly their commitment to this statement.
2. Learn the new philosophy: top management and everybody.
3. Understand the purpose of inspection, for improvement of processes and reduction of cost.
4. End the practice of awarding business on the basis of price tag alone.
5. Improve constantly and forever the system of production and service.
6. Institute training.
7. Teach and institute leadership.
8. Drive out fear. Create trust. Create a climate for innovation.
9. Optimize toward the aims and purposes of the company the efforts of teams, groups, staff areas.
10. Eliminate exhortations for the workforce.
11. a. Eliminate numerical quotes for production. Instead, learn and institute methods for improvement.
b. Eliminate M.B.O. instead, learn the capabilities of process, and how to improve them.
12. Remove barriers that rob people of pride of workmanship.
13. Encourage education and self-improvement for everyone.
14. Take action to accomplish the transformation.

Deming cycle: The Plan, Do, Check, Act (PDCA) cycle is an all-encompassing improvement methodology given by Deming.

- Plan what to do.
- Do the experimentation.
- Check the solutions.
- Act on the results.

His famous books include: *Out of Crisis* and *Quality, Productivity and Competitive Position.*

Juran's Legacy

Dr. Joseph M. Juran, the son of an immigrant shoemaker from Romania, began his industrial career at Western Electronics' Hawthorne plant before World War II and later he worked at Bell Laboratories in the area of quality assurance. Juran is the creator of many of the basic concepts of statistical quality. Juran believed that management and the system are responsible for quality improvement. One of the most enduring lessons for managers given by Juran is his 85-15 rule which states that when things go wrong, there is roughly about 85% of the time the system is at fault and only about 15% of the time individual employee is at fault (Juran, 1989). He developed a perpetual spiral of progress or continuous striving towards quality.

Juran's concept of quality includes the managerial dimension for *quality planning, quality control and quality improvement* (known as Juran Trilogy) and focuses on the responsibility of management to achieve quality. He has also developed a ten step procedure for quality improvement (Table 1.5).

Table 1.5: 10 Steps to Quality Improvement

1. Build awareness of the need and opportunity to improve set goals for that improvement
2. Create plans to reach the goals
3. Provide training
4. Conduct projects to solve problems
5. Report on progress
6. Give recognition for success
7. Communicate results
8. Keep score
9. Maintain momentum
10. Build an annual improvement cycle into all company processes.

Cost of quality: Juran suggested that by implementing his theories of quality improvement, not only higher quality products could be produced, but also the actual costs could be brought down. His cost of quality principle is known as 'Gold in the Mine'. The costs can be:

- **Failure costs:** Scrap, rework, corrective actions, warranty claims, customer complaints and loss of custom.
- **Appraisal costs:** Inspection, compliance auditing and investigations.
- **Prevention costs:** Training, preventive auditing and process improvement implementation.

Juran's famous books include: *Quality Control Handbook, Quality Planning and Analysis* and *Juran on Leadership for Quality.*

Ishikawa's Legacy

Prof. Kaoru Ishikawa (1915-89) is more popularly known as the 'Father of Quality Circles' for his role in launching Japan's quality movement in the 1960s. As the President of JUSE, he was instrumental in developing a unique Japanese strategy towards total quality, i.e. the broad development of the entire organisation in its total sense—every worker, every process, and every job.

Ishikawa (1985) has identified several basic tools that are indispensable for the success of total quality control (Table 1.6).

Table 1.6: Seven Quality Control Tools

1. Pareto Analysis
2. Fishbone diagram
3. Stratification
4. Tally charts
5. Histograms
6. Scatter diagrams
7. Control charts

He has also identified few critical factors for achieving quality.

- Participation by all members of the organisation in the company-wide quality control activities.

- Education and training in all aspects of total quality, which often accounts to 30 days per year per employee.
- Use of quality control circles to update standards and regulations, which are in constant need of improvement.

Ishikawa believed that the management practices should be democratic. The top management must provide guidelines to guide people and implement the policies so that they are uniformly followed by all.

Feigenbaum's Legacy

A.V. Feigenbaum is best known for coining the term Total Quality Control and for his pioneering 850-page book on the subject (Feigenbaum, 1983). His teachings center around the integration of people-machine-information structure in order to economically and effectively control quality and achieve full customer satisfaction. In his book, he uses the concept of the "9M's" to describe the factors that affect quality: (1) Markets, (2) Money, (3) Management, (4) Men, (5) Motivation, (6) Materials, (7) Machine and Mechanisation, (8) Modern information methods, and (9) Mounting product requirements. These methods led to increased quantification of total quality programme improvements during the 1970s and 1980s.

He has identified nine crucial elements of TQ to enable a totally customer focus (Table 1.7).

Table 1.7: Nine Elements of Quality

1. Quality is the customers' perception of what quality is, not what a company thinks it is.
2. Quality and cost are the same not different.
3. Quality is an individual and team commitment.
4. Quality and innovation are interrelated and mutually beneficial.
5. Managing Quality is managing the business.
6. Quality is a principal.
7. Quality is not a temporary or quick fix but a continuous process of improvement.
8. Productivity gained by cost effective demonstrably beneficial Quality investment.
9. Implement Quality by encompassing suppliers and customers in the system.

His famous books include: *Total Quality Control* and *The Power of Management Capital.*

Crosby's Legacy

Unlike the other quality gurus, Philip Crosby, who hailed from the rank of an Inspector and ultimately became the Corporate Vice-President of a company, is known for his motivational talks and style of presentation. A very important and famous statement 'quality is free' is given by Crosby. According to him, quality is not:

- goodness or luxury
- intangible
- unaffordable

He has also developed the concept of Zero Defects while working as a Quality Manager at Martin Marietta Corporation in Orland, Florida. Crosby believed that Zero Defects motivated the workers to turn out perfect products. Crosby has contributed four absolutes of quality management:

He has developed fourteen steps for a quality improvement programme, which are given in Table 1.8.

Table 1.8: Crosby's Fourteen Steps to Quality Improvement

Step–1	To make clear management's commitment to quality.
Step–2	To set up quality improvement teams with representatives from each department.
Step–3	To set in place quality measurement to provide a display of current and potential non-conformance problems.
Step–4	To determine the 'cost of quality' and explain how to use it as a management tool.
Step–5	To raise the level of quality awareness and personal concern for the company's quality reputation for all employees.
Step–6	To take corrective action on the problems raised in the previous steps.
Step–7	To plan a zero defect programme.
Step–8	To train the supervisors actively to carry out their part in the total quality improvement process.
Step–9	To hold a zero defects day to create an event that will let all employees through a personal experience that there has been a change.
Step–10	Goal setting and encouraging individuals and groups to set improvement goals.
Step–11	To encourage employees to communicate to management the difficulties they have in achieving their improvement goals in the error-cause removal campaign.
Step–12	To recognise and appreciate all those who participate in the programme.
Step–13	To establish quality councils to communicate on a regular basis.
Step–14	To do it all over again to emphasise that quality programmes never end and that they are indeed a journey not a destination.

Crosby's basic elements of improvement include: determination, education and implementation. By determination, he meant that the top management must be serious about quality improvement. Everyone should understand the absolutes and this could be accomplished only through proper education and guidance. Finally, every member of the management team must understand the implementation process.

His famous books include: *Quality is Free, Quality Without Tears, Let's Talk Quality.*

Importance of Quality in Different Sectors

American Society of Quality (ASQ) has identified the reasons why quality is required in different sectors like service, healthcare, education, government, etc.

- Why quality in service? Service industries face a special challenge: meeting customer needs while remaining economically competitive. While automated processes can make an impact, service industries are still labour-intensive and there can be no substitute for high quality personal interaction between service employees and customers. Competitive advantage rests with those organisations which successfully provide customer value through the most efficient use of technology and people. Thus, service industries put emphasis on:
    - o Understand and improve operational issues
    - o Identify problems quickly and systematically
    - o Establish valid and reliable service performance measures
    - o Measure customer satisfaction and other performance outcomes

- Why quality in healthcare? Healthcare professionals across all segments are required to take care of:
  - o Quality of care
  - o Patient safety and satisfaction
  - o Organisational efficiencies
  - o The bottom line

For qualitative enhancement in profession, healthcare organisations invest a lot of resources in providing resources, training, certification and networking opportunities of its professionals.

- Why quality in education? Quality is not just for manufacturers. Quality in education means:
  - o High standards of achievement
  - o Create a foundation of teaching methods that work
  - o Create a system of accountability to measure results

Education institutions utilise a rich menu of available quality tools and resources that can help institutions and teachers in improving teaching, learning and the documentation of classroom processes. The common quality issues in education are:

- o Accountability
- o Alignment
- o Assessment
- o Student requirement

- Why quality in government? In today's economic and political climate, even government find ways to trim costs and manage cash-flow while continuing to deliver excellent customer service. Elected officials are challenging the departments under their purview to increase efficiency, prevent errors and provide their constituents with more resources. Government agencies take full advantage of performance-improvement tools to measure, track and improve internal processes and customer satisfaction.

Misconceptions about Quality

In spite of many efforts wrong notions about the role of quality still persist in the international arena like:

- Higher quality may cost more;
- The emphasis on quality leads to loss in productivity;
- The quality is affected by the work culture of the labour force; and
- Quality can be assured by strict inspection only.

Unless these misconceptions are thrown out of mind, no amount of effort can bring total quality management.

Chapter Overview

In this chapter, we have discussed about the concept of quality. The definitions given by prominent researchers, quality gurus are also discussed. Different approaches to quality have been cited and also the legacies of quality gurus such as Deming, Crosby, Ishikawa, etc. are highlighted. Quality can be an input in the system, to result in the desired output through qualitative process. TQM needs to address all the stages. Although quality is a natural given property, yet through human contribution it can be converted to greater use.

Discussion Questions

1. Define 'quality' and explain the concept of quality citing suitable examples.
2. Discuss different approaches to quality.
3. Describe the legacies of quality gurus.
4. Explain the importance of quality in different sectors with illustration.

***Appendix* 1**

Approaches to Define Quality

Sl. No.	Approach	Major Focus	Definitions	Source
I.	Transcendent	'Quality is a simple, yet unanalysable property which can be recognised only through experience'.	• "Quality is neither mind nor matter, but a third entity independent of the two...even though quality cannot be defined, you know what it is". • "...a condition of excellence implying fine quality as distinct from poor quality.... Quality is achieving or reaching for the highest standard as against being satisfied with the sloping or froudent". • "Innate excellence".	1 2 3
II.	Product-based	'Quality as a precise and measurable variable'.	• "Difference in quality amounts to differences in the quantity of some desired ingredient or attribute". • "Quality refers to the amounts of the unpriced attributes contained in each unit of the priced attribute".	4 5
III.	User-based	'Quality lies in the eyes of the beholder'.	• "Quality consists of the capacity to satisfy wants". • "...the quality of a product depends on how well it fits patterns of consumer preference". • "...the goods that best satisfy consumers' preferences are the ones having the highest quality". • "Quality has led to the notion of ideal points: precise combinations of product attributes that provide the greatest satisfaction to a specified consumer. • "Quality differences are captured by shifts in a product's demand curve".	6 7 8 9 10
IV.	Manufacturing-based	'Quality is concerned with engineering and manufacturing practices, i.e. the supply side of the equation.'	• "Quality is the degree to which a specific product conforms to a design or specification". • "Quality improvements (which are equivalent to reductions in the number of deviations) laid to lower costs for preventing defects is viewed as less expensive than repairing or reworking them".	11 12
V.	Value-based	'Quality in terms of costs and prices'.	• "Quality is the degree of excellence of an acceptable price and the control of variability at an acceptable cost". • "Quality-product is one that provides performance on conformance at an acceptable price or cost".	13 14

Sources:

1. Prising, Robert M. (1974) *Zen and the Art of Motorcycle Maintenance*, Bantam Books, New York, pp. 185-213.
2. Tuchman, Barbara W. (1980) "The Decline of Quality", *New York Times Magazine*, November, Vol. 2, p. 38.
3. Prising, Robert M., *op. cit.*, pp. 183-228; and Tuchman, Barbara W., *ibid.*, pp. 38-41.
4. Abott, Lawrence, *Quality and Competition*, Columbia University Press, New York, pp. 126-27.
5. Leffler, Keith B. (1982) "Ambiguous Changes in Product Quality", *American Economic Review*, December, p. 256.
6. Edwards, Carwin D. (1968) "The Meaning of Quality", *Quality Progress*, October, p. 37.

7. Kuchn, Alfred A. and Ralph L. Day (1962) "Strategy of Product Quality", *Harvard Business Review*, Nov-Dec., p. 101.
8. Edwards, Corwin D., *op. cit*., pp. 36-39; and Kuchn and Day, *ibid*., pp. 100-10.
9. Kuchn and Day, *op. cit*., pp. 101-08; and Johnson, Richard M. (1971) "Market Segmentation: A Strategic Management Tool", *Journal of Marketing Research*, February, pp. 13-18.
10. Chamberlain, Edward H. (1953) "The Product as an Economic Variable", *Quarterly Journal of Economics*, February, pp.1-29; Dorfman, Robert and Steiner, Peter O. (1954) "Optimal Advertising and Optimal Quality", *American Economic Review*, December, pp. 822-36; and White, Lawrence J. (1972) "Quality Variation when Prices are Regulated", *Bell Journal of Economics and Management Science*, Autumn, pp. 425-36.
11. Glimore, Harold L. (1974) "Product Conformance Cost", *Quality Progress*, June, p. 16.
12. Campanella, Jack and Frank J. Corcoran (1983) "Principles of Quality Costs", *Quality Progress*, April, p. 21.
13. Broh, Robert A. (1982) *Managing Quality for Higher Profits*, McGraw Hill, New York, , pp. 3-4.
14. *Ibid*.

Notes

1. This conclusion was drawn from a survey of consumer's perception of quality conducted in 28 product categories. For details see, *The Consumer Network Inc., Brand Quality Perceptions, Consumer Network*, Philadelphia, August 1983.
2. A number of authors have divided the history of the quality movement in distinct periods, although they have frequently used only two categories, quality control and quality assurance. For details see, Abbot and Leaman, 1982; Adam, 1984, ASQC, 1986; Dorsky, 1984; Owens, Undated; and Reddy, 1980.
3. While the initial breakthroughs involving interchangeable parts have often been associated with Eli Whitney, recent research suggests that his role has been overrated. For details see, Woodbury (1960).

Total Quality Management

2

Chapter Outline

- Roots of TQM
- Defining TQM
- Understanding TQM
- Principles of TQM
- Approaches to TQM
- Models of TQM
- Traditional Quality Management and TQM
- Reasons for Growth of TQM
- Chapter Overview
- Discussion Questions

Chapter Objectives

After completion of this chapter, the reader will be able to:

- Identify the roots of TQM
- Explain the concept of TQM
- Define TQM
- Discuss various approaches to TQM
- Differentiate between traditional quality management and TQM

Roots of TQM

Till 1970, quality was mostly confined to ensure product quality as determined by the customer alone. During the 1970s, Western companies started putting more emphasis on quality to retain and recapture their market position thereby laying the ground for TQM to take shape. Finally, the concept gained momentum during the 1980s. TQM encompasses not only product, service and process improvements but also those relating to costs and productivity and to people involvement and development. Its added advantage is that its main focus is on customer satisfaction (Dale, 2004).

TQM to a great extent is influenced by Japanese management style but it cannot be treated as 'Made in Japan'. Majority of its operational elements have roots in theories and practices of management developed in America. Schmidt and Finnegan (1992) suggest that TQM's roots include:

1. *Scientific management*—Finding the best way to do a job.
2. *Group dynamics*—Enlisting and organizing the power of group experience.
3. *Achievement motivation*—People get satisfaction from their accomplishment.
4. *Employee involvement*—Employees should have some influence on the organisation.
5. *Socio-technical systems*—Organisations operate as open systems.
6. *Organisation development*—Helping organisations to learn and change.
7. *Training and development*—Investing in human capital.
8. *Corporate culture*—Beliefs, myths and values that guide the behaviour of people throughout the organisation.
9. *The new leadership theory*—Inspiring and empowering others to act.
10. *The linking pin concept organisations*—Creating cross-functional teams.
11. *Strategic planning*—Determining where to take the organisation and how and when.

Defining TQM

One of the problems in the discussion of TQM is the apparent lack of a generally accepted description of what it actually consists of. Authors argue that there is confusion as to what different writers mean when they discuss TQM. Spencer (1994) provides a thorough review of the TQM literature arguing that different quality experts emphasise different aspects of it. For example, TQM is described as a new way of thinking about the management of organisations (Chorn, 1991), a comprehensive way to improve total organizational performance and quality (Hunt, 1993), a systematic approach to the practice of management (Olian and Rynes, 1991), an alternative to management by control (Price, 1989) and as a paradigm shift (Broeding in Spencer, 1994).

Despite that, the concept lacks any universal definition. Practically, every management author, consultant or practitioner has a different meaning for TQM (Luthans, 1993). Table 2.1 lists out some of the important definitions of TQM propounded by famous quality gurus and management experts.

Table 2.1: Some Definitions of TQM

Definitions	Source
"A dynamic process involving all levels in an organisation to promote never ending improvement in the effectiveness and efficiency of all elements of business".	1
"The system of activities directed to achieving delighted customers, empowered employees, higher revenues, and lower costs".	2
"Continuous, customer-centered, employee-driven improvement".	3
"TQM means that the organisation's culture is defined by and supports the constant attainment of customer satisfaction through an integrated system of tools, techniques, and training. This involves the continuous improvement of organisational processes, resulting in high quality products and services".	4
"The TQM concept refers to company-wide quality assurance from suppliers to customers (external and internal) using systems approach of documented sets of procedures and control of process variability in a team spirit with top-management commitment".	5
"TQM refers to continuous profitability improvement".	6

Definitions	Source
"TQM is an integrated organisational approach for delighting the customers (both internal and external) by meeting their expectations on a continuous basis through everyone involved with organisation working on a continuous improvement in all products, services along with proper problem solving methodology".	7
"TQM is an organisational strategy with accompanying techniques that deliver quality products and/or services to customers".	8
"Continuous improvement in quality through men and every other operational aspect of the organisation with customer at the centre of its activities".	9
"TQM as a corporate business management, philosophy which recognizes that customer needs and business goals are inseparable.... It involves every department, function and process in a business has the active commitment of all employees to meeting customer needs".	10
"TQM as an integrated organizational approach in delighting customer (both internal and external) by meeting their expectations on a continuous basis through everyone involved within the organisation, working on a continuous improvement in all products. Services and processes with proper problem solving methodology".	11
"TQM is a business discipline and philosophy of management which institutionalises company-wide planned and continuous business improvement through employee participation and involvement with the purpose of satisfying the customers in the marketplace".	12

Sources:

1. Deming, W. Edwards (1986) *Out of the Crisis*, Cambridge University Press, Cambridge.
2. Juran, J.M. and F.M. Gryana (1995) *Quality Planning and Analysis*, 3rd edition, Tata McGraw Hill, p. 13.
3. Schonberger, R.J. (1992) "Total Quality Management Cuts a Broad Swath Through Manufacturing and Beyond", *Organisational Dynamics*, Spring, p. 18. Also see, Denton, D.K. (1995) "Creating a System for Continuous Improvement", *Business Horizon*, January-February, pp. 565-84.
4. Sashkin, M. and K.J. Kiser (1993) *Putting Total Quality Management to Work*, San Francisco, Berrett-Koehler, p. 39.
5. Oakland, J.S. (1989) *Total Quality Management*, Heinemann Publishing Co., Oxford.
6. Stein, Robert E. (1994) *The Next Phase of TQM*, Marul Dekkel Inc., p. 4.
7. Anandaram, K.S. (2001) "Total Quality Management: A Goal for Organisations", *Indian Journal of Training and Development*, Vol. XXXI, No. 2, April-June, pp. 44-53.
8. Luthans, Fred (1995) *Organisational Behaviour*, McGraw Hill International Editions, Seventh Edition, Singapore, p. 30.
9. Khan, Praveen (2001) "Training Employees for Total Quality", *Indian Journal of Training and Development*, Vol. XXXI, No. 2, April-June, pp. 55-62.
10. British Quality Association, 1989.
11. Indian Statistcal/Institute Training Material.
12. Hill, S. (1991) "Why Total Quality Circles Failed but Total Quality Management might Succeed, *British Journal of Industrial Relations*, 29(4), pp. 541-68.

These definitions capture in a few words what the objectives of a modern organisation should be. Thorough examinations of all these definitions reveal that TQM is an integrated organisational approach to bring continuous improvement in products, services, and processes by using proper tools, technology and training to meet customers' expectations on a continuous basis through total employees' involvement.

Understanding TQM

TQM has been variously defined over the years, thus creating a great deal of confusion. Some say that 'total quality is a business strategy'. Others consider it to be a 'new management philosophy'. Still others say, "It's more than a programme, it's a state of mind", or "It's not a programme, it's a process" (Kelda, 1996). Even if such definitions cannot be dispelled completely, the concept of total quality must be defined in more concrete and measurable terms. Just as the concept of *quality* has been a source of debate, so is the concept of TQM. The acronym Total Quality Management represents three facets of an organisation-wide quality management. The best way to understand TQM is to look at each aspect of the concept separately, i.e. Total, Quality, and Management.

The TOTAL Aspect of TQM

Total quality is different from traditional quality in the sense that customer determines whether a product/service is totally qualitative or not. If quality is achieved in totality, it leads to customer satisfaction which is the focus of TQM and also of every organisation.

The 'conformance to specified standard' constitutes the very base of traditional approach to quality. Under it the concept of quality includes only the user perceptions and consequences as far as use of a product is concerned. But the concept of total quality extends to every aspect of an organisation (Bourds et al., 1994).

According to Kelly (2000), total in TQM means that quality is integral to every phase of a company's business. The various functions within a business that way get interrelated. Quality in purchasing is just as important as quality in production. Billing can be just as crucial a factor in a customer's perception of quality as sales.

Under Total Quality (TQ) workers are generalists rather than specialists. Therefore, efforts need to be made towards a value analysis as well as the operation method of developing products and for without this maximization of value to the stakeholder, whether customers, employees or shareholders cannot be possible. Making of better products inherently underlines the search better ways in this regard. The significant way to ensure this can only be through remaining conversant with the ground reality and the best way to make a right move in this regard is possible through communication, feedback, interaction, etc. As Lewis and Smith (1994) rightly point out that TQ is more than an attempt to make better products; it is also a search for better ways to make better products.

Ishikawa (1985) states: "narrowly interpreted, quality means quality of product. Broadly interpreted quality means quality of work, quality of service, quality of information, quality of process, quality of division, quality of people including employees, managers and executives, quality of system, quality of company, quality of objectives etc."

Total Quality (TQ) is a people-focused management system that aims at continual increase in customer satisfaction. It is a total system approach (not a separate area or programme), and an integral part of high-level strategy which works horizontally across functions and departments by involving all employees from top to bottom and extending backward and forward to include the supply chain and the customer chain (Rampey and Roberts, 1992). The foundation of TQ is philosophical: the scientific method of TQ includes systems, methods and tools. TQ is anchored in values that stress the dignity of the individual and the power of community action (Procter and Gamble, 1992).

Wakhlu (1994) has defined the term 'total quality' taking into consideration not only product quality, but also encompassing all aspects of the organisation. It deals with organisational performance in the long run. He has defined total quality as, "performance superiority in delighting customers. The means used are people, who are committed to employ organisational resources to provide value to customers by doing the right things, right at the first time, and every time".

This definition contains some important phraseology, which is discussed below:

Phrase 1. Performance superiority—An organisation that is on the path of total quality has to strive towards being the 'best in the entire industry'. This is possible by constantly providing value to customers, which is possible only when the organisation is responsive to changes in customer requirements, technology and any other environmental factors that have a bearing on its ability to provide its customers the desired value.

Phrase 2. Delighting customers—Today only those organisations excel who can anticipate their customers' requirements and strive to exceed them. This not only delights customers, but also provides firms with advantages to emulate, since they have a head start in figuring out what their customers seek.

Phrase 3. Provide value—If a customer perceives that the product or service that he buys provides him value, then it can be assumed that quality of the goods relative to the cost incurred by the customer must be higher than that of competitors. The cost incurred by a customer could be the price or even the lifecycle cost, depending on the product. Thus, value may be defined as the ratio between quality and cost. Thus,

$$\text{Value} = \frac{\text{Quality}}{\text{Cost}}$$

Phrase 4. Doing the right things—It emphasizes the importance of ensuring that only those things be done in the organisation that add value to the final output. All else is wasted effort.

Phrase 5. Right the first time—This suggests that organisations have to define their processes in such a way that the output is provided to the customer exactly the way it has been planned, and without errors of any kind.

Achieving Total Quality

In order to achieve TQ, quality has to be 'built-into' and not 'inspected into' the product right from the quality at source to quality in manufacturing process to quality in customer's hands. In TQ, quality flows through different stages of the 'quality loop' as shown in Fig. 2.1. This loop conceptualises that 'total quality' is an outcome of flow of quality through different activities, namely marketing, designing, engineering, purchasing, manufacturing, supervision and shop operation, inspection and testing, packing, distribution, installation and servicing to customer.

The leading quality expert, Feigenbaum (1983) of General Systems Company Inc., USA has described seven characteristics of managing TQ. These characteristics are:

(i) TQ is not a technical function of a department, but a systematic process that extends throughout the company.

(ii) TQ must be organised to recognise that while it is everybody's job in the company, it will become nobody's job unless quality process in the company is correctly structured to support both the quality of work of Individuals and quality teamwork among departments.

(iii) TQ improvement must take place in marketing, development and engineering, in manufacturing and particularly in service department not merely in the production department.

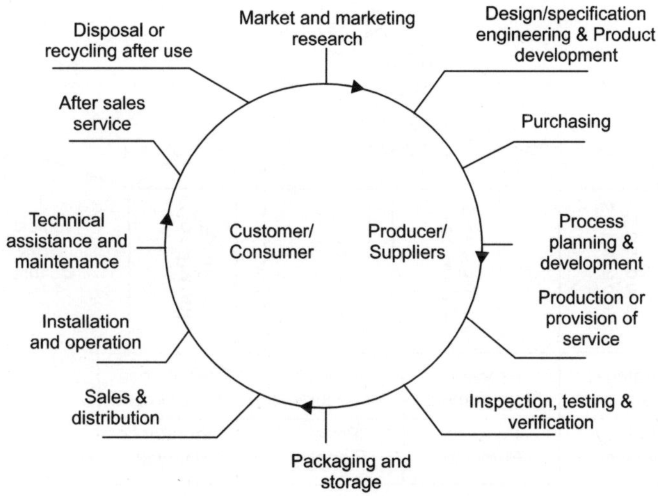

Fig. 2.1: The Total Quality Loop

Source: Bureau of Indian Standards (1991)

(iv) TQ must be perceived to be what the buyer wants and needs to satisfy his requirements, not what the company needs to satisfy its requirements for marketing and production efficiency.

(v) TQ improvement requires applications of new technology ranging from quality design techniques to computer-aided quality management measures and control.

(vi) TQ improvement is achieved only through the help and participation from all the men and women in the workforce, not from just a few specialists.

(vii) For TQ attainment, the company has to establish a clear and customer-oriented quality management system throughout the organisation which people can understand, believe in and want to be part of.

The House of Total Quality

The House of Total Quality presents an overview of the total quality philosophy and provides a comprehensive frame of reference, integrating key aspects of organisation design and operations. It consists of six components as shown in Fig. 2.2. They are as follows:

(i) The *roof* or superstructure consists of four organisational systems within which the actual work of any organisation takes place: the management, social, technical and educational sub-systems.

(ii) The four *pillars* of quality: customer satisfaction, continuous improvement, speaking with facts, and respect for people.

(iii) The four *foundations*: strategy management, process management, project management, and individual task management.

(iv) The four *cornerstones*: strategic planning, process planning, project planning and performance planning.

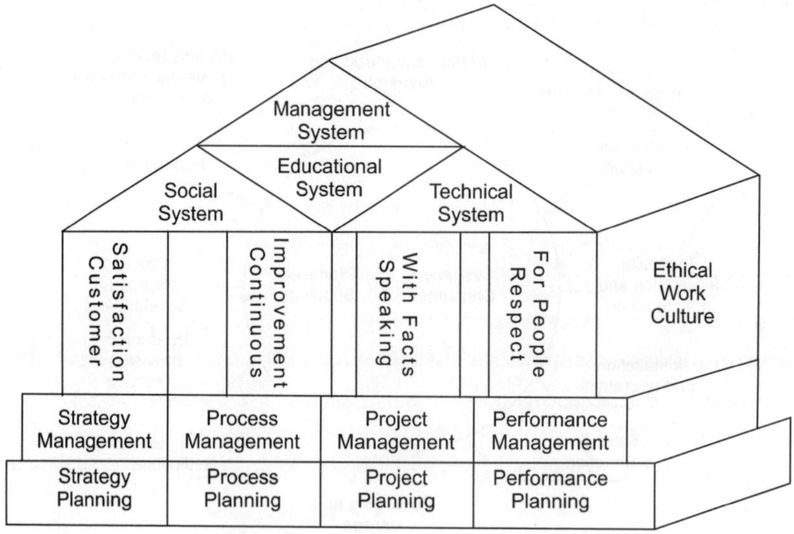

Fig. 2.2: The House of Total Quality

(v) The *mortar* of deployment between the joint of the roof, the pillars, the foundations and the customers is the ethical work culture.

While the House of Total Quality provides the height and breadth of TQ, the organisational ethical work culture provides its depth and determines what it "feels like" to internal and external stakeholders who dwell there (Petrick and Furr, 1995). The ethical work culture of an organisation determines, whether the house becomes a home—a place where respect, cooperation, trust, caring, justice and high performance standards prevail. Organisations with highly developed ethical work cultures demonstrate organisational integrity, which can be defined as "the collective alignment of moral awareness, judgment, intention and conduct around principled standards" (Petrick and Quinn, 1996; and Paine, 1996).

The QUALITY Aspect of TQM

When a company adopts TQM, it begins to define quality according to the needs of its customers, and not by parameters of production. Quality is designed into the products/services. It is not merely an add-on, it flows from company's processes and culture (Kelly, 2000).

The MANAGEMENT Aspect of TQM

The 'M' in TQM implies that it is a management approach, and not just a narrow quality control or quality assurance function. Someone from the quality control function may head-up and coordinates the TQM efforts, but to get away from this more traditional, and limited perspective, it would be more appropriate for someone from another department, someone who is respected and is a good communicator and "doer", to be the TQM project manager. The manager ideally should not only thoroughly understand and be able to train others in TQM, but also be a strong advocate and report directly to the General Manager/CEO (Luthans, 1995).

Management is a crucial part of the TQM concept. First the impetus for TQM must come from top managers; second TQM in some senses turns every worker into a manager by pushing decision-making down to the most effective level.

Principles of TQM

There are variations in the language and scope of TQM program. Different quality experts highlight upon different TQM principles. For instance, some have identified four common TQM principles:

(i) do it right the first time to eliminate costly rework;

(ii) listen to and learn from customers and employees;

(iii) make continuous improvement on everyday matter; and

(iv) build teamwork, trust and mutual respect (Bowen and Lawler III, 1992).

Some others have identified six common TQM principles (McShane, Steven and Glinow, 2001). Discussed below are these six principles that capture common themes in the field.

Customer Focus (CF)

Quality is always defined in terms of customers. A customer is anyone outside or inside the organisation to whom the employee supplies products, services or information (Goetsch and Davis, 1997; Milakovich, 1995; and Flood, 1993). The goal of satisfying customers is fundamental to TQM and is expressed by the organisation's attempt to register decision and deliver products and services that fulfill customer needs. By being close to internal and external customers, employees feel a stronger sense of responsibility to ensure that the product/service is defect-free. Moreover, if internal customer satisfaction level is high in an organisation then automatically external customer satisfaction level is enhanced.

Employee Involvement (EI)

EI a logical follow-up of the CF for ensuring quality naturally evolves on everything the employees do in an organisation instrumental behind the product and associated service. Quality management through EI therefore inheres such necessary aspects like decision making, including making suggestions for improvement, planning, goal setting, and monitoring performance. EI comes in different forms, but teamwork is distinct.

EI is of strategic importance in TQM because employees necessarily have the best information to identify quality problems and take corrective actions. EI also helps to minimise resistance to change. Through necessary forms of career progression, EI increases employee motivation and performance, which in turn improves customer satisfaction.

Continuous Improvement (CI)

TQM is a never-ending process. CI is often called 'Kaizen', a Japanese word that literally means "good change" (Burlage, 1997). In his book *Kaizen*, Masaaki Imai, who in fact coined the term, states that "Kaizen means improvement. It means continuing improvement involving everyone—managers and workers alike" (Imai, 1986). He also indicates "a Kaizen strategy maintains and improves the working standard through small, gradual improvements". He further adds "improvement can be defined as Kaizen and innovation, where...innovation calls forth radical improvements as a result of large investments in technology and/or equipment".

The 1995 Malcolm Baldrige National Quality Award criteria booklet states that the term 'continuous improvement' refers to both incremental and 'breakthrough' improvement'. CI is also treated as a significant part of the 'lean management' philosophy that is currently sweeping the manufacturing sector (Niepce and Molleman, 1998). No matter what title is used, the idea is to continually improve the effectiveness and efficiency of activities and processes in order to provide added benefits to the customer and organisation; the improvement may be incremental (steady progress, step by step, each problem solved in order) or breakthroughs (big jumps).

Today, many firms have used Kaizen blitzes in order to encourage the continuous improvement process. Kaizen blitzes are intense team-based events in which employees are given a fixed time to review specific work activities, so that they can further reduce waste.

Defect Prevention (DP)

TQM is built on the adage that 'a stitch in time saves nine'. A defect or error should stopped at its source, as the cost of repair increases exponentially as the defect moves further along the process. Thus, a central tenet of TQM is 'do it right the first time'. This quality philosophy also pushes towards zero defects because even the smallest defect made may have sizeable consequences.

Performance Measurement (PM)

Performance measurement is the main driver of CI and defect prevention. By measuring the efficiency of work process and organisational outcomes, quality problems become apparent and employees can see how their efforts are reducing these problems (Milakovich, 1993). This is consistent with the trend towards fact-based management, i.e. using objective rather than subjective information to assess quality and make corporate decisions.

Continuous Learning (CL)

'Learning' refers to acquiring knowledge, leading to new goals or approaches, and adaptation to change. TQM requires knowledgeable employees who have the ability to work in teams and adapt themselves to the dynamic work environment. In other words, TQM requires a heavy investment in employees' training and education. It envisages that learning should be a regular part of employees' daily work so that they can seek to eliminate problems at their source and be driven by opportunities to do better.

Approaches to TQM

There is no internationally recognized 'standard' approach to TQM, although the key implementation factors can be identified to distinguish one approach from other. Research studies show three key factors, viz. *organisation, approach* and *motivation* which are common to any enterprise (Sharma, 2002). Among the critical *organizational decisions* are:

(a) how the TQM process be started?;

(b) what type of improvement teams should be employed?; and

(c) what should be the mechanism for creating cultural change?

The *approaches* those can be adopted are:

(a) technical-led (problem solving, statistical process control, etc.);

(b) guru-led (Juran, Deming, etc.); and
(c) vision-led (customer satisfaction).

The *motivation* for TQM can be provided from a number of sources. It may be:

(a) leader driven (CEO);
(b) champion driven (quality manager);
(c) quality control driven (group of individuals); and
(d) corporately driven (external corporate level objectives).

Kelemen (2003) has viewed TQM from five distinct metaphorical perspectives. The metaphor is a central sense making mechanism by which 'humans forge their experience and knowledge of the world in which they live' (Morgan, 1986). The metaphors are as follows:

1. TQM and *machine* metaphor: This metaphor sees organisations as displaying the characteristics and behaviour of machines. TQM's final goal is to increase profits through conformance to technical requirement.
2. TQM and the *organic* metaphor: It sees organisations as having the characteristics and behaviour like that of organisms. TQM works to improve communication between the company's departments and between individual employees via empowerment programmes and better communications. On the other hand, TQM acts as a buffer between the company and its external environment in both technical and symbolic ways.
3. TQM and the *cultural* metaphor: It sees organisations as networks of shared values, beliefs and attitudes. TQM is seen to be a culturally enacted phenomenon, negotiated and maintained through the use of rituals, stories, etc.
4. TQM and the *change and transformation* metaphor: It suggests that organisations are in constant flux and transformation. TQM could be seen as a change programme.
5. TQM and the *political* metaphor: It views organisations as coalitions of actors with different interests and aspirations. TQM may serve to enhance the already dominant perspective and vision in the organisation held by managers and quality professionals and may push other voices to the margin.

The first two metaphors subscribe to a managerial approach to quality, while the last three take a critical view of quality.

There are two broad approaches to TQM:

1. The *hard* approach emphasizes continuous improvement by the use of statistical methods. This approach is associated with the earlier management gurus whose work primarily focuses on improving productivity and profits.
2. The *soft* approach focuses on leadership, emotional intelligence and cultural change. This approach was popularized by American gurus and its aim is to create a strong organizational culture aligned to the demands of the customer.

Models of TQM

I. *Integrated Model*

Sohal, Tay and Wirth (1989) have discussed quality in terms of Total Quality Control rather than TQM. But the five elements they include in the system of TQ control are equally emphasized in TQM. It is done to refer control to the management of quality at various stages of the process. The model is given in Fig. 2.3.

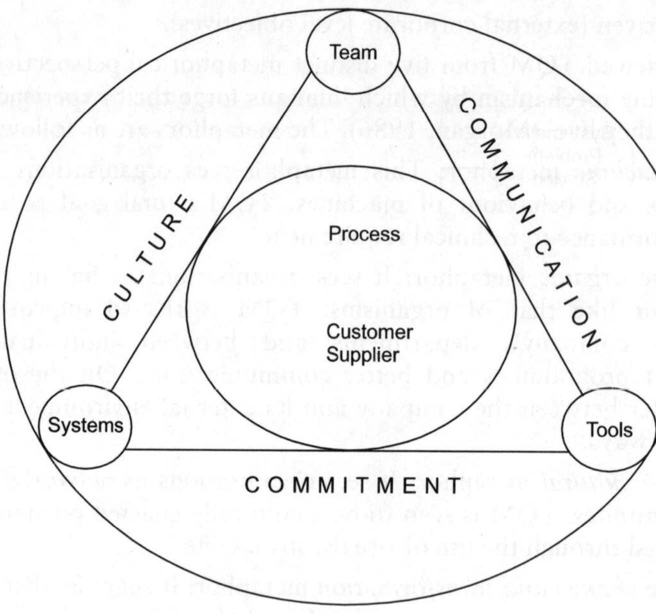

Fig. 2.3: The Integrated Model of TQM

II. *Oakland's Model*

The Oakland's (1989) model describes TQM as a pyramid representing five distinct components (Fig. 2.4).

- Management commitment;
- Customer-supplier chains;
- Systems approach to documented sets of procedures and standards;
- Statistical Process Control (SPC) tools; and
- Teamwork and continuous improvement.

At the heart of the model is the establishment of customer-supplier chains, where the interplay of supplier and customer processes determine the strategy for continuous improvement through process feedback and customer feedback.

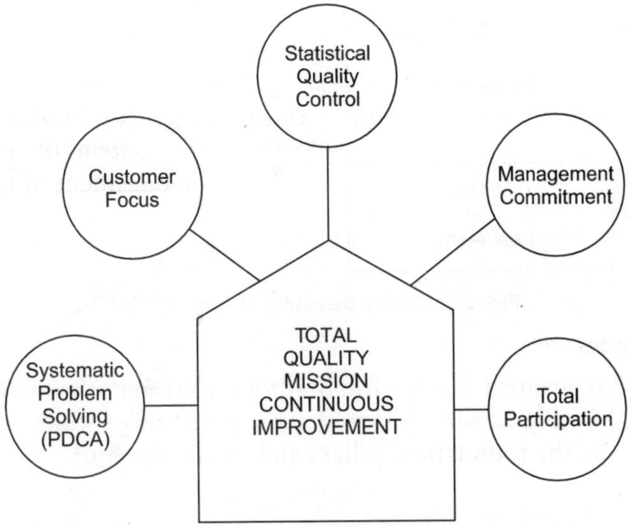

Fig. 2.4: Oakland's Model

Oakland has enumerated the following thirteen strategies to represent a gradual progression towards implementing a TQM-based culture. These are:

- Understanding quality
- Commitment to quality
- Policy on quality
- Organisation for quality
- Measurement costs of quality
- Planning for quality
- Design for quality
- System for quality
- Capability for quality
- Control for quality
- Teamwork for quality
- Training for quality
- Implementation of TQM

III. *Quality-Sweating Theory*

Kano (1989) has propounded the "Quality Sweating Theory" (Fig. 2.5). The model states that TQM is an effective tool for improving quality. As the very name suggests the success of TQM depends on making many employees sweat. This theory encompasses two alternative approaches: CLSQ (Crisis Consciousness and Leadership make people Sweat for Quality) and VLSQ (Vision and Leadership encourage people to Sweat for Quality).

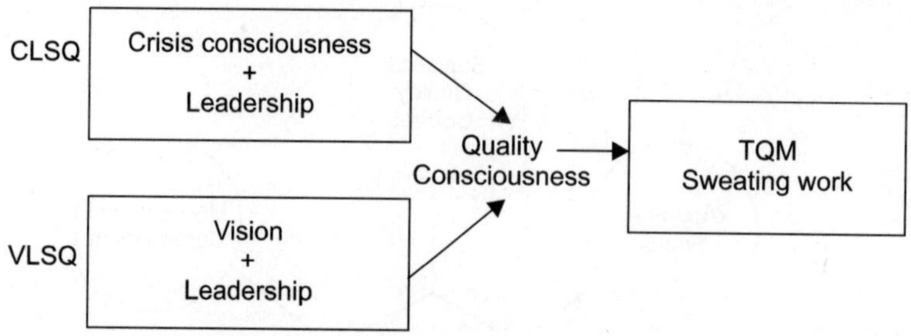

Fig. 2.5: Quality Sweating Theory of TQM

IV. *Building Blocks Model*

Zairi (1991) at the Management Centre for Bradford University has developed the 'Building Blocks Model of TQM' (Fig. 2.6). This model proposes three kinds of building blocks to develop total quality, viz. the foundation, pillars and finally the roof.

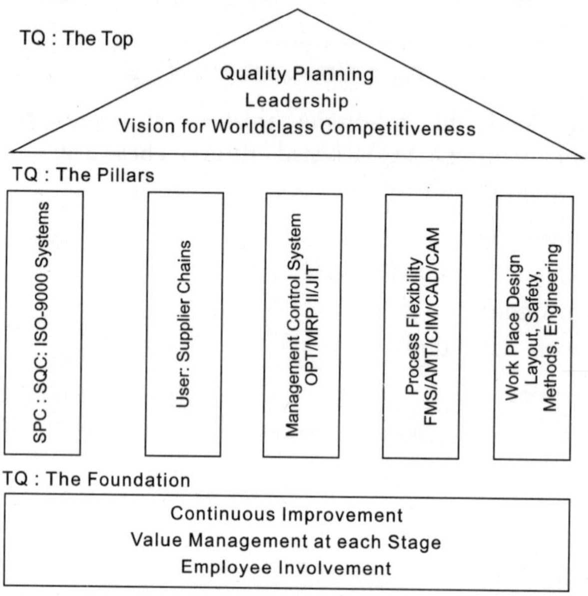

Fig. 2.6: The Building Blocks Model of TQM

The Foundation of TQ: The three elements that constitute the foundation of TQM are:

- Continuous improvement;
- Value addition at each stage of every operation; and
- Employee involvement.

The Pillars of TQ: Pillars are the means by which the human creativity inputs can be converted into outputs for the benefit of the end customers. These are represented by various quality systems such as procedures, documentation, use of Statistical Process Control (SPC), management control system, process flexibility provided by the use of computers, workplace design, ergonomics, and customer (both internal and external) supplier chain.

The Top of TQ: The topmost building block should shield the organisation from adverse external factors and protect it all the time. It should be weather proof (not affected by adverse changes in market place) and tangible (organisations are dynamic in nature and have to adapt to new market patterns). In this context, the senior managers must assume the responsibilities for:

- Quality planning;
- Leadership; and
- Vision for world-class competitiveness.

V. *Theoretical Model*

Anderson et al. (1994) have developed the 'Theoretical Model of Total Quality Management' on the basis of 'Deming's Management Method'. The theoretical essence of the Deming Management Method uncovers the creation of an organisational system that fosters cooperation and learning to facilitate the implementation of process management practices. This in turn leads to continuous improvement of processes, products, and services and to employee fulfilment, which are critical to customer satisfaction and ultimately, to the survival of the organisation. The relational diagram of the theory of total quality management underlying the Deming Management Method is shown in Fig. 2.7.

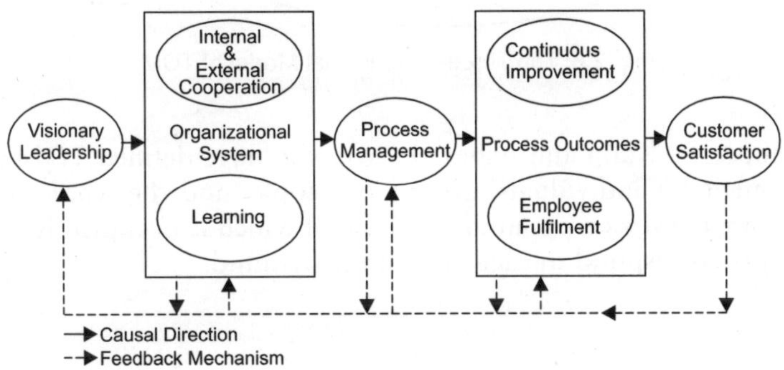

Fig. 2.7: The Theoretical Model

The key concepts underlying the Deming Management Method are as follows:

- Visionary leadership;
- Internal and external cooperation;
- Learning;
- Process management;
- Continuous improvement;
- Employee fulfilment; and
- Customer satisfaction.

VI. *Three-dimensional Model*

This model was developed by Joseph N. Kelda (1996) which emphasises upon the following three dimensions of TQM (Fig. 2.8).

(i) The Human Dimension: psychological and political.

(ii) The Logical Dimension: rational and systematic.
(iii) The Technological Dimension: mechanical and systematic.

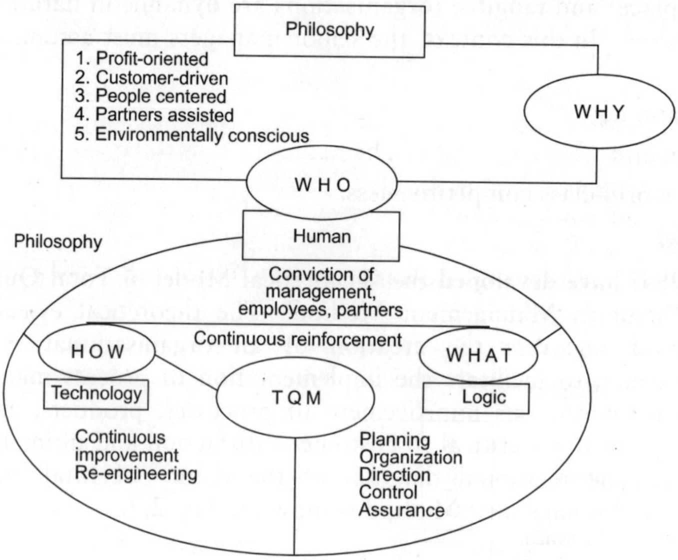

Fig. 2.8: The Three-dimensional Model of TQM

VII. *Pyramid Model*

This model is developed by Kanji and Asher (1996), who have defined TQM as, "a continuous process of improvement for individuals, groups of people, and the whole organisation". The model (Fig. 2.9) shows TQM as a pyramid, the base of which is occupied by the four principles and two core concepts correspond to each side of the pyramid.

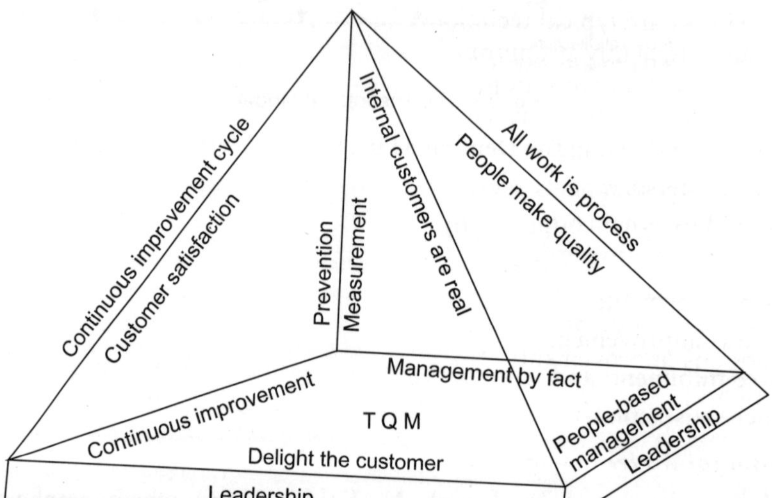

Fig. 2.9: The Pyramid Model of TQM

The model also indicates that organisation has to be guided through the TQM principles and core concepts of top management leadership.

VIII. *The House of TQM*

This model is developed by Kano (1997), which mostly deals with the structure of TQM (Fig. 2.10). From the figure, it is evident that the floor of TQM House symbolizes "motivational approach" and the roof shows "customer satisfaction/quality assurance"—which is the ultimate purpose of TQM. The base is the "intrinsic technology", which refers to the driving technology specific to an industry. "Concepts" are of the pillars of the house which show how to proceed from a particular perspective when a given intrinsic technology and motivational level already exist. "Concepts" consist of both a theory of quality (such as "quality is the satisfaction of the customer") and a theory of management (such as "PDCA cycle").

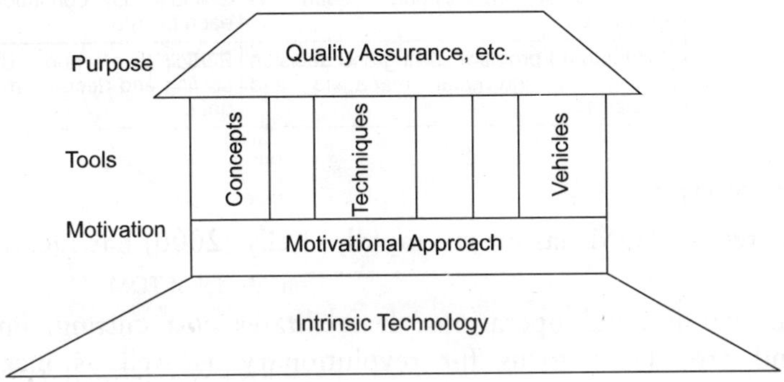

Fig. 2.10: The House of TQM

When actual activities based on these concepts begin, some "techniques" (the second pillar) for collecting and analysing the data become necessary. The seven QC tools (details are given in next chapter) are typical techniques that are applied here. At this point, some methods for effectively and efficiently promoting all of these activities within the organisation become necessary. Promotional organisation, education and training, quality circles, team activity, management by policy, daily management are different methods that can be called "vehicles" (the third pillar) since they quicken and facilitate promotion.

A review of all these models reveal that they share eight common features (Nilakant and Ram Narayan, 1998). These are:

(i) Focus on the customer;
(ii) Strategic leadership;
(iii) Processes and systems;
(iv) Continuous improvement;
(v) Teamwork;
(vi) Empowerment;
(vii) Learning and experimentation; and
(viii) Complexity[1]

Traditional Quality Management and TQM

The differences between traditional management and TQM are highlighted in the following Table 2.2.

Table 2.2: Traditional Quality Management and TQM

SL. No.	Aspect	Traditional Quality Management	TQM
1.	Quality definition	(a) products meet specification (b) focus on post product inspection	(a) products fit for customer use (b) focus on building quality into work process
2.	Customers	Ambiguous understanding of customer requirements	Systematic approach to seek, understand and satisfy internal and external customer
3.	Errors	A certain margin of error, waste and rework is tolerable	No tolerance for errors; do it right the first time and every time approach
4.	Improvement emphasis	Technological breakthrough such as automation	Gradual but continuous improvement of each function
5.	Problem solving	Unstructured problem solving and decision making by individual managers and specialists	Participative and disciplined problem solving and decision making based on hard data.

Source: Sharma (2002)

Reasons for Growth of TQM

World wide interest in TQM has grown rapidly. Kelly (2000) has identified three reasons for this trend.

1. TQM improves internal operations: It facilitates cost cutting, improves employee morale and provides a focus for revolutionary as well as incremental leaps in productivity.
2. TQM improves competitive position: A formal, company-wide quality system reassures customers. In a highly competitive market, TQM can give your company an edge. It is a visible signal of your commitment to quality.
3. Customers demand it: The growth of TQM has been a natural chain reaction. As companies adopt the principles of TQM and see the benefits, they begin to require that their suppliers do the same.

Chapter Overview

TQM is a holistic organisational approach to bring continuous improvements in organisational activities, processes and products to satisfy the customers. Quality experts have propounded different TQM models describing various components, core methods and principles of TQM. A review of all these models reveal that 'customer' is the heart of TQM and the interplay of customer and supplier determines an organisation's strategy for its continuous improvement. But as far as the applicability of models is concerned there is no one most widely accepted model. The models are situation specific—as per the requirement of the organisation.

TQM encompasses certain basic principles such as focus on customer, employee involvement, continuous improvement, defect prevention, performance measurement, and continuous learning. These principles can be put into practice by using suitable TQM methods.

Discussion Questions

1. Define TQM and identify its roots.

2. Explain the concept of TQM.
3. Discuss various approaches to TQM. Which approach is best suitable for your organisation and why?
4. Differentiate between traditional quality management and TQM.
5. Explain the concept of TQM citing suitable examples.

Note

1. In TQM jargon, complexity refers to unnecessary work or activities that do not increase quality. These could be extra process steps that are required to deal with external or internal errors. Reduction of these errors will eliminate unnecessary process steps leading to higher productivity. For details see, Fuller (1985).

Total Quality Management and Continuous Improvement

3

Chapter Outline

- Improvement Process
- Customer
- Approaches to Improvement
- Tools and Techniques of TQM
- TQM Methods
- Chapter overview
- Discussion questions

Chapter Objectives

After completion of this chapter, the reader will be able to:

- Explain the improvement process
- Discuss various approaches to improvement
- Describe about different TQM methods

Improvement Process

Improvement is the heart of TQM and every organisation needs to improve continuously in contemporary times showing fast changing customer needs and highly volatile competition for survival in the market. In such a scenario, anybody who is associated with the organisation is required to do certain activities in the improvement process.

While TQM is a general process, improvement targets specific goals. There is a great deal of commonality between TQM and improvement. Indeed both are to a great extent the two sides of the same coin. Hence, TQM methods do develop with the improvement tools to a great extent. Like TQM the customers, their needs and expectations and explorations and use of appropriate tools and techniques for problem solving and continuous improvement are well included within the strategy improvement.

Customer

In this section, we view customers from three angles, i.e. who are they?; what they need?; and how to satisfy them? If we see organisation as a system the products/services that the customer receive is the output. To achieve the result the suppliers as the input must identify the needs and expectation of both the internal and external customer. If you have customer then you are automatically a supplier and your suppliers will view you as their customers. Hence, the point is assessing everyone's need for improvement.

The words 'needs', 'expectations' and 'wants' have become interchangeable in the customer context. Customer needs are seen as basic requirements like empathy, reassurance and security, whereas customer expectations tend to be based on what the customers believe they should receive and customer wants implies fulfilling the customer requirements. However, in the organisational context, we view customer needs/expectations/wants as:

- Value for money
- Products/services that work
- Delivery on time
- Friendly service (Management Extra, 2005).

Organisations use different techniques and methods to satisfy or delight their customers. Some of the commonly used methods are:

- Making customer satisfaction as their employee's objectives and organisation's mission
- Setting standards for customer satisfaction
- Providing education and training to employees to achieve customer delight
- Setting up specialised customer care department
- Improving communication channel
- Providing tailor-made services to customers
- Developing flexible pricing, delivery methods
- Making everything customer friendly
- Improving communication channels

Approaches to Improvement

There are mainly two approaches to quality improvement:

1. Breakthrough improvement
2. Continuous improvement

Breakthrough improvement is a sudden change in the organisation's normal way of operation. This may come through introduction of new technology, structural change or implementation of any new system or combination of any of the above. The best examples of breakthrough improvement can be Business Process Re-engineering (BPR), Six Sigma Technique.

Continuous improvement is incremental and gradual as compared to breakthrough improvement. This approach is popularly known as Kaizen. In Japan, it means continuous improvement by involving everyone in the organisation. Famous TQM guru Deming has presented the continuous improvement as a cycle known as PDCA Cycle or Deming Wheel. PDCA stands for Plan, Do, Check, Act.

Tools and Techniques of TQM

Tools and techniques of TQM can be categorised depending upon their usability and utility. Broadly, they can be categorised as: (a) Tools for quality improvement and (b) Tools for problem solving. The category (a) is generally used by teams/groups and (b) is used at individual level. In this section, we will discuss the most common and popular tools used by practitioners under both categories.

Category (a): It comprises the following popular techniques.

1. **Flow chart:** It is a diagrammatic representation of any process, using standard symbols like rectangle, arrow, square, etc. that shows tasks, decisions, relations, outcome, and feedback in a sequence they occur. Flow chart provides historical information as well as future projects. It is useful to represent how a system works. It helps the team to improve quality quickly and at low cost.
2. **Arrow diagrams:** It is a graphical method for planning and controlling projects and other related activities. It is also used to detect delays in planned schedules and suggest remedies to prevent recurrence. Numericals and arrows are used to show the activities and the sequence. It helps in effective resource utilisation to achieve the goals of the organisation.
3. **Histograms:** These are the visual representation of the distribution or spread of data (frequency distribution). The measures of central tendency can be in the form of mean, median and mode. The information presented in the histograms is represented by a series of rectangles or bars which are related to the groups of data. These are used to measure the consistency and suggest ways of keeping a process in control.
4. **Run/Control charts:** It is a graphic representation which illustrates how a process changes over a period of time. Line graphs are used to track a process trend or performance. The control chart provides a picture of how the operations withstand or fail to continue within the control limits.
5. **Affinity diagram:** This is a graphical tool to generate, organise and consolidate gathered information. It helps to give a sense of the ideas that a group has concerning a given issue, non-judgmental format for gathering group input. It also provides information about the similarity and dissimilarity of thoughts.
6. **Brainstorming:** It is a process of open and uninhibited generation of ideas by a group. The purpose is to generate a wide variety of ideas, to ensure that everyone on the team gets involved, to assure that nothing is overlooked and to provide an atmosphere in which creativity can flourish breaking out of conventional thought process. Group input is a vital issue in this.
7. **Nominal group technique (NGT)/Light voting:** It is a structured group process used to help teams make decisions without falling into voting or other decision-making modes that can divide the team. It gives everyone on the team an equal voice in the decision

and reduces the pressure of traditional decision-making model to confirm. It is used anytime a team needs to generate or choose a course of action for improvement.

8. **Lotus diagram**: It is a tool to expand thinking around single topic. This expansion may include types, categories, details or questions around a theme. It is a simple, effective way to organise the output around brainstorming. It is a good choice to organise the output of brainstorming around any central theme.

Category (b): It comprises the following popular techniques.

1. **Fishbone diagram**: Also known as Ishikawa diagram is a cause and effect diagram which is employed as a diagnostic exercise in quality improvement. When the diagram is completed with the causes and effects it looks like a fishbone. It helps to see the problem in totality and also makes it clear that the problem has been thoroughly investigated.
2. **Check sheets or graphs**: These are the graphs designed to figure out defect—occurrence patterns. Graphs can be single or multi line or bar charts, even pie—diagrams which give a clear picture of the source-wise contribution of variations or defects in quality improvement.
3. **Pareto analysis**: It is named after the 19th century Italian economist Vilfredo Pareto who noticed that 80 percent of the wealth of his country was owned by 20 per cent of the population (Pareto's 80-20 law). This is a diagnostic tool commonly used for separating the vital few causes that account for dominant share of quality loss. It ranks data in categories from largest to the smallest in terms of frequency of occurrence, cost, or time. It evaluates related measures of a problem or category.
4. **Scatter diagram**: It is graphical representation to show relationship between two variables. It helps to institute requisite control over certain operations or processes based upon the relationship study. Also, it evaluates the relative importance of process factors for control based on their strength of relationship.
5. **Force field analysis**: This is a tool to assess the likelihood of accomplishing a change. The tool defines driving forces, or any resources, attitudes and experience and so on that will support the change and restraining forces in all these regards that will cause the change to be stopped or delayed.
6. **Stratification**: This is a process by which data collection is structured with respect to the possible sources of variation or defects in the product or process. Different factors like machines, shifts, etc. are strata with respect to which the study of variations is conducted for diagnosis and possible prevention of variation or its control.
7. **Tree diagram**: It identifies the tasks and methods needed to solve a problem and reach a goal. It systematically traces the means and clarifies the problem to be solved by exposing its complete structure. From this analysis, the problem-solving method can be identified.
8. **Matrix chart**: This chart shows the relationships among various groups of data. It yields information about the relationships and the importance of those task/method elements of the subjects.

9. **Programme chart:** This is used for contingency planning. It focuses on possible sequences to help lead to a desirable result. It was developed to plan for the future while still in the development stage of problem solution planning.

TQM Methods

Basing on the TQM principles, as discussed in the previous chapter and using the above discussed improvement tools and techniques TQM can be put into practice by using suitable methods. However, adopting the right kind of method is one of the most important jobs of the senior management and the degree of its success largely depends upon their knowledge and understanding of these methods. All these methods can be classified into four major categories:

- Management methods;
- Analytical methods;
- Idea generation; and
- Data collection, analysis and display (Kanji and Asher, 1996).

A descriptive analysis of some of the important TQM methods is given below.

Design of Experiments (DOE)

DOE was first developed by Ronald Fisher in England in the 1920s to evaluate agricultural experiments in the natural conditions and was further developed by Taguchi in 1950s.

Purpose: DOE is a branch of applied statistics dealing with planning, conducting, analysing and interpreting controlled tests to evaluate the factors that control the value of a parameter or group of parameters. It is often used in conjunction with Quality Function Deployment.

Process: The following steps are important in using DOE:

- Obtain management support for the implementation of an experiment and approval for the required resources.
- Select a simple product and process to practice teamwork, methodology and interpretation of results.
- Organise the experiment team with people possessing both technical expertise and operating knowledge of the product and process to be studied.
- Establish team objectives, kinds of data and measurements required and method of operating.
- Perform the process analysis using appropriate QC tools to select the input factors for study.
- Formulate the experiment design and data sheets.
- Manipulate the process and run the experiment.
- Analyse the results and draw conclusions.
- Make an experimental confirmation run and identify requirements.

Benefits: DOE provides data that:

- Allow engineers to optimise the design characteristics so that performance variation can be minimised in the manufacturing and customer-use environments.

- Make products less sensitive to variations in their internal components.
- Identify best material, design or method that provides adequate performance.
- Provide the lowest cost design (avoid over-design).

Quality Function Deployment (QFD)

QFD took shape in 1972 at the Mitsubishi's Kobe Shipyard site. Toyota began to develop the concept shortly thereafter and it has been used since 1977. Today, companies like GM, Ford, Xerox, and IBM are using QFD very successfully.

Purpose: QFD is a structured method in which customer requirements are translated into appropriate technical requirements for each stage of product development and production. The QFD process is often referred to as listening to the voice of the customer.

Process: QFD is a five-stage process that takes a design from customer requirements into a plan and schedule (Bossert, 1991; Day, 1993):

1. Identifying customer needs or wants.
2. Translating requirements into technical specifications through the use of technical experts.
3. Turning the technical specifications into end-product specifications. These are called 'critical part characteristics'.
4. Designing the process to deliver the product or service.
5. Planning the activities necessary to produce the required output.

Benefits:

- QFD encourages organisations to focus on the process itself rather than just on the product or service.
- Improved communications and teamwork among all constituencies in the organisation.
- QFD helps to determine the causes of customer dissatisfaction.

Re-engineering

Re-engineering has been a popular activity and another name for making major organisation-wide improvements. These are decisions by management based primarily on cost reduction.

Purpose: Re-engineering is "the fundamental rethinking and radical redesign of business processes to achieve dramatic improvements in critical contemporary measures such as cost, quality, service and speed" (Hammer and Champy, 1992). Breakthrough redesign and process improvement, not structure reorganisation, are the common objectives of re-engineering (Cartin, 2000). Table 3.1 shows key re-engineering concepts.

Process: There are usually two methodologies to re-engineer business activities: (i) Critical Redesign Activities, and (ii) High-level Reengineering Activities. Both the methodologies are listed in Table 3.2 and Table 3.3.

Table 3.1: Key Re-engineering Concepts

Topic	Concept
• **Re-engineering**	• Fundamental rethinking • Radical redesign • Process • Dramatic improvement • Measures • Return • Risk
• **Process**	• Activities • Customers • Measures • Work ordering • Time • Space • Beginning • Ending • Inputs • Outputs • Structure • Action • Baseline
• **Redesign**	• Process configuration • Design flows • Process transformation • Redesign alternatives

Source: Cartin (2000)

Table 3.2: Critical Redesign Activities

Understanding and improving existing processes
1. Describe the current process flow 2. Measure the process in terms of the new process objectives. 3. Assess the process in terms of the new process attributes. 4. Identify problems with, or shortcoming of the process. 5. Identify short-term improvements in the process. 6. Assess current information technology and organisation.
Designing and prototyping a new process
1. Brainstorm design alternatives. 2. Assess feasibility, risk and benefit of design alternatives. 3. Select the preferred process design. 4. Prototype the new process design. 5. Develop a migration strategy. 6. Implement a new organisational structures and systems.

Table 3.3: High-level Re-engineering Activities

1. Identifying process for innovation.
2. Identifying change levers (that is enabling or transformation technologies).
3. Developing process visions.
4. Understanding and improving existing processes.
5. Designing and prototyping the new process.

Benefits:

- Re-engineering helps in clarifying the responsibility between organisation functions about how work actually gets done, what processes are needed and how they should relate.
- It eliminates work not contributing to goals.

Just-in-Time (JIT)

JIT usage began in the USA in the late 1980s. The first success with JIT occurred in Japan, i.e. in Toyota Company.

Purpose: JIT is an optimal material requirement planning system for a manufacturing process in which there is little or no manufacturing material inventory on hand at the manufacturing site and little or no incoming inspection.

Process: The themes and concepts of JIT are Total Quality Control, inventory reduction and employee involvement and their interrelationships. All are treated as integral parts of JIT's application. The major elements of JIT are visibility, people development, process improvement, uninterrupted flow, continuous improvement, and manufacturing excellence, elimination of waste, simplicity and flexibility.

Benefit: JIT helps to eliminate stocks in order to prevent unproductive stock cost.

Zero Defects

Zero Defects is a performance standard developed by Philip B. Crosby (1984) to address a dual attitude in the workplace. People are willing to accept imperfection in some areas and at the same time they expect the number of defects to be zero. This dual attitude had developed because of the recognition of the fact that people are human beings and are prone to mistakes. However, the zero defects methodology states that if people commit themselves to watching details and avoiding errors, they can move closer to the goal of zero.

Purpose: Zero Defects allows teams to experience the success involved in meeting more demanding target without demotivating them by not achieving absolute success at once.

Processes: Zero Defects is a very simple concept described by Crosby using the team approach:

1. Identify and agree the current level of performance.
2. Agree a target and time-scale for the target to be met with milestones.
3. Monitor performance against the target and publish the results.
4. If the target is met on time, recognise the team's performance and step 2 is to be repeated.

Benefit:

- Zero Defects give a way of setting tougher targets and recognising the success of teams that meet them, so as to encourage future efforts.

Benchmarking

The concept of benchmarking was developed by Xerox in 1979 and subsequently it has been widely adopted by other companies. Benchmarking is an improved process in which a company measures its performance against that of best-in-class companies. It determines how those companies achieved their performance levels and use the information to improve their own performance. The subjects that can be benchmarked include strategies, operations, processes and procedures.

Purpose: Benchmarking identifies and fills gaps in performance by putting in place best practice. Thus, it establishes superior performance.

Process: There are three distinct types of benchmarking which can be used by an organisation progressively to stimulate the improvement process. These are:

1. **Internal benchmarking:** It is the comparison between functions, departments or similar organisation as a means of improving performance.
2. **Competitive benchmarking:** It is a cross-comparison within one industry sector aimed at establishing best practice through the identification of gaps between own and competitor's performance.
3. **Comparative benchmarking:** It is the comparison across all business sectors aimed at establishing best practice in all areas of operation.

Benefits: Benchmarking accrues several valuable benefits such as:

- Highly motivating for an organisation to know that it is performing as well or better than the best.
- Provides an introduction to the idea of measurement.
- Helps organisations to move away from being introspective towards being externally focused and close to their markets.

Figure 3.1 shows an eleven-step process based on implementation of benchmarking as a sequence or a process.

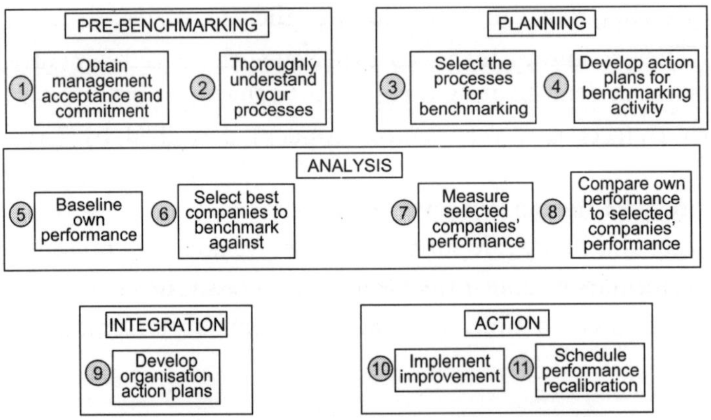

Fig. 3.1: Eleven Step Process of Benchmarking

Concurrent Engineering (CE)

CE refers to the cross-functional integration and concurrent development of a product or service and its associated processes (Swink, Scandvig and Mabert, 1996; Zangwill, 1993; Owen, 1992).

Purpose: CE is a methodology for the design, development and manufacture of products that meet the market/customer demand for high quality, low cost and fast delivery.

Process: Generally, CE occurs by assigning product development to a cross-functional project team consisting of people from the key functional organisations like marketing, re-engineering, manufacturing, quality engineering and suppliers. Figure 3.2 makes a comparison between how the product development process traditionally works and works under CE.

Benefits: The results as demonstrated by Japan and companies initiating CE in the West reveal that CE products are:

- More desired in the marketplace;
- More competitive;
- Involve lower engineering and manufacturing costs; and
- Shorter design delivery cycle times (Cartin, 2000).

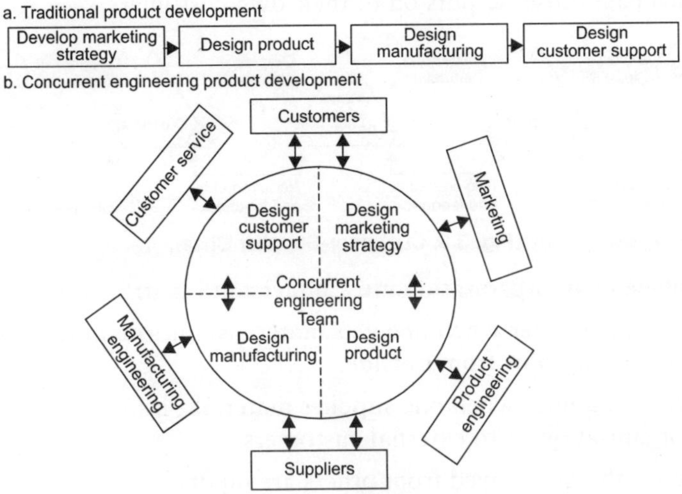

Fig. 3.2: Traditional and Concurrent Product Development

Suggestion Schemes

Purpose: To generate ideas for improvement.

Process: The following are guidelines for successful administration of suggestion schemes.

1. Set up a steering group to oversee the process.
2. Delegate as far down as practical the decision on whatever or not to implement the suggestion.
3. Give awards to supervisors and managers whose employees generate most ideas.
4. In the early stages go for quantity of ideas, rather than quality.
5. To generate ideas in manageable numbers try to set themes for ideas and change the themes regularly.
6. Ensure that all ideas are acknowledged quickly and that the person generating the idea is told whether it is to be implemented or not, what is the reason.

7. Look for reasons to say 'yes' rather than 'no'.
8. In the early stages be prepared for ideas to be about environmental aspects rather than operational ones.

Benefit: Suggestion schemes provide a way of moving to continuous improvement via small incremental changes.

Internal Customer Satisfaction (ICS)

Purpose: The purpose of ICS is to build positive relationship between customers and suppliers both inside and outside the organisation. In a quality organisation, employees must realise that providing outstanding service to the internal customers also enables the organisation to provide outstanding service to external customer.

Process: The customer-supplier chain given in Fig. 3.3 shows that any work can be seen as a customer-supplier chain in which customers receive inputs from their suppliers, value to those inputs and then pass those outputs on to their own customers.

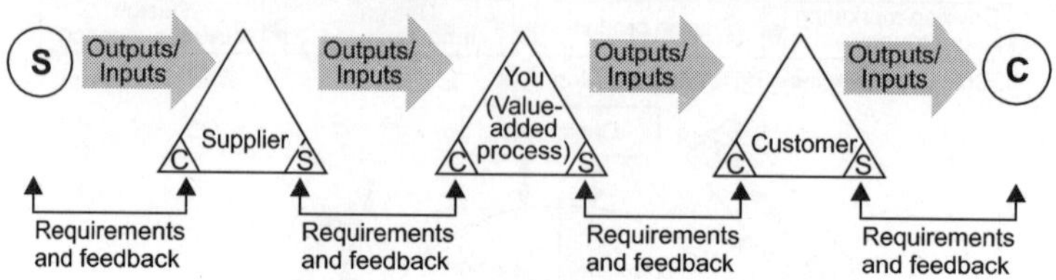

Fig. 3.3: Customer-Supplier Chain

Therefore, everyone in an organisation must understand that:

- One becomes a customer when one gets materials, information or services from others inside the organisation or from outside.
- One becomes a supplier when one supplies materials, information or services to others inside the organisation or to external customers.
- As a customer, things received from others are inputs.
- As a supplier, things that are supplied are outputs.
- Customers and suppliers exchange information about their requirements and provide one another with feedback on how to meet the stipulated requirements.

Benefits:

- Building positive relationship between customer and supplier which ultimately leads to doing right things right which is the key of adding value to the inputs.
- Workflow becomes smoother.

Teamwork

Teams are groups of two or more people, who interact and influence each other, and are mutually accountable for achieving common objectives and perceive themselves as a social entity within an organisation (Cohen and Bailey, 1997).

Purpose: To provide expression to employee empowerment and involvement.

Process: There are several elements to consider while designing teams, but the main elements are organisation and team environment that influence team design, processes and outcomes.

Benefit: Teamwork helps to develop a quality strategy or to achieve solutions to a problem that is vital to the company.

Chapter Overview

This chapter gives an overview about the improvement process and its importance for TQM. There are two approaches to improvement, i.e. continuous and breakthrough. There are various tools and techniques of TQM which can be used for problem solving at individual level and decision making at group level. Different TQM methods are also discussed along with their purpose, process and benefit.

Discussion Questions

1. Explain the improvement process and the approaches.
2. Discuss various problem solving tools and techniques with illustration.
3. Describe about different TQM methods indicating how they work and what is the purpose.
4. Discuss the importance of the concept of customer in TQM.

Total Quality Management in Education

4

Chapter Outline

- Quality in Education
- Approaches to TQM in Education
- Concept of TQM in Education
- Customers of Education Institutions
- Models/Plans/Roadmaps for TQM Implementation
- TQM Implementation in Education and its Outcome
- Barriers to TQM in Education
- Critical Success Factors (CSDs) for TQM in Education
- Chapter Overview
- Discussion Questions

Chapter Objectives

After completion of this chapter, the reader will be able to:

- Analyse quality in education
- Outline the reasons for TQM in education
- Describe the concept of TQM in education
- Explain approaches to TQM in education
- Identify customers of education institution
- Outline different TQM implementation models
- Discuss the barriers and Critical Success Factors (CSFs) to TQM implementation in education

Quality in Education

Education involves processes and outcomes that are defined qualitatively in the Jomtien Declaration in 1990. The Dakar Framework for Action 2000 recognised the quality of education through the factor as to whether Education for All is achieved or not. More specifically the second of the six goals set out in the Dakar Framework commits nations to the provision of primary education 'of good quality'. Moreover, the sixth goal includes commitments to improve all aspects of education quality so that everyone can achieve better learning outcomes 'especially in literary, numeracy and essential life skills'. UNICEF strongly emphasises what might be called desirable dimensions of quality, as identified in the Dakar Framework. Its paper "Defining Quality in Education" recognises five dimensions of quality: learners, environments, content, processes and outcomes, founded on the rights of the child, his survival, protection, development and participation (UNICEF, 2000).

While discussing about the quality of education it is useful to know about different approaches to quality. The educational outcomes and the processes leading to them have deep roots and are reflections on educational thought.

A. Humanist Approach to Quality

- Standardised, prescribed, externally defined or controlled curricula are rejected. They are seen as undermining the possibilities for learners to construct their own meanings and for educational programmes to remain responsive to individual learner's circumstances and needs.
- The role of assessment is to give learners information and feedback about the quality of their individual learning. It is integral to the learning process. Self-assessment and peer assessment are welcomed as ways of developing deeper awareness of learners.
- The teacher's role is more that of a facilitator than an instructor.
- Social constructivision, while accepting these tenets, emphasizes learning as a process of social practice rather than the result of individual intervention.

B. Behavioural Approach to Quality

- Standardised, extremely defined and controlled curricula, based on prescribed objectives and defined independently of the learner are endorsed.
- Assessment is seen as an objective measurement of learned behaviour against preset assessment criteria.
- Tests and examinations are considered central features of learning and the main means of planned and delivering rewards and punishments.
- The teacher directs learning, as the expert who controls stimuli and responses.
- Incremental learning tasks that reinforce desired associations in the mind of the learner are favoured.

C. Critical Approach to Quality

- Critical theorists focus on inequality in access to and therefore on unequal outcomes of education and an educator's role in legitimising and reproducing social structures through transmission of a certain type of knowledge that serves certain social groups.
- Equate good quality in the education that prompts social change.
- A curriculum and teaching methods that encourage critical analysis of social power relations and of ways in which formal knowledge is produced and transmitted.
- Active participation by learners in the design of their own learning experience.

Given the diversity of understanding and interpretation of quality evident in the different approaches discussed above, we might characterise the central dimensions influencing the course of process of teaching and learning as follows:

- learners' characteristics and dimensions
- contextual dimension
- enabling inputs dimension
- teaching and learning dimension
- outcomes dimension

Figure 4.1 shows the above-mentioned dimensions and their relationships.

Two principles characterise most attempts to define quality in education: the first identifies learner's cognitive development as the major explicit objective of all education systems. Accordingly, the success with which systems achieve this is one indicator, of their quality. The second emphasises education role in promoting values and attitudes of responsible citizenship and in nurturing creative and emotional development (EFA Report, 2005).

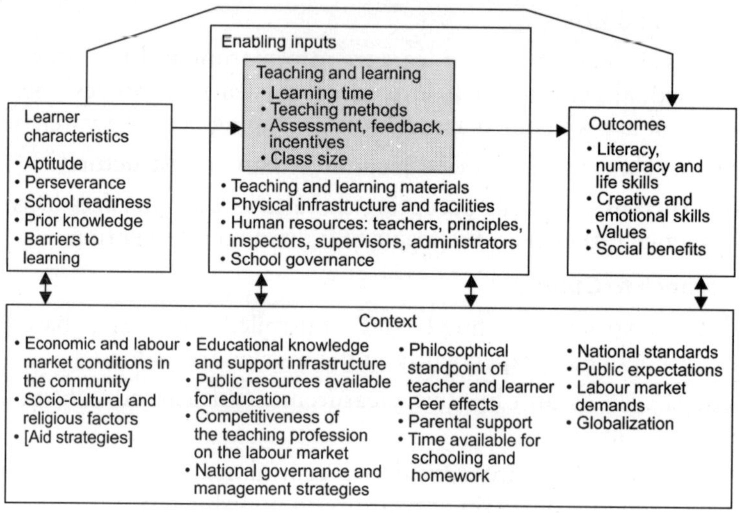

Fig. 4.1: Framework for Understanding Education Quality

Source: EFA Global Monitoring Report (2005)

Defining quality in education is never found an easy task. Mukhopadhyay (2005) has viewed quality education as goal-oriented and with reference to following goals:

- Excellence in education;
- Value added in education;
- Fitness of educational outcome;
- Conformance of education output to planned goals specifications and requirements;
- Defect avoidance in education process; and
- Meeting or exceeding customer's expectations of education.

Liston (1999) has identified the principles for quality in education as commitment to:

- continuous improvement in teaching, research and community interactions;
- continuous improvement in staff and student relationships;
- staff development and resource management to ensure continuous improvement; and
- evaluation and review of all activities to seek continuous improvement.

Barrow (1991) has emerged with a 'suggestive' definition of 'quality' in higher education as: a high evaluation accorded to an educative process where it has been demonstrated that, through the process, the students educational development has been enhanced; not only have they achieved the particular objectives set for the course but also, in doing so, they have fulfilled the educational aims of autonomy, of the ability to participate in reasoned discourse, of critical self evaluation and of coming to a proper awareness of the ultimate contingency of all thought and action.

De Jager and Nieuwenhuis (2005) point out that according to Harvey (1995), quality as fitness for purpose is defined as quality in terms of fulfilling a customers' requirements, needs or desires. Theoretically, the customer specifies requirements. In education, fitness for purpose is usually based on the ability of an institution to fulfil its mission or programme of study to fulfil its purpose. Murgatroyd and Morgan (1993) explain quality in the educational context with a practical example, mentioning that lecturers are assigned specific duties and tasks at the beginning of each academic year. These assignments or duties represent a contract of work between the lecturer and the institution. Educational quality is therefore assessed by whether or not and how will the duties performed. Following these notions, De Jager and Nieuwenhuis (2005) define quality education as a process of continuous improvement by systematically and collectively evaluating and refining the system, practices and culture of education institutions in order to meet the needs of the customers.

Although the issue of quality seems to be common sense, as Dick Budd, a quality development manager in a service industry explains it's basic things we often forget of someone to have received a good quality service, it is important to thank the provider so they know they are getting it right (Biles, 1995). Hence, Garbutt (1996) identifies that schools need to: look at the way services are provided, identify the factors which the way a service is delivered, and offer feedback, advice and question staff as to how try see "quality" operating in their area. Such procedures help them to assess their quality.

The Quality in Higher Education Project, based in Birmingham found that there are widely different conceptualisations of quality in education (Harvey, 1994). However, these can be grouped into five discrete but interrelated ways of thinking about quality (Harvey and Knight, 1996).

(i) Quality in education can be viewed, first as "exceptional", with three notions in terms of "being distinctive, as exceeding very high standards and as passing a set of required standards", with each of these being subject to debate.

(ii) A second approach to quality of education, views in terms of "consistency", especially of the processes involved through specifications, to be achieved through a "zero defects approach and a quality culture". But the very basis poses limitations and may be questioned with regard to whether there is a consistent conformity to standards in education (Harvey and Knight, 1996), especially given the fact that such standards of conformance are achieved by the students.

(iii) A third approach to quality views quality, in relation to the "purpose of the produce/service" (Crawford, 1991), which again raises three issues—"fitting the customer specifications, mission, based on fitness for purpose and customer satisfaction", each being subject to debate.

(iv) The fourth approach to quality views it as "value for money through efficacy and effectiveness" (Schrock and Lefevre, 1988), clearly linked to accountability and with emphasis on performance indicators, but, here again, the very emphasis on performance indicators is debatable.

(v) The final approach, which views quality as, "transformative" in terms of qualitative change or form, to include cognitive transcendence, wherein education is believed to be an ongoing process of transformation that includes empowerment and enhancement of customer.

Green (1994) refers to quality as "an elusive" concept difficult to articulate. He has identified different concepts and approaches to quality in education as discussed below:

- Quality is "conformance to specification or standards". He points out that, while this approach gives all education institutions an opportunity to aspire quality, with different standards being set for different types of institutions, it sets no basis/criteria to be used to set standards. Further, with a heavy emphasis or measurable and quantifiable standards, this approach may not be amenable for education institution.
- Quality as "fitness for purpose" is one definition that is adopted in education. The fact is that different stakeholders may have different views as to what the purposes should be and education may have multiple purposes, some of which may be conflicting.
- Quality as "effectiveness in achieving institutional goals", implies efficiency in the use of resources or effective management and has significant implications for education.

Given the varied approaches, Green (1994) points out that it is not possible to deal with quality as a unitary concept, and the best that can be achieved is to define clearly the criteria that each stakeholder uses when judging quality and take into account the competing views when assessment of quality is undertaken.

Mortimore and Stone (1990) emphasised quality in education as "an attribute or defining essence; a degree of relative worth; a description of something good or excellent; and a non-quantified trait".

TQM in Education

Keeping in view the changing demands of various stakeholders, education institutions (EIs) world wide are emphasising on shifting the trend from quantitative expansion to qualitative output. From the earlier discussions, it is very much clear that high quality products/services are the success formula for achieving customer satisfaction. Once again customer satisfaction is the way to survival of any organisation (including EIs) in this turbulent and competitive environment. So, this can be viewed as a vicious circle starting at customer demand and ending at customer satisfaction following the path of quality. In Chapter 1, we have seen the quality movement, where it has finally reached the stage of TQM. Industries throughout the globe have utilised this concept and have shown remarkable success in business. Following this trend, leaders in education institutions have realised the need for a renewed concept of quality, i.e. shifting from QA to TQM. The reason for the shift may be due to varied reasons. Thakkar, Desmukh and Shastree (2006) have identified the reasons as:

- pressures from industry for continuous upgrading of academic standards with changing technology;
- government schemes with allocation of fund, which encourage research in the field of quality;
- increasing competition between various private and government academic institutions; and
- a reduction in the pool of funds for research and teaching, implying the only reputable institutions will have a likely chance of gaining access to various funds.

Lewis and Smith (1994) emphasised that the renewed focus on quality stems from several sources:

- over the past decade numerous books, reports, and commentaries have expressed an increasing dissatisfaction with the performance of education system;
- the world in which institutions of education operate is changing dramatically;
- increased market forces and competition in education;
- competition among colleges and universities will be encouraged by technological developments and the reality of long distance education; and
- projected conditions of the general economy strongly suggest or continuation of limited economic growth for the focusable future.

EIs have opted for TQM due to escalating number of students, lack of consistent leadership style, increasing need for accountability to the public and changing attitudes towards universities (Kwan, 1996). De Cosmo et al. (1991) have pointed out resource constraints and increasing pressures as the reasons.

Borahan and Ziarati (2002) have observed that there is a strong correlation between a country's competitiveness and quality of education provided within that country.

David (1991) has enlisted the reasons why EIs should adapt TQM? It can help:

- EIs to focus on the proper needs of their market
- EIs to achieves top quality performance in all areas
- Produce systems for achieving quality performance
- Examine and remove non-productive aspects
- To develop measures of achievement
- To remain competitive
- To develop team approaches
- To improve communication
- To reward outstanding achievement
- To enable a continual review process to operate

Smith (2004) has identified several source of quality being significant in EIs. They are dissatisfaction with the performance of EIs, increasing competition for student enrolments, the growth in distance and online learning and increased demands for public accountability.

Vazzana et al. (2000) observed that proponents of TQM can hardly be ignored in EIs due to reasons: problems in EIs require attention, teaching and learning need to be assessed and processes should be adopted to improve the quality of education, increase constituent involvement, empower faculty and focus on customer.

According to Tuttle (1994), a growing number of universities are embracing TQM for the same reasons that led industry and government to embrace it: "management systems are outmoded and can no longer ensure success in an increasingly competitive world".

Oblinger and Rush (1997) pointed out that rising costs, reductions in funding and fluctuating enrolments combined with public demands for higher quality are raising a number of questions on university campuses:

- how can administration be made more effective and responsive while avoiding or reversing staff expansion?
- how can the efficiency and quality of instruction be improved?
- how can we appeal to a new generation of students?
- how can we be more student (customer) oriented?
- how can we be more responsive to the changing needs of those who employ our graduates?

To address these issues and improve performance, a number of universities have started TQM initiatives.

Bresler (1993) explained that "TQM's practical process based approach is attractive to many education administrators who find themselves increasingly challenged to offer a higher quality 'product' at a more affordable price".

Kanji and Tambi (1999) after making a survey of the practice of TQM in UK, EIs have identified 32 causal factors for quality management. They have identified one unique causal for college, i.e. resolve current problems and overcome weaknesses. The unique causal factors for universities are image building, increasing market share, encourage teamwork, etc.

Realising the growing importance of TQM, EIs throughout the globe have started implementing the same. Loads of literature is available on the implementation of TQM in EIs and related issues such as models of implementation, the customers of EIs, what exactly TQM means to EIs, factors responsible to make it a success, principle and approaches to TQM in EI, outcome of implementation and barriers. Some of them are reviewed discussed below to get an overview of the existing TQM scenario in education sector.

Approaches to TQM in Education

Shifting further from quality assurance in EIs towards TQM in EIs includes new approaches and concepts of quality. In the earlier paragraphs we have already discussed what exactly quality in EIs means, let us now move towards TQM in EIs.

According to Haris (1994), there are three generic approaches to TQM in EIs: a customer focussed approach, where the idea of service to students is fostered through staff training and development; a staff focussed approach concerned to value and enhance the contribution of all the members of staff to the effectiveness of school; and the third that takes a service agreement focus and seeks to ensure conformity to specification at certain key measurable points of the education process. Kanji and Tambi (1999) opine that the new approach for assessing the quality of EIs is based on the quality assurance method, hence its name the quality assurance framework. In quality management perspective, the quality assurance method has the weaknesses of relying or inspection and corrective action. This results in inefficiency because of tediousness and high cost. TQM, however, emphasises prevention and continuous improvement. Therefore, costs will be minimised and EIs will improve their effectiveness over time.

Sahney et al. (2002) have identified multifaceted approach to TQM in education. It believes in the foundation of an educational institution as a systems approach, implying management system, a technical system and a social system all based on principles of quality, to be implemented throughout. It aims at satisfying the needs of various stakeholders, through the design of a system based on certain principles and practices. It includes within it the quality of inputs from students, faculty, support staff and infrastructure; the quality of process in the form of learning and teaching activity; and the quality of outputs in the form of enlightened students that move out of the system.

Lewis and Smith (1994) have given the open systems approach of total quality improvement. It provides a means for developing an integrated quality assurance system for EI through three stages, viz.: inputs, transforming processes and outputs. Such determinations are made from knowledge of teaching and the learning process.

According to Miller (1991), many schools have raised concerns that have led to a questioning of outcomes, educational process and student assessment. These have made the schools to undertake a move to a skill-based or outcomes-based approach to education. These approaches provide measurable outcomes, which is an essential element for a TQM programme. Having measurable outcomes also implies an accountability to meet these outcomes and accountability is another element of TQM implementation.

Spanbauer (1995) provides us an approach that tells improvement of systems through process management as a key feature of TQM implementation. The goal is to improve systems and processes by creating an environment where faculty and staff examine customer needs and do their jobs in the most efficient manner possible. Garbutt (1996) has insisted that schools must adopt a TQM approach that continually looks to improve the effective use of resources, maximise the opportunities for pupil, develop their staff and fulfil the needs of the community. Mukherjee (1995) proposes the use of TQM in education through customer orientation, management commitment, continuous improvement and innovation.

Concept of TQM in Education

Dahlgard et al. (1995) define TQ education as, "...an educational culture characterised by increased customer satisfaction through continuous improvement in which all employers and students actively participate". By amalgamating ideas from TQM with a system's approach (Tanner and Dectro, 1992). Cheng (1996) defines education quality as, "...the character of the set of elements in the input, process and the output of the education system that provides services to completely satisfy both internal and external strategic contributors by meeting their expectations". Govinda and Varghese (1992) have conceptualised quality in education in a contextual manner, taking into account the external environment in which the teaching-learning process takes place and the home environment of the learners.

Holmes and McElwee (1995) recognise that TQM is concerned with promoting organisational effectiveness through the excellence, reliability and quality of an organisation's goods and services. It is associated with every aspect of organisations activities requiring the total commitment of every member. Its objectives are to create a quality culture and develop the principles of error free work. For EIs this is appropriate where getting it right first time may be in the support function but not in the teaching and learning function.

Chizmar (1994) defines TQM in education as the collaborative and holistic application of the ideas of industrial model to teaching and learning. It focuses attention on the management function that transforms teacher and student effort into learning. The power of TQM teaching/learning model lies in its ability to suggest hypothesis concerning teaching strategies that enhance learning and its emphasis on the quality of product, orientation to students, advocacy of teamwork and a continuing desire to improve.

According to Vazzana (1997), TQM in education is an integrated approach, with the students overall professional development based on outcomes tied to marketable skills and work performance, which guides the learning process and connects graduates to employers.

TQM is an all-inclusive quality management strategy that involves support staff as well as academic staff; it focuses on all organisation activities, including teaching, research, managing, catering and housekeeping; as the name implies, it is a total approach that encourages concentration on the core activity of universities while endeavouring towards embedded quality within a culture (Lomas, 2004).

Customers of Education Institutions

TQM is customer focussed and revolves around the concept of customer satisfaction (Walsh et al., 2002). Then automatically a question arises, who are the customers of EIs and who should measure the quality of outputs? Several researchers have tried to answer this question and some of them are discussed here. Zairi (1995) suitably answers these questions: students who are the recipients of the service (acquiring knowledge/information) are the ones who should measure the quality of the output, similarly to the industrial context, the customer is the ultimate judge of quality.

Moreover, EIs are increasingly recognising that Higher Education (HE) is a service industry and are placing greater emphasis on meeting the expectations and needs of their customers, i.e. the students (De Shields et al., 2005). Wiers-Jenssen et al. (2002) state that student satisfaction approaches may be a tool for building a bridge between more traditional and academic views on how to improve HE.

According to Sirvanci (2004), in some EI TQM models students are treated as customers, their role as customers is a debatable issue. There is an analogy between EIs and production plants. Once admitted students move through the various courses required for a degree as raw material flows through the successive stages of the manufacturing process. As the finished product carries the brand name and label of the manufacturer, graduating students are issued with diplomas certifying that all the requirements for their degree have been completed.

Graduates may be interpreted as the finished product and the employers as the customers of EIs.

Table 4.1: Production Analogy for EIs

Higher Education	Production
Schools	Suppliers
Admitted graduates	Raw material
Student	Product in process
Courses	Process stages
Graduate	Finished product
Employers	Customers
No. of graduates employed	Sales
Starting salary	Price

Source: Sirvanci (2004)

The measurement of quality in service sector is based on customer's perceptions of the service and is highly multi-dimensional (Lovelock, 1983). The customer is usually involved in the delivery of service and his/her perceptions of quality depend on contentment and satisfaction with regard to the result of the service and the service process itself. However, the very definition of the "customer" is debatable, given the large number of complementary and contradictory customers that the educational system has. In education, the criteria for quality and therefore the customer requirements involve a much greater number of interested parties—students, staff, faculty, industry, parents and the society (Sahney et al., 2000).

Downey et al. (1994) remark that the primary customer in an education system is the student: who is both an internal and an external customer. While in the system, the student is an internal customer, participating in the learning process; he/she becomes an external customer when he or she leaves the system. He/she then, becomes the ultimate external customer, functioning effectively in the society. The external customer includes EIs, business, industry and society.

Madu et al. (1994) refer parents and students as input customers, the faculty as the transformation customer and the corporations and society as the output customers. Spanbauer (1995) remarks that customers are of two types—external (students, employers, the community at large, tax payers, other educators from different institutions) and internal (other instructors, service department staff).

Kanji et al. (1999) classify the customers of EI into primary internal customer (both teacher and student) and secondary external customers (student, industry and parents).

According to Sallis (1993), learner is the primary external customer; parents and employers are secondary external customers; the labour/job market, government and society are the tertiary external customers.

Some researchers have been sceptical about the students being referred to as prime customers of education (Marchese, 1991; Rhodes, 1992). Ewell (1993) views the students as customers, only when they are recipients of services and not when they are recipients of education. Pitman et al. (1995) refer to students both as customers and product (cited in Sahaney et al., 2004).

In education, unlike most businesses product and primary customer are essentially the same. Students are with the products of efforts and the primary customers or users of efforts (Macy et al., 1998).

Most of the contemporary researchers and writers in the field of quality in education assign the role of external customers to students, employers and the society as a whole. Any person next in line within the organisation in reference who adds value to the educational service, i.e. teaching and support staff is assigned the role of internal customer (Siegel and Byrne, 1994; Sallis, 1993 cited in Varnavas and Soteriou, 2002).

Sahney et al. (2004) had conducted an empirical study on select EIs of India to assess the importance assigned to various customer groups and they found that "delighting customers" is one of the core elements of TQM, which emphasises the service relationship between an institution and its customers.

Table 4.2 shows how Lewis and Smith (1994) have summarised the customers of EIs.

Table 4.2: The Customers of Higher Education

Customers	Needs
Internal customers—academic students	Knowledge, skills, and abilities to pursue personal and professional goals; joy in learning
Faculty	Continuous personal growth, security, joy in work, information and input
Programmes/departments	Continuous improvement, information exchange (input/output), cooperation, and collaboration
Internal customers—administrative students	Service provided when requested, question answered when asked
Employees	Continuous personal growth, security, joy in work, information and input
Units/departments, divisions	Continuous improvement, information exchange (input/output), cooperation, and collaboration
External customers—direct employers	Competent employees, productive performance
other colleges, universities	Students capable of advanced learning and research
External customers—indirect	Be elected or re-appointed, compliance, make a contribution
legislature (state, federal)	Competent workforce, leaders and followers, volunteers in community services, politically active citizens
Community	Compliance with established criteria and standards
Accrediting agencies	Pride in having attended, continuing education
Alumni	Awareness of both the quality and needs of the college/university, appropriate acknowledgement of a donation
Donors	

Source: Lewis and Smith (1994)

Models/Plans/Roadmaps for TQM Implementation

Policymakers and authors have identified alternate plans to implement TQM in educational institutions. Some of them are discussed here.

Sekthivel et al. (2005) have developed a model, "5-C TQM Model of Academic Excellence". This model establishes a link between five TQM variables: commitment of top management, course delivery, campus facilities, courtesy and customer feedback and improvement and students' satisfaction of academic performance.

Chizmar (1994)'s "TQM Teaching/Learning" model highlights teaching and learning strategies that involve students actively in their own learning through the creation of learning communities and increased use of collaboration. This model features continuous improvement, discerning feedback, empowering teachers, empowered students and ubiquitous teamwork.

Macy et al. (1998) have developed a "Continuous Process Improvement (CPI) Model" which is used to apply TQM principles to educational process. The components of the model are: outcomes and criteria, curricular and co-curricular instruction, student performance, assessment and feedback.

Spanbauer (1995) has identified seven key elements: customer service, leadership education and training, organisational climate, scientific methods and tools, meaningful data and team problem solving. If these key elements are taken care efficiently application of TQM in EIs becomes easier.

Scrabec Jr. (2000) presents a "Total Quality Education (TQE) Model" based on who benefits and on quality education attributes. It also embodies the principal criterion of being beneficiary driven but recipient focussed. This model shows recipient or student satisfaction as a result of TQE approach, but not the main feedback to improve the system. A student is both a recipient and a beneficiary. Further, the model uses internal auditing to improve the education process continuously.

Vazzana et al. (1997) have developed a "TQM—Assessment Model" for continuous process improvement at Missouri University. This model comprises eleven components: the vision, focus on quality, customer-driven approach, teamwork, making processes work better, training and self-improvement, extending the mindset, discipline of information, eliminate rework, empowering people and leadership.

De Jager and Nieuwenhuis (2005) have used the "outcomes based-education (OBE)" approach to implement TQM in EIs. The OBE approach is learner-centred and result-oriented. It is characterised by active learners, assessment on an ongoing basis, integration of knowledge, innovative and creative lecture, flexible timeframes, critical thinking, reasoning and action. The key principles of OBE in relation to TQM are customer (learner) services, optimise learners abilities, education and training, framework and outcomes, market needs, clearly defined standards and group work (quality problem-solving).

Leeds Metropolitan University uses "EQSEL (Excellence through Quality, Service, Empowerment and Leadership) Model" to implement TQM. The model comprises three phases, i.e. aims (mission), actions (quality, people and processes) and achievements (customers, Employees and shareholders) (Hazel, 1993).

Crawford (1990) has recommended eight steps for implementing TQM in EIs. Frazier (1997) has suggested a six-step roadmap: prepare, assess, plan, deploy, sustain and breakthrough. Navaratnam (1997) has offered a six-stage quality journey.

Mukhopadhyay (2005) has proposed a seven step strategic plan: (i) belief, vision, mission, goals; (ii) learner's need assessment and client education; (iii) institutional assessment and SWOT analysis; (iv) quality policy and intervention plan; (v) cost of quality; (vi) planning for implementation; and (vii) evaluation and feedback. He has also developed a "spiralling" model for TQM implementation process. As TQM is a continuous search for new breakthrough, this model accommodates the spirit of continuity.

Crumrine and Runnels (1991) offer a model for implementing TQM in vocational-technical school or similar institutions. It has five phases: commitment, organisation development, customer focus, process orientation and continuous improvement. Kanji and Tambi (1999) have reported about several TQM models which exist in EIs in many parts of the world. The models include those developed at Auburn University (Burkhalter, 1996), Aston university (Clayton, 1995) the "LEARN" model, Samford University (Baugher, 1991) "FVTC" (Spanbauer, 1989), "HETQMEX", Leicester Business school (Ho and Wearn, 1996) and the "Business Excellence Model" (Kanji, 1998).

The Oregon State University (OSU) TQM model is also a landmark in this regard. It is a seven step model consisting of: (i) TQM goal setting; (ii) assessment; (iii) strategy management and concept development; (iv) process management development; (v) project management development; (vi) task management implementation; and (vii) evaluation (Lewis and Smith, 1994).

Now, the obvious question that arises is whether the models are contextual or transferable to certain extent? Although some authors have acknowledged the application as situation, yet most of them have advocated that TQM can be applied uniformly to all organisations (Juran, 1986, cited in Skikin, 1994).

TQM Implementation in Education and its Outcome

Initial efforts made to pass from the traditional management in educational institutions to a management based on total quality are indicative of the new orientation. Many adopted the TQM principles in education (Barnalee, 1995; Murgatroyd and Morgan, 1993; Schmoker and Wilson, 1993; Weller and Hartley, 1994; Crawford and Shuttler, 1999; Sallis, 1996). However, the main problems with the implementation of TQM are that on the one hand that TQM's efficiency in education are yet to be proven and on the other, many educators express their strong reservation towards its implementation (Konidari and Abernot, 2006).

In response to growing concerns from stakeholders about poor or inconsistent quality, EIs are increasingly seeking ways to improve education quality. Many universities and colleges have looked to apply lessons from industry and adopt some type of TQM system (Hubbard, 1994; Vazzana et al., 1997). For instance, Northwest Missouri State University experienced significant improvements in student enrolment and academic performance, faculty recruitment and retention and budgetary matters as a result of implementing TQM programme (Hubbard, 1994, cited in Lawrence and McCollough, 2001).

The quest for quality is apparent in most educational reforms undertaken in different countries throughout the world. A number of successful stories about incorporating TQM principles in education setting have been reported (Dobyns and Crawford-Masori, 1991; Coate, 1994, cited in Varnavas and Sateriou, 2002). For example, one of the most publicised TQM success stories is that of Oregon State University (OSU) (Coate, 1990), where TQM was successfully applied to a number of different processes within OSU.

Macy et al. (1998) have conducted a study on implementation of TQM approach at Central Missouri State University (Central) of TQM. They have observed that focused on educational outcomes and the assessment processes TQM at Central has led not just to an extensive re-examination of the faculty's approach to Education but also to many significant changes in practices. The faculty at Central believes the improvement from the TQM model over the traditional model has been worth the investment.

Lozier and Teeter (1996) from a survey of post-secondary institutes in the USA found that 11 per cent of universities had active TQM groups or had applied TQM, whereas a further 60 per cent had "limited activity" with TQM initiatives. They noted that successful TQM tended to be confined to the administrative sector of the universities rather than the teaching sector. In the survey of EIs in the UK, Kanji and Tambi (1999) have reported that only four institutions implemented TQM. A postal survey by Owlia and Aspinwall (1996) was carried out and a majority (94 per cent) believed that quality measurement was very important to TQM.

A number of authors have documented case studies on TQM in EIs. For example, Billing (1996) documents the strive for quality at the University of Westminister, Clayton (1995) for Aston University, Morris and Haigh (1996) at the University of Texas (cited in Hills and Stewart-David, 2001).

Brigham (1993) has reported that although often overlooked, medical and dental schools were early adopters of TQM. One study of 32 EIs found that administrators and stakeholders believed that their TQM programmes were making a great contribution to organisations effectiveness and that the benefits were greater from the costs (Elmuti et al., 1996).

Montano and Utter (1999) observed that "while implementing TQM and quality improvement endeavors at educational institutions can be difficult, the results can be extremely beneficial for all involved". Aly and Akpovi (2001) study reveals that more than half of the California Public Universities are implementing TQM in one form or the other. Universities which have implemented TQM almost unanimously reported some improvement as a result of this implementation.

According to Wiklund et al. (2003), during the last years, the debate has covered themes, or parts of TQM such as continuous quality improvement (e.g. McGettrick et al., 1997; Peterson et al., 1997), TQM in class room (e.g. Hansen and Jackson, 1996; Wiklund and Sandvik Wiklund, 1999a, b; Wiklund, 2000; Wiklund, 2001), the university as a learning organisation to facilitate TQM (e.g. Meade, 1995; Cleary, 1999) and external quality reviewers (e.g. Harvey, 2002). Parts of TQM and quality assurance system based on TQM have also been tried out in EIs in recent years, e.g. the UK, Australia and the USA (Williams, 1993; Cowles and Gilbreath, 1992; Landquist, 1997).

Mukhopadhyay (2005) finds the applicability of TQM in education from many authors such as De Cosmo et al. (1991), Sherr and Lozier (1991), Bonser (1992) and Kwan (1996). He also claims that several experiments on TQM in EI have substantiated Deming's claim regarding the relevance and applicability of TQM in education.

Cole (1995) concluded that the application of TQM has resulted in improvement process in optimizing job definition and improving recruitment technologies, creating better alignment between faculty needs and expectations. Yodof and Busch Vishniac (1996) have found three significant potentialities that TQM can offer to education: (a) TQM offers a justification and a technique for continuous search for quality and excellence; (b) it develops willingness and hence a culture for change related to that, organisations learn to be more flexible and responsive; and (c) TQM makes qualitative shifts in decision making.

Barriers to TQM in Education

Hills and Stewart-David (2001) have reviewed plethora of papers on TQM in EIs and they have concluded that there appear to be general reasons for the lack of case studies in EIs first due to barriers in implementation (e.g. Bergman, 1995; Kells, 1995; Billing, 1996; Lozier and

Teeter, 1996) and second due to the complexities of educational setting (Westgaard, 1991), especially the identification of "customer" and stakeholders (Spanbauer, 1995; Kanji and Tambi, 1999).

According to several researchers (Coate, 1990; Axland, 1991; Entin, 1993; Schargel, 1993; Stern and Tseng, 1993; Chappel, 1994), the main reason why TQM has not been successfully implemented is due to lack of commitment of upper management of an organisation (Motwani et al., 1996).

Authors like Mathews (1993) and Bass et al. (1996) have reported that TQM efforts in academia have been limited to administrative and support functions and its extension to teaching processes have to be a major challenge.

According to Hubbard (1994), faculty have had a difficult time understanding exactly how TQM principles should be applied in the classroom and are genuinely concerned about a loss of rigor in the class room (Franz, 1998).

Coate (1992) has reported that Oregano State University is committed to TQM but its deployment "was more challenging than many of us realized at first" and described seven barriers for this: (i) skepticism (ii) time (iii) language (iv) middle management (v) university governance (vi) dysfunctional units and (vii) attitude.

Freeston (1992) has found few attitudinal barriers (Table 4.3) while implementing Newton model of TQM.

Table 4.3: Attitudinal Barriers to Quality

The Word Quality itself	Soon by many as a platitude unobtainable and overused by advertisers
The Corporate World as the Model	Skepticism about corporate example, rejection of customer orientation
Leadership	Low confidence in leader commitment, scant examples of quality-oriented leaders
Just Another Change	Regarded as another trend that will pass
One Year at a Time	Quality is a long-range commitment and schools plan on a one year basis
I Know that Already	Base perception that there is nothing new in a quality orientation
Students Don't Value School	If only the students work harder we wouldn't need to improve schools
N's Not My Fault	Changed social context of families presents insurmountable barriers to successful schools
A Question of Culture	Belief that quality management is only achievable in Japan's culture
Teacher as Self-Employed Entrepreneur	Teaching is an independent, isolated profession without the collaboration needed for a quality approach

Critical Success Factors (CSFs) for TQM in Education

Although Kanji (1998) has never used the term CSFs, he emphasized that the HE system has to be guided through the TQM principles and core concepts by top management leadership in order to achieve business excellence. He has identified four principles: delight the customer; management by fact; people-based management; and continuous improvement. Each principle is divided into two core concepts: (a) delight the customer-customer satisfaction and internal customers are real; (b) management by fact—all work is process and measurement; (c) people-based management—teamwork and people make quality; (d) continuous improvement—continuous improvement cycle and prevention. Leadership serves as prime.

Kanji and Tambi (1999) have made a survey on TQM in the UK EIs and in that they have identified nine CSFs that influence TQM (Table 4.4).

Table 4.4: Ranking of CSFs at Planning Stage and during Implementation of TQM

CSFs	Rank
Leadership	2
Continuous improvement	1
Prevention	9
Measurement of resources	8
Process improvement	6
Internal customer satisfaction	7
External customer satisfaction	3
People management	4
Team work	5

Source: Kanji and Tambi (1999)

Coate (1990) suggests six key recommendations for the successful implementation of TQM in education: (i) support from the top (ii) just do it! (iii) teams are everything! (iv) you need a champion (v) breakthrough (Hostin) planning helps vi) try the service or administrative side first.

According to Marchese (1991), "taken piecemeal, TQM does not have a chance in being successful, but if used correctly, it can help achieve efficiencies, raise morale, slow good stewardship of funds and in public trust". He has pointed out the CSFs of TQM as: customer focus; continuous improvement; management by fact; benchmarking; people; and organizational structures.

Garbutt (1996) has pointed out that TQM is about efficiency, productivity, long-term success and adopting an attitude that all individuals can contribute to the pursuit of continuous improvement. Whatever the institution, achieving total quality is an attitude of mind. It is about encouraging people to educate and develop themselves to work in teams. Everyone needs to believe in quality and contribute towards it by constantly improving his/her standards.

Waller and Ahire (1996) have identified 'management commitment' is the most important factor affecting TQM implementation in education.

Chaffe and Tierney (1988) identified nine areas of sensitivity that provide a broad context within which to consider application of TQM:

(i) find internal contradictions;
(ii) develop comparative awareness;
(iii) clarify the identity of the institution;
(iv) communicate;
(v) act on multiple, changing forms;
(vi) treat every problem as if it has multiple solutions;
(vii) treat every solution as a fleeting solution;

(viii) look for consequences in unlikely places; and

(ix) be aware of any solution that levels people or undermines strong values.

Chapter Overview

I. Reasons for Implementing TQM in Education

- Increased market force and competition
- Need for accountability
- Demand for quality performance
- To improve review process
- Growth in distance learning
- Focus on stakeholders
- Reduction in funding
- Fluctuating enrolment
- Image building

II. Concept of TQM in Education

- Increased customer satisfaction
- Total commitment of employee
- Employee empowerment
- Continuous improvement
- Teamwork
- Defect prevention
- Feedback
- Leadership
- Data analysis and problem sharing
- Learner centered
- Result-oriented

III. Approaches to TQM in Education

- Customer focused approach
- Employee focused approach
- Prevention and continuous improvement
- Open systems approach
- Outcomes based approach

IV. Customers of Education

- Student
- Employees (faculty and staff)
- Parents
- Society
- Industry/business house/employer

V. Models/Roadmaps/Plans for TQM Implementation

- 5-C TQM Model of Academic Excellence
- Teaching/Learning Model
- Continuous Process Improvement Model
- Total Quality Education Model
- Assessment Model for Continuous Process Improvement Model
- EQSEL Model
- Crawford's Eight Step Model
- Fracies's six step roadmap
- Novaratman's six stage quality plan
- Mukhopadhyay's seven step strategic plan
- Oregon State University Model
- HETQMEX Model

VI. TQM Implementation and its Outcome

- Significant improvement in student enrolment and academic performance
- Massive changes in academic practices
- Enhanced contribution to organizational effectiveness
- Optimizing job requirement
- Better alignment between faculty needs and expectation
- Institutions become more flexible and responsive
- Qualitative shift in decision making
- Commitment towards continuous search for quality and excellence

VII. Barriers to TQM in Education

- Academic culture not receptive to TQM
- Complexities of educational sitting
- Identification of customers and stakeholders
- Skepticism about students being treated as customers
- Lack of commitment of top management
- Difficulty in understanding TQM and its applicability in education
- Attitudinal barriers

VIII. CSFs for TQM in Education

- Leadership
- Customer satisfaction
- Teamwork
- People management
- Communication
- Quality culture
- Employee empowerment

- Training
- Recognition
- Breakthrough planning
- Employee involvement
- Employee commitment

Discussion Questions

1. What are the different approaches to quality in education?
2. Identify the reasons for TQM in education. According to you, which one is the prime reason and why?
3. Who are the customers of EIs? Do you accept student as a customer? Justify your answer with valid reasons.
4. Enlist different models of TQM implementation which one is the best according to you and why?
5. Discuss various critical success factors of TQM implementation in education.

Quality Scenario in Distance Education

5

Chapter Outline

- Distance Education: Genesis and Growth
- Quality in DEIs: An Overview
- Chapter Overview
- Discussion Questions
- Appendix-1: Growth of DE: International Scenario

Chapter Objectives

After completion of this chapter, the reader will be able to:

- Discuss the growth and genesis of distance education world wide
- Outline the quality culture in different distance education institutions
- Assess the need of TQM in distance education institutions

Distance Education: Genesis and Growth

What is Distance Education (DE)? It is not an easy task to define DE, because there is no single meaning of this term. Along with its growth, it is known by a variety of names, viz. correspondence education, home study, external study, off-campus study, open-learning, flexible learning, resource based learning, distributed learning, etc. (Reddy, 1987; Lockwood, 1998; Inglis et al., 1999; Lockwood and Gooley, 2000). DE has been defined by several researchers and the most widely accepted ones are as follows:

- "The family of instructional methods in which teaching behaviours are performed apart from learning behaviours including those that in a contiguous situation would be performed in the learner's presence, so that communication between the teacher and learner must be facilitated by print, electronic, mechanical or other devices."—Moore (1973)
- "A method of imparting knowledge, skills and attitudes which is rationalised by the application of division of labour and organisational principles as well as by the extensive use of technical media, specially for the purpose of reproducing high quality teaching material which makes it possible to instruct great number of students at the same time wherever they live. It is an industrialised form of teaching and learning."—Peters (1973)

- "The various forms of study at all levels which are not under continuous, immediate supervision of tutors present with their students in lecture rooms on the same premises, but which nevertheless, benefit from planning, guidance and tuition of a tutorial organisation."— Holmberg (1981)

Keegan (1986) has identified the following typical characteristics of DE:

- Quasi-permanent separation of teacher and learner throughout the length of learning process, which distinguishes it from conventional face-to-face education.
- Influence of an educational organisation both in planning and preparation of learning materials and learner support services.
- Use of technical media to unite teachers and learners and carry the context of the course.
- Provision of two-way communication to initiate and get engaged in dialogue.
- Quasi-permanent absence of learning groups through art the length of the learning processes.

DE in the global scenario began at the school level. The first three Open Learning Institutes were set up in Australia, Canada and New Zealand in 1916, 1919 and 1922 respectively (Mukhopadhyay and Philips, 1994). In the form of higher education, University of South Africa (UNISA) is generally considered to be the oldest and first ever dedicated DE University set up in 1946. With the establishment of British Open University in 1969, it is believed that a landmark in the field of DE has been made. The Appendix 1 gives an overview of growth of DE throughout the globe.

DE has passed through five generations based on the mode of delivery (Taylor, 1995; 1999; and 2001) (Table 5.1).

Table 5.1: Generations/Models of DE and Related Delivery Technologies

Generation/Model	Delivery Technologies
First Generation/The Correspondence Model	• Print
Second General/Multi-media Model	• Print • Audio Tape • Video Tape • Computer based learning • Interactive Video disk
Third Generation/The Tele-learning Model	• Audio teleconferencing • Video conferencing • Audio graphic communication • Broadcast TV/Radio and audio teleconferencing
Fourth Generation/The Flexible Learning Model	• Interactive multi-media • Internet • Computer mediated communication
Fifth Generation/The Intelligent Flexible Learning Model	• Interactive multimedia • Internet • Computer automated response • Metadata • Learning objects

There are mainly three types of DE Institutions (DEIs) world wide: Dedicated Open Universities (e.g. IGNOU, Athabasca, UKOU, etc.), Dual Mode Universities (e.g. University of Nairobi, University of Delhi, University of Zambia, etc.) and Mixed Mode Institutions (e.g. Deakin University, Murdoch University, etc.).

DE is gaining momentum significantly throughout the globe. A good number of conventional universities seem to invest in technology to move with the pace in this regard. But the most notable challenge for the DEIs is either perform or perish. The phenomenal growth of ICT urges DEIs to give the best possible output (e.g. quality of course material, learner support service, conforming to the demands of graduates in the market, innovative and upmarket programmes, etc.). Further all these are measured in terms of quality because of the growing number of service providers in the market. DEIs are already in terms with this scenario and are adopting mechanisms to provide quality output. So far the major landmark studies available in this field are conducted by Deshpande and Mugridge (1994), Jung (2004; 2005); Tait (1997) and Koul and Kanwar (2006). The overall picture of quality management and the quality culture as evident through these studies are presented below. The Part B of the book carries eight case studies in detail in this regard. Besides, the following section gives an overview of the quality culture in 14 other DEIs world wide derived from secondary sources.

Quality in DEIs: An Overview

Norway

Quality assessment (QA) and assurance are matters of continuous concern for distance educators in Norway. Under the law of 1948, government takes care of the quality control of DEIs by way of accreditation and financial support. In order to deliver quality products and satisfy customers. Norwegian Association for Distance Education (NADE) has developed guidelines for QA with DE. The quality activities are divided into four main categories: information and counselling; course development; course delivery; and organisation. Each of the main categories is again divided into four phases: conditions and constraints; implementation; results; and follow up (Bo, 1997).

Israel

The Open University of Israel has a small internal faculty, who quite efficiently manage the QA activities. The QA activities range from course development to monitoring the learning, tutoring and teaching process (Guri-Rosenblit, 1997).

Japan

Establishment of a new DEI or programme is regulated by university establishment standards and related regulations. A new higher education QA system in Japan evaluates the institutes at the time of establishment and reaccredit them every seven years thereafter. Standards for establishing a distance teaching university specify methods of delivery, calculation of unit credit, requirements for graduation, inclusion of a variety of interaction mechanisms in case of e-learning and student-teacher ratio (Jung, 2004).

Korea

In principle, the establishment of a distance teaching university is required by the Higher Education law to be approved by Ministry of Education. The establishment of e-learning institutions (virtual universities) is required by the Lifelong Education Law, 1999 to be approved by the Ministry. However, Korea National Open University (KNOU) has been the only DE University without having external QA and evaluations and reviews. KNOU's competitive power in providing high quality education entirely depends on an internal QA mechanism (Jung, 2001).

Botswana

The Revised National Policy on Education (RNPE) is the reference point for major educational advancements in Botswana. The Botswana College of Distance and Open Learning (BOCODOL) instituted by an Act of Parliament in 1998 and guided by RNPE has the underlying central theme, i.e. "quality education". QA policy (QAP) of the college was developed by a committee appointed by the College Director. The QAP was implemented in a phased manner like: sensitise action meetings, documentation and development of instruments. Although the QA initiative proved to be quite phenomenal, some challenges were also to be dealt with (Tau, 2006).

Uganda

Kyambogo University's (KYU) notion of QA as a whole is still in its infancy and is yet to adopt a QA system across the board. The Department of Distance Education (DDE) in KYU defines quality as providing the best materials and supporting those studying the materials with the best support system which can be manageable. DDE's mechanisms for maintaining quality involve the monitoring and review of materials and systems. To do this they use participatory teamwork approach. DDE's quality control and assurance activity by considering the four aspects of quality that Norman (1984) identified: products (courses and materials, number of graduates, examination pass rate and equivalent results in public examinations); processes (learning and teaching, application registration and examination, advising students, record keeping and coordinating groups of external writers); production and delivery systems (course production, print production, audio production, scheduling and progress chasing, warehousing and stock control, getting materials to students); and as a general philosophy or ethos (policy statements, attitudes of staff, management and training of staff, motto or slogan and/or images and messages). Central to quality improvement in KYU's DE programme is the training of its staff and the network of tutors and staff. One of the pleasing advantages from KYU has been the increasing recognition of its staff and programmes offered through DE (Binns and Otto, 2006).

Nigeria

QA at the National Teachers' Institute (NTI), Kaduma, Nigeria took more than two decades to evolve and are continuously being subjected to critical reviews and transformations in response to new technological developments and changes in the socio-economic and political environment in which the institute operates. There are two dimensions of QA at NTI: internal and external. Internal QA refers to those processes and practices that are designated and executed by the NTI in order to ensure that its products are of high quality and are comparable with those of the conventional universities in the country; while external QA refers to procedures carried out by accreditation bodies set up by the government, notably the National Commission for Colleges of Education (NCCE). The institute's internal QA mechanisms cover the operational areas: admission policies, course approval and review assessment regulations and mechanisms, monitoring and feedback processes, staff selection and development, and staff appraisal. QA procedures and practices have helped the institute in development of self-instructional modules of high quality, enhancing the efficiency and effectiveness of monitoring process, capacity building increased use of examiners and moderators, use of a decentralised programme management and delivery system. These modest achievements are not without problems such as inadequate funding and the need for more staff who are sufficiently grounded in the methods and techniques of ODL (Umar, 2006).

South-eastern Louisiana University (SLU)

SLU recognises the advantages of providing learning opportunities to students not restricted by time, place, or method of delivery. At the same time, the university recognises that new approaches to instruction must meet the same high quality standards that exist for traditional classroom-bound education and has institutionalised quality standards for the delivery and assessment of DE. The university has set standards for Curriculum and instruction; student learning assessment and evaluation; student services; technology; and planning, budgeting of policy development. The university has developed standardised form and fact sheets for assuring quality at every stage (www3.selu.edu).

African Virtual University (AVU)

AVU has adopted a mixed mode of delivery for all programmes in order to maximise stimulus, variation and enhance opportunities for teaching and learning. Different modes of delivery include: internet, intranet, CD-ROM, email, satellite TV broadcast and video and digital library. Hence, the biggest challenge is to ensure quality. The QA of AVU's academic programmes is based on specific indicators: need for programme; educational design including appropriate graduate capabilities; well designed programmes with clear learning objectives and outcome; equity in selection, transition and teaching support for students; appropriate delivery system; and management of programmes with respect to processes of student communication, input and feedback to ensure that the programme remains relevant for all stakeholders. AVU has set up quality indicators, processes and procedures involved in improving the quality of teaching and learning (Juma, 2003).

Virginia Polytechnic Institute and State University

To successfully address the needs of learners, Virginia Tech adopted an academically oriented holistic view to DE through establishment of its Institute for Distance and Distributed learning in January 1999. Virginia Tech's holistic approach to DE has matured over the past seven years to quality focussed six dimensional model: learning effectiveness, student satisfaction, faculty satisfaction, access, cost effectiveness and system effectiveness. The six dimensions intersect with stakeholders: students and faculty (primary stakeholders), instructional designers, technical support personnel, admission registration; library personnel; and institutional leaders who make decisions for DE. Consortia partners, funding agencies and governmental and accrediting agencies are other stakeholders. The holistic view of DE taken by Virginia Tech can be shown as a holistic thread that serves as a DNA like structure, providing building blocks for development, delivery and support of quality DE courses and programmes. Each DE course passes a common set of quality traits, while still being individually unique in its design. Similarly, programme managers connect organisational distance learning activities to the institutional plans based on common quality traits ensuring that their efforts are integrated into institutions strategic thinking (Wilkinson, 2006).

South Africa

South African Institute of Distance Education (SAIDE) revised the 1998 *Criteria for Quality Distance Education in South Africa* in the light of changes in the DE landscape both nationally and internationally, growth in understanding of DE through research and evaluation and the emerging quality emphasised in the Higher Education Quality Committee's (HEQC) criteria for programme accreditation and institutional audit. In accordance with that, National Association of Distance Education Organisations of South Africa (NADEOSA) conducted a workshop and developed a document representing a comprehensive set of criteria for quality DE agreed upon by the South African DE community. The criteria were developed under following parameters of DEIs: policy and planning; learners; programme development; course design; course materials; assessment; learner support; human resource strategy management and administration; collaborative relationships; quality assurance; information dissemination; and results (Welch, 2003).

Yashwantrao Chavan Maharashtra Open University (YCMOU), India

YCMOU has recently been awarded the Commonwealth Institutional Excellence Award. YCMOU's quality perspective consists of five components: institutional commitment and support; curricular flexibility; flexibility in learning strategies; learner support and assessment and evaluation. The institutional commitment covers: sensitivity to the needs of learners; sustained effort at developing relevant academic programmes; a concern for creating a trained and qualified workforce; a focus on upgrading recourses to cope with advances in technology; a strong orientation towards systemic research and an openness towards objective appraisal of institutional practices. Flexibility in curricular offerings has been introduced both in order to maintain the spirit of "openness" as well as to provide for cultural contextualisation so that learning materials become appealing to diverse users. In addition to developing programmes that are relevant, periodic enrichment and updating is undertaken. YCMOU has moved ahead steadily but cautiously with regard to learning strategies. The nature of course content and the technological readiness of learner groups have largely determined the learning-teaching strategy adopted. In order to provide the resources and necessary support for the academic success of learners, YCMOU has established an extensive network of connectivity located study centres that are served by appropriately qualified and trained staff. The accompanying issues of equity and access have also been dealt with by adopting a sound rationale. In the context of learner evaluation, YCMOU has developed a systematic approach for ensuring objective and reliable assessment of student learning.

QA has been viewed by the university as an ongoing endeavour with possibilities always available for improvement. QA initiatives taken by the university have very good impact but with constraints which are shred across the globe (Deshmukh, 2006).

The University of New England (UNE)

UNE has a long and successful DE history. Staff is experienced in teaching student at distance. It has well-established procedure for developing, producing and dispatching DE learning materials. However, the growth of e-learning created a need for new procedures and associated QA systems.

The university adopted an institutional approach to e-learning QA, featuring:

- A university policy on online teaching that specifies an online learning management system.
- Classification and description of web use level for different courses.
- A high level of technical, administrative and pedagogical support for staff.
- Basic training for all online teaching staff.
- A team approach to e-learning materials development comprising an educational designer, teacher, academic developer, university copyright officer, programmer and graphic designer.
- Procedures for e-course development that follow university approval guidelines, including submission to the Academic Board.
- Clear designation of online courses in the university handbook and all other public documents, to ensure students are aware of technology requirements before enrolling.
- Complete design and technical verification of e-learning materials before teaching begins, including editorial checks for technical problems such as broken links.
- Course materials approval and "sign off" by the academic supervisor before being made available.
- Extended below desk and phone support hours for staff and students.
- Service agreements with the university's Division of Information Technology designate e-learning a mission critical activity, ensuring problems are resolved immediately.
- On course review on a three cycle, using criteria equivalent to print course reviews.
- Regular external peer review of selected online courses (Kirkpatrick, 2005).

Open University Malaysia (OUM)

As the first private University in Malaysia, and the first to offer open and distance learning there, OUM needed to show the public that it provided educational products, experiences and outcomes of ensured quality that were at least equal to that delivered to the students on campus universities.

While OUM's quality management system addresses key performance areas of corporate culture, improving and monitoring quality curriculum and courseware development are at the heart of its QA effort.

OUM adopted a strategy of putting the customer and providing quality services and products, featuring:

- Identified best practice standards in Open and Distance Learning management through benchmarking visits to renowned international open universities.
- Academic standards for programmes set by external regulators, ensuring quality and equivalence.
- Well developed procedure for courseware development.

- To ensure viability and that course will meet client needs; a market survey is conducted before any academic programme is developed.
- First drafts of any curriculum formulated by a team comprising deans of faculties, lecturers and experts from professional bodies.
- Feedback on curriculum drafts by Board of Studies comprising experts from academia, government and industry. Drafts are then scrutinised by the university's Academic Board, comprising senior faculty member and academic stakeholders.
- Curriculum approval from the private educational department and national accreditation board at the Ministry of Education.
- Development of learning materials by a team of subject matter, experts, academic moderators, module writers, tutors and consultants (Kirkpatrick, 2005).

The preceding cases give a clear indication that quality culture exists in all the DEIs. The institutions either have external QA (i.e. accreditation), internal QA mechanisms or both. QA is limited to academic function (like course materials preparation, multimedia use, etc.) and few student support system (like student enrolment, counselling). The administrative functions are not yet coming under the purview of quality in any of the DEIs. Further some of the institutions use continuous improvement tools and techniques and also assessment and feedback are not given much importance. Although quality is assured, it is not managed totally. Gaining an insight from the HEIs (we have already discussed in Chapter 4), the DEIs should move forward towards TQM for better outcome and stability in the competitive environment.

TQM is nothing but QA plus continuous improvement (CI) leading towards delighting the customers (Fig. 5.1).

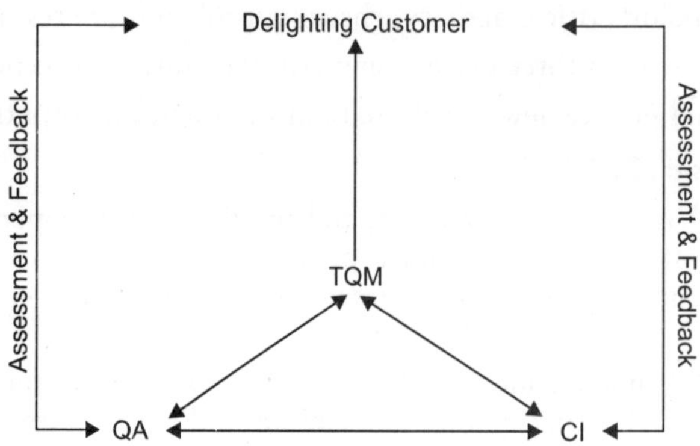

Fig. 5.1: TQM

The components which are missing in the existing quality practice of DEIs are:

- Environment analysis
- Customer need analysis
- Use of CI tools and techniques
- Assessment and feedback
- Evaluation
- Accountability

If these components can be synergised with the existing quality culture then total quality culture (i.e. TQM) can be attained. To attain TQM, a systematic and consistent process needs to be followed. The following four pronged strategy provides way out in this regards (Box 5.1).

Box 5.1: Four Pronged Strategy to Implement TQM in DEIs

- Environment (internal and external) analysis (Where are we now?)
- Vision, mission, goal, and objectives (Where we want to be?)
- Policy, plan, strategy, tools and techniques (How we will get there?)
- Assessment, evaluation, feedback and improvement (Did we get there?)

In the light of DEIs the above-mentioned steps have to be consistently followed by all the functions/components of the institution, namely learner support (information, counselling, etc.), programme development (course material and multimedia, etc.), material production and distribution and delivery, learner registration, and evaluation, HRM, research, training and development, finance and general administration (Fig. 5.2).

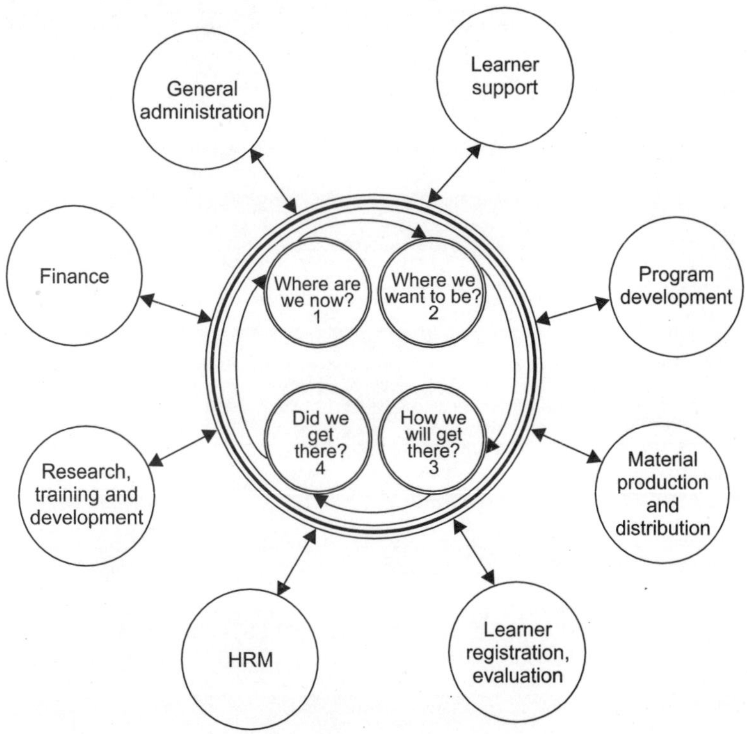

Fig. 5.2: TQM in Distance Education

Chapter Overview

The chapter highlights the scenario of DE from a global perspective. Broadly, it gives an idea about the DE system, its mode of delivery and importance of quality. Fourteen short case studies are presented to familiarise the existing quality culture of DEIs. After analysis, the gap between total quality culture and existing quality culture has been identified. To bridge the gap, four steps are suggested for achieving TQM in DEIs.

Discussion Questions

1. Given an historical overview of growth of distance education.
2. What are the generations/models of distance education?
3. Discuss the existing quality culture of DEIs citing suitable example.
4. Describe the steps to make the existing quality culture into total culture in DEIs.
5. Enlist the components of DEIs, where quality needs to be aligned.

***Appendix* 1**

Growth of DE: International Scenario*

Continent/Country	Name of the Institution	Year of Establishment
Africa		
Nigeria	Correspondence and Open Studies Institute	1973-74
South Africa	University of South Africa	1946
Sudan	Open Learning Institute	1984
Tanzania	Tanzania Open University	1992
Zimbabwe	Zimbabwe Distance (Correspondence) Education College	1980
	African Virtual University	1997
Asia		
China	Central Radio and TV University	1978
	National Open University of China	1986
Hong Kong	Open University of Hong Kong	1989
India	Dr. B.R. Ambedkar Open University	1982
	Indira Gandhi National Open University (IGNOU)	1985
	Yashwantrao Chavan Maharashtra Open University (YCMOU)	1989
	Kota Open University	1987
	Nalanda Open University	1987
	Madhya Pradesh Bhoj Open University	1992
	Karnataka State Open University	1996
	Netaji Subhas Open University	1997
	Uttar Pradesh Rajarshi Tandon Open University	1999
	Tamil Nadu Open University	2002
Indonesia	University of Terbuka (Indonesia Open University)	1984
Korea	Korea National Open University	1982
Malaysia	Open University of Malaysia	2000
Pakistan	Allama Iqbal Open University	1974
Sri Lanka	Open University of Sri Lanka	1980
Thailand	Sukhothai Thammathirat Open University	1978
Turkey	Anadolu University	1958
Australia	Gippsland Institute of Advance Education	1972
	Mibchell College of Advanced Education	1974
	Victoria College	1976
	University of Southern Queensland	1967
Europe		
England	Open University	1969
	Open College of Arts	1986
	Open College	1987
	Open School	1989
France	Centre de tele-Enseignment a Distance (CNED)	1986
Germany	German Institute of Distance Education	1965
	Fern Universitat	1979
Italy	Consorgio per I Universita a Distanza (CUD)	1984
Netherlands	Netherland Open University	1984
Norway	Norwagian Association for Distance Education	1985
Spain	Universidad National de Education a Distancia (UNED)	1972
Sweden	Hermodes	1966
USSR	Russia Open University	1990
North America		
Canada	Athabasca University	1987
	University of Alberta	1987
Costa Rica	Universidad Estatala Distancia	1977
Venezuela	Venezuela Open University	1977

* The list is not covering all the DEIs. The idea is just to show the historical development.

Total Quality Management of Distance Education

6

Chapter Outline

- Strategy for TQM Implementation
- Stage 1: Where are we now?
- Stage 2: Where we want to be?
- Stage 3: How we will get there?
- Stage 4: Did we get there?
- Barriers to TQM Implementation
- Chapter Overview
- Discussion Questions
- Appendix 1: Quality Culture of the Institute
- Appendix 2: Customer Satisfaction Survey
- Appendix 3: Employee Participation Survey
- Appendix 4: Institutional Process Climate
- Appendix 5: Leadership Quality Analysis
- Appendix 6: Evaluation of TQM Implementation

Chapter Objectives

After completition of this chapter, the reader will be able to:

- Explain the stages of strategic framework for implementing TQM in DEIs
- Describe the barriers to TQM implementation

Strategy for TQM Implementation

On learning different models of TQM in HEIs and experiences from industries, the author proposes a strategic framework (Fig. 6.1) for implementation of TQM in DEIs. The framework would dwell upon four stages:

- Where are we now?
- Where we want to be?
- How we will get there?
- Did we get there?

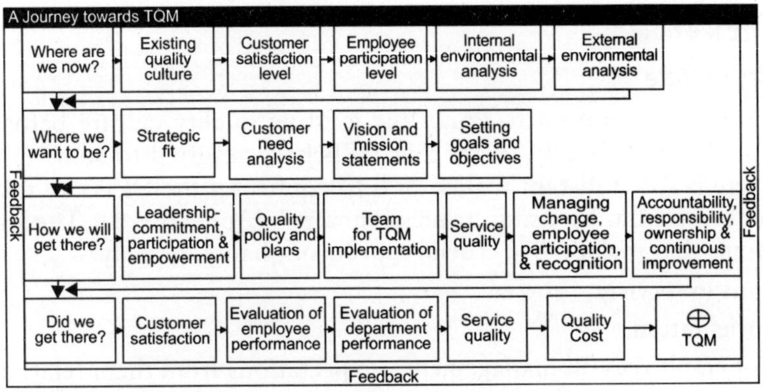

Fig. 6.1: Framework for TQM Implementation in DEIs

Figure 6.1 shows the stages and its sub-stages as follows.

Stage 1: Where are we now?

(a) Existing quality culture
(b) Customer satisfaction
(c) Employee participation
(d) Internal environment analysis
(e) External environment analysis

Stage 2: Where we want to be?

(a) Strategic fit
(b) Customer need analysis
(c) Vision and mission statements
(d) Setting goals and objectives

Stage 3: How we will get there?

(a) Leadership
(b) Quality policy and plan
(c) Teamwork
(d) Organising workshop
(e) Managing change
(f) Accountability

Stage 4: Did you get there?

(a) Overall Institutional Performance
(b) Evaluation of TQM implementation
(c) Cost of quality

Stage 1: Where are we now?

(a) Existing Quality Culture

It is crucial for the institution to know the existing quality culture before moving ahead with anything else. We are already aware that DEIs have resorted to some quality culture but total quality culture is still a distant reality. Still to confirm it the DEIs can take an account of their existing quality profile by using a questionnaire* (Appendix 1). The questionnaire has five sets of questions that include five crucial aspects of quality, namely:

- Deviations in services.
- 'Fix it' orientation.
- Clarity of employees on management's expectations from them relating to quality.
- Management's awareness of the price of non-conformance to quality.
- Belief of management relating to the cause of quality problems.

(b) Customer Satisfaction

Delighting customer is the ultimate aim of TQM. We have already discussed about customer satisfaction in previous chapters. Customer of any distance education institute includes learners, employees, parents and society. Customer includes both internal and external. So, before starting TQM implementation, it is imperative to know the existing customer satisfaction level. Hence, to know the satisfaction level the questionnaire in Appendix 2 can be used.

(c) Employee Participation

Existing employee participation refers to the degree that the employee shares information, knowledge and power throughout the institution. The level of participation ranges from an employee providing the information without knowing the problem to a work team having control over all the phase of decision-making process. Employee participation is promoted at all levels to cultivate commitment and involvement of employees to different participative group activities. Apart from the above, power is delegated in different degree at all levels across the institution so that the individual responsibility is discharged in commensurate with authority. The employee participation level can be assessed by using the questionnaire given in Appendix 3.

(d) Internal Environmental Analysis

Internal environmental analysis helps an institute to know its own departments' strengths and weaknesses. It is as important as external analysis in strategy formulation. Basically, there are four types of approaches that institutions follow for internal environmental analysis: resource-based approach; performance analysis approach; value chain analysis; and functional analysis approach.

In resource-based approach, an institution's competitive advantage is determined by its resources and capabilities. The basic elements of this framework are:

- Defining institution's resources that present internal strengths and weaknesses.
- The institution's combined resources form a number of capabilities.

* The questionnaire was developed by Crosby (1987) that has been modified by the author as per the suitability of DEIs.

- These resources and capabilities provide a sustainable competitive advantage.
- This sustainability derives from linking the institution's unique resources to different types of strategies that exploit these resources and capabilities across time.
- The characteristics of resources and capabilities (durability, transferability and replicability) are important in sustaining competitive advantage and in identifying resource gaps (Grant, 1991).

Another way of doing internal analysis is by performance analysis. There are many ways of doing this, i.e. by financial and non-financial. In an institution apart from financial performance analysis, non-financial analysis can be done by calculating the student enrolment, student retention, employability of graduates, etc.

Value chain analysis framework has been developed by Porter (1985) to examine the nature and extent of synergies, if any, among the internal activities of an institution. According to Porter, an organisation is a collection of activities that are performed to design, produce, promote, deliver and support its products. All these activities can be represented using five primary activities and four support activities using a value chain concept (Fig. 6.2).

The internal analysis of an institution using this framework can be undertaken as:

- Examination of each service line's value chain in terms of various activities involved in rendering the service.
- Examination of linkages within each service line's value chain.
- Examination of the potential synergies among the value chain of different services.

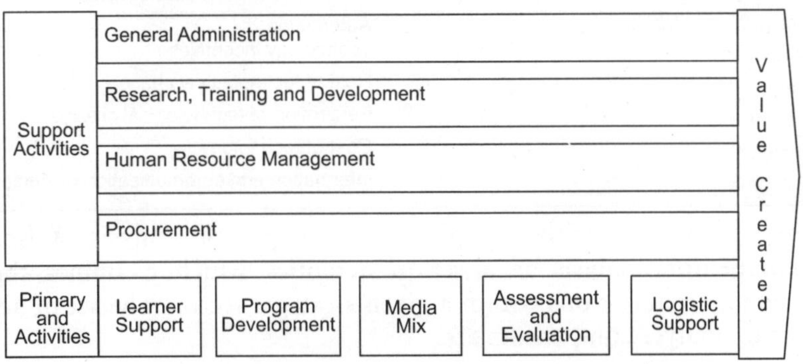

Fig. 6.2: Sample Value Chain Analysis in DEIs

In a functional analysis approach, a company's skills and resources are organised in accordance with its functions. The company's resources include not only financial and physical resources but also the ability of people in each area to formulate and implement necessary functional objectives, strategies and policies. If properly used, these functional resources become the strength of the institution.

(e) External Environmental Analysis

The key external factors affecting strategy formulation can be of six broad types: customers; economic; social and cultural; political and legal; technological; and competitive.

The external factors do not directly touch upon the short run activities of the institute but can influence its long run strategic decisions.

The external factors can be analysed in different ways, the most notable being the PEST (Political, Economical, Social and Technological) framework (Table 6.1). The institute should identify and examine the possible impact of the external factors and analyse its outcome. This information helps the institution to build a roadmap through which it can develop various strategies to exploit opportunities and reduce the threats. The result of PEST analysis varies from country to country depending upon variations in the PEST scenario among the countries.

Another way of doing external environment analysis is by using Porter's five forces model (1979). This model suggests that competition extends beyond the institute to include new entrants, substitutes, customers and suppliers. A strong force may be regarded as a threat, while a weak force may be regarded as an opportunity for the institute.

Table 6.1: Sample PEST Analysis in DEIs

Political	Social
Political stability	Population growth rate
Government policy on education	Literacy rate
Impact of laws	Career attitudes
Impact of environmental regulations	Attitude towards change
Decision-making structures	Society expectation
Government fund/grants	Demographic profile
Economic	**Technological**
Economic growth and stability	Automation
Interest rates	Technology incentives
Inflation rate	Rate of technological change
Trade agreements	Perception of technological change
Budget allocation	Cost of technology
Per capita income	Information and communication technologies

Another aspect of external analysis is perceptive competitor analysis. Wilson and Gilligan (1997) define competitor analysis as a set of activities which examines the comparative position of competing organisations within a given strategic sector. The set of activities that an institute may take to analyse competitors are:

- Identifying institute's competitors
- Understanding competitor's objectives
- Identifying competitor's strategies
- Assessing competitor's strengths and weaknesses
- Estimating competitor's reactions
- Selecting competitors to attack and/or those to avoid

Stage 2: Where we want to be?

(a) Strategic Fit

A systematic way of integrating internal and external environment analysis helps to find a 'strategic fit' between what the environment wants and the institution has to offer and vice versa. SWOT (Strengths, Weaknesses, Opportunities and Threats)/TOWS (Threats, Opportunities, Weaknesses and Strengths) analysis or situational analysis is an important tool for analysis of strategic fit. SWOT analysis is a common management technique used mainly for organizational diagnosis. It is an effective way of identifying strengths and weaknesses, which can lead to examination of the available opportunities and possible strengths. There are several ways of carrying out SWOT analysis like fill in blank SWOT sheets, open discussion or through data collection by questionnaire administration or tests. The following table is a sample SWOT analysis in DEIs.

Table 6.2: Sample SWOT/TOWS Analysis for DEIs

SWOT/TOWS ANALYSIS	**Opportunities** Collaborations with international institutions Introduction of latest courses Up to date course material Use of different medium of course material Develop staff skills and capabilities Placement of graduates Encouragement of e-learning Accreditation	**Threats** Loss of identity Loss of strength and reputation Competitive market Mushrooming growth of DEIs Absence of accreditation Retention of efficient staff High average of staff learning to superannuating Pressure for teacher and staff union Outdated course material
Strengths Enthusiastic management team Excellent result Timely result Ample no. of courses Flexibility High quality course materials Efficient student support system Support of government Counselling	**Strategy - 1 (SO)** Collaborations with international institutions Introduction of latest courses Up to date course material Use of different medium of course material Develop staff skills and capabilities Placement of graduates Encouragement of e-learning Accreditation	**Strategy - 2 (ST)** Example: The institution can leverage its strength 'efficient student support system' to ward off the threat 'loss of identity' a strategic fit.
Weaknesses Poor faculty and staff Lack of recognition Inadequate and outdated course Poor examination result Weak student support system Absence of counselling Insufficient budget	**Strategy - 3 (WO)** Example: The institution can overcome its weakness 'lack of recognition' with the emerging opportunity for 'accreditation' a strategic fit.	**Strategy - 4 (WT)** Example: The institution can minimise the weakness like 'poor faculty and staffs' to avoid threat of competition.

(b) Customer Need Analysis

Satisfying customers and creating customer enthusiasm through understanding their needs and future requirements is the crux of TQM and all institutions are dependent on having satisfied customers (Dale, 2003). Understanding customer needs and wants is not an easy task. It is more difficult for a service provider to correctly understand the customer's needs. The service provider should distinguish between five types of needs (Kotler, 2005):

1. Stated needs
2. Real needs
3. Unstated needs
4. Delight needs
5. Secret needs

In DEIs, the need can be pursuing education to acquire a degree. While the real need can be to pursue education along with job, the unstated need can be career growth. The need varies from customer to customer, hence understanding customer need is very important.

Stamatis (1993) has developed a generic model for complying with the needs of customer. The model has six steps as follows:

1. Identify the added value of service that is to be rendered to the customer.
2. Identify the customer and clearly determine his or her expectations.
3. Identify the institution's critical needs that are required for customer satisfaction.
4. Define the process required to perform the work in order to ensure quality customer service.
5. Zero-defect the process and eliminate wastefull efforts.
6. Ensure continuous improvement by obtaining continuous feedback from the customer, in order to produce continuous total quality results as output.

(c) Vision and Mission Statements

Vision statement outlines what an institute visualises to be in the future. It is more specific of objectives and goals. The strategic point for TQM is to set a shared vision. Hence, institution by involving all the stakeholders should make the vision statement. Once the vision statement is ready, several mission statements have to be articulated. The vision statement can galvanize the people to achieve defined objectives, even if these may appear to be little stretched out. It needs to be SMART, i.e. Specific, Measurable, Achievable, Relevant and Time bound.

Mission is always futuristic and directional—statements of purpose of an institution. It typically explains what it provides to its customers. It provides institutional identity externally and internally unanimity of purpose. The important elements of a mission statement are: philosophy/beliefs, aspirations and values of the institution; services/products; customers; market or geography of operation; technology; employee; and public image. There should be a well-documented mission statement of the institution. Each mission may have several tasks in the form of goals.

Vision and mission statements are foundation stones for implementing a successful strategy. Vision and mission statements should not only be developed but should also be properly communicated to all the stakeholders of the institution. These are the long-term objectives of the institution and if clearly prepared will not require infrequent changes. A good vision statement reflects what the customer wants rather than what the institute offers to the customers.

Sample of vision and mission statements of an open university is given in Box 6.1.

Box 6.1: Sample Vision and Mission Statements

Open University Malaysia

Vision

- To be a leader and innovator in open learning

Mission

- To be the leading contributor in democratising education
- To develop quality education through multimode learning technologies
- To develop and enhance learning experiences towards the development of a knowledge-based society

Source: University website

(d) Setting Goals and Objectives

Goals are missions unbundled. Each goal contributes to the achievement of mission. Goals determine the tasks, programmes, activities and processes of an institution. The term 'objective' is used to refer to what is to be achieved and covers the range of desired outcomes to achieve a goal. The objective could be short term or long term, critical or non critical, strategic or operational. Based on the inputs from 'strategic fit' the institution could frame its objectives for implementation of TQM.

An objective to be acceptable should be flexible and appropriate for the planning horizon, it should be measurable and achievable, and if it is achievable it should be challenging enough to be motivating, and it should be suitable to the current position of the organization and suitable in the context of the organization's mission. A well-stated and meaningful objective should be understandable to all stakeholders. Sample of objective statements of an open university is given in Box 6.2.

Box 6.2: Objectives of Indonesia Open University

1. To offer various educational programs of high quality at the level of higher education by using distance education system that can be accessed by the whole society.
2. To produce high quality learning materials for higher education using various media.
3. To offer different forms of learning support to increase the quality of learning and graduates.
4. To conduct valid and reliable evaluation of the process and learning output.
5. To create partnership and cooperative efforts with various institutions, locally, nationally and globally.
6. To utilize various technologies including the communication and information technology, to carry out education, research and distribution of research information.
7. To develop human resources who are competent in distance education, especially distance higher education institution and other knowledge.
8. To build an effective and accountable distance education higher institution which is accredited nationally and internationally.
9. To conduct research in distance education, especially in distance education higher institution and other knowledge as well as distribute the results in innovative and sustainable manner.

Source: University website

Stage 3: How we will get there?

Before implementing TQM, it is essential to make an objective assessment about the readiness of the institute for implementation. The process climate of an institution adds evidence in support of/against TQM implementation. The process climate may be exploitative, impoverished, supportive or total quality. Although the total quality climate is the most desirable one, the supportive climate also nourishes the TQM effort. In order to assess the process climate of the institute, a survey can be made by administrating a well-structured questionnaire (Appendix 4) developed by Petrik and Quinn (1996).

TQM can be implemented by using eight steps (Fig. 6.3).

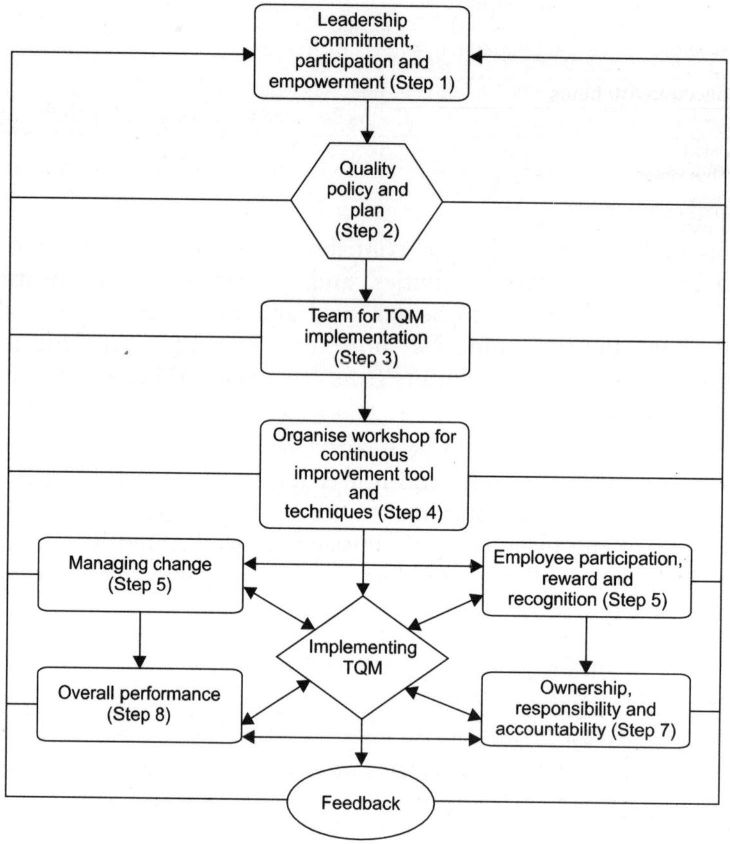

Fig. 6.3: TQM Implementation Flowchart

(a) Leadership

Leadership plays a vital role in implementation of TQM in any organization/institution. It is the responsibility of the top management to take the initiative or recognize the demand of an initiative for TQM. While TQM is a participative management with a concern for all the persons of the institution, it needs someone or a group to think continuously on quality issues and mobilize others and so on.

Rather than keeping all these dimensions with the head of the institution, a core team of the most efficient staff can be formed. One member can be chosen as the TQM master for a specified time. The team should be given the responsibility of TQM environment building across all the sections of institution and among all the levels of employees.

Leadership can be analysed from eight different angles: commitment; participation; learning; empowerment; encouragement; role model; pursuit of long-term success; and management by fact. A questionnaire is provided in Appendix 5 to analyse the leadership quality in the institution.

Some of the essential leadership attributes for effective TQM implementation are given in Table 6.3.

Table 6.3: Essential Leadership Attributes for Effective TQM Implementation

Leadership Attributes	Description
• Leadership vision o Creating TQM vision o Communicating the vision o Modelling the vision o Building commitment	o Shape a strategic vision in consultation with employees, customers, suppliers and other constituents. o Communicate the meaning and elevate the importance of the visionary goals to the employees. o Legitimise the vision by enacting on it. o Build a contagious enthusiasm to energise people. Involve people in the process of shaping the vision.
• Leadership motivation o Power o Responsibility o Resource allocation	o Share power through participative management. o Delegation and joint decision-making. o Allocation of sufficient resources—human, material and finance.
• Leadership drive o Achievement motivation o Ambition o Initiative o Energy o Tenacity	o Sky is the limit o Being the best o Overcome the eventualities, be determined and dedicated. o 8-day week, chasing opportunities. o Struggling to accomplish the new.
• Honesty and integrity o Ethical standards o Using connections (Blat)	o Personal trust, transparency, approachability o Greasing palms, but learning to achieve the TQM outcome straight.
• Self-confidence	o From cynicism to over promising.

Source: The idea is derived from Puffer (1994)

(b) Quality Policy and Plan

Articulation of quality policy is dependent upon the current status of the institution and where does it want to go. The quality policy differs according to the situation of the institution: crisis, normal running or already in good position. In a broader context, in quality policy specific interventions are chosen and quality plan provides instruments and practice of interventions. There are seven Key Business Drivers (KBDs) that form the nucleus of a company's quality policy and its strategic quality planning process. These seven KBDs are: customer satisfaction; employee satisfaction; process optimization; fair profit; growth and survival; environmental consciousness; and external relations (quality and effectiveness of interactions with suppliers, community and other external agencies).

The following issues and action points are worth considering in the quality plan:

- Develop long-term (7 to 10 yrs), medium-term (3 to 4 yrs) and short-term (1 yr) plans.
- Identify intervention mechanisms
- Prioritise area of intervention
- Identification of resources
- Provide training and development
- Provision of feedback and review

To become total quality cultured institution the following actions are proposed:

- Generate more commitment among people towards TQM by providing TQM trainings, and organizing more TQM workshops.
- Find out the reasons for deviations in the desired behaviours.
- Create a climate where everyone is prepared to accept his/her assigned responsibilities.
- Help people perceive quality as a super-ordinate goal.
- Communicate the voice of customers to all employees through interaction.
- Reinforce the system for information sharing, suggestion scheme, monitoring result, and the accountability as well as the feedback system.

(c) Teamwork

Good teamwork constitutes the base of TQM. Teamwork requires the spirit of cooperation, complementation and synergetic relationship among members. Work teams have a much greater chance of being effective, if they are nurtured and facilitated by the institution. In order to make teamwork TQM-oriented, the institution can take the following measures:

- Creating purpose of the team in concert with the institution strategy.
- Creating a culture in the institution that values team participation and autonomy.
- Providing appropriate training to team members.
- Reinforcing teamwork by reward system of institution.

Table 6.4 contains few recommendations that may be useful for the institution to make teamwork more effective.

Table 6.4: Recommendations to Facilitate Teamwork in the Context of TQM

• Clear purpose	The mission, vision, objectives or task of the team must be clearly defined and accepted by everyone. The purpose needs to be in concert with the institution's purpose and strategy.
• Climate	The climate needs to be informal, comfortable, or relaxed. There should be no tensions or signs of boredom.
• Participation	There should be much discussion, and every one should be encouraged to participate.
• Listening	The members should be good listeners*.
• Consensus decisions	As far as possible, reach decision through open discussion of every one's ideas and avoid rating or easy compromises. Do not over emphasise on results, or achieving quick results.
• Open communication	Team members should feel free to express their views on matters concerned. Develop good interpersonal skills (assertive rather than aggressive communication).

• Clear roles and work assignments	Fairly distribute work among team members. Clearly explain the role expectations.
• Shared leadership	The team may have a formal leader, but the leadership functions should shift from time to time depending on the circumstances, the needs of the team, and the skills of the members.
• External relations	The teams should spend more time in developing outside relationships, mobilizing resources, and building credibility with important players in other parts of the institution or other teams.
• Self-assessment	Periodically, the team should make a self-assessment of how well it is functioning, and what are the barriers to their effectiveness.

*Note:** indicates every member must be trained in making effective use of listening techniques such as avoiding interruptions, maintaining interest, postponing evaluation, organizing information, showing interest, and providing feedback.

(d) Organising Workshops

To appreciate the need for TQM, and to make aware about the continuous improvement (CI) tools and techniques, institute should arrange regular workshops. The TQM facilitators and the top management should ensure that all the employees are aware of the tools and techniques. Pocket books, leaflets, manuals should be prepared and distributed in these workshops.

(e) Managing Change

Any institution wishing to implement TQM must be clear at the outset that TQM is not merely a management technique; it is also a change management programme. No matter how technically or administratively perfect a proposed change may be, people may make it or break it. People make it when they perceive it as a 'basket of opportunities', and break it when they perceive it as a 'bundle of threats'. People are the creatures of habit and it is highly difficult for them to try new ways of doing things at workplaces. Therefore, they resist changing and resistance occurs at all levels. However, all people do not resist TQM. Whether people resist or accept TQM as a change initiative depends upon the individual employee, who is subject to such change processes (Palo, Panigrahi and Padhi, 2002).

Implementation of TQM and the accompanying changes in the process bring large scale transformation. Sometimes, it becomes too difficult for people to adapt to such changes, therefore they do resist TQM implementation. However, failed TQM efforts would be very costly in terms of money and resources, lowered probability of achieving goals, decreased employee loyalty, etc. Therefore, resistance must be carefully managed. 'Managing resistance to change' is one of the most troubling and challenging tasks faced today. The TQM manager must learn the skills of juggling tasks, striking a delicate balance between individual and collective actions, paying attention to the context as well as process of TQM, etc. Some strategies like employee empowerment and recognition can be effective to manage resistance to change.

(i) **Empowerment**: "Empowerment is moving decision-making down to the lowest level, where a competent decision can be made" (Hodgettes, 1996). The keys to empowerment are through sharing of information, freedom of action, involving employees in decision-making, etc. Therefore, as TQM is a change initiative, employees should be made responsible for its implementation, share power with them through participative management, providing training for new skills required for TQM implementation, etc. The institute should formulate a good empowerment plan and implement it. The proposed empowerment plan has been given in Box 6.3.

Box 6.3: Empowerment Plan

Information Sharing
• Share company performance information even with lower-level employees. • Help people understand the business process. • Build trust through information sharing. • Create self-monitoring possibilities.
Rebuilding Institutional Structure
• Flat and team-based structure. • Clear goals. • Role clarity.
Rearranging Institutional Processes
• Create a clear TQM vision in consultation with employees. • Create new decision-making rules that support performance management processes. • Clear communication. • Job rotation. • Job enrichment.
Re-engineering HRM Practices
• Provide direction and training for new skills. • Provide encouragement and support for change associated with TQM implementation. • Acknowledge the fear factor. • Have managers, who do not hesitate to share power with their subordinates.

(ii) **Rewards and Recognition:** Rewards are the centrepiece of institutional life. Both extrinsic (financial, material and social) and intrinsic (self-granted and psychic such as deriving pleasure from the work itself, experiencing a sense of competence, or self-determination) rewards motivate people to join and contribute to the quality efforts of an institution. However, the relative importance of extrinsic and intrinsic rewards is a matter of personal values and tasks. The top management may keep the following tips in their mind while administering a good reward system in the institution:

- Rewards should be tied to contributions/performances of both individual and team.
- Reward system should be based on clear and consensual exchange norms.
- Reward teamwork whenever possible.
- Reward teamwork behaviour (such as mutual support, cooperation, and group problem solving). Introduce team-based pay incentives to avoid overload and frustration.
- Create a pay plan that blends individual achievement and team incentives.
- Provide reward having a long-term motivational impact on people.
- Every reward must have an 'appreciative effect'.

(f) Accountability

Accountability often used synonymously with such concepts as answerability, enforcement, responsibility, blameworthiness, liability and other terms like account-giving, etc.

(http://en.wikipedia.org/wiki/Accountability). Implementation of TQM and subsequent goals and objectives increases accountability for all the employees including top management. TQM makes every employee responsible for institution-wide quality practice. The institutional level vision and mission are cascaded down to the divisional and functional level by setting goals and objectives at each functional level. Consequently, individual employee's target is also set. The employee target can be directly linked with the performance management of the institute. By this, the institution creates a cycle between individual employee's performance and overall institutional performance. The framework for accountability is given is Fig. 6.4.

There are two sub-systems in the framework, i.e. planning cycle and the accountability cycle. The planning cycle begins with the broad vision and mission statements set by the institution and is connected with functional and employee target and with performance. The accountability cycle starts at individual employee and is linked to the individual performance and provides input to the planning cycle by means of review.

One of the widely used performance management tool is Balanced Scorecard. Kaplan and Norton (1992, 1996) introduced the Balanced Scorecard as a tool to measure and evaluate performance of the company and individual. It has four perspectives: financial; customer; internal process; and learning and growth.

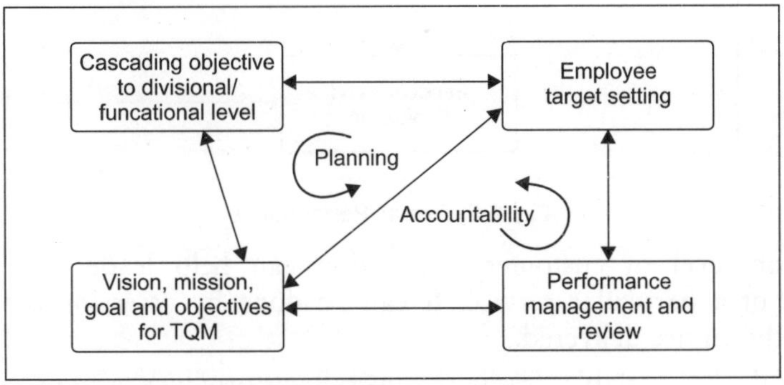

Fig. 6.4: TQM and Accountability

By this the employee will identify himself with the institutional objectives and have a sense of ownership.

Stage 4: Did we get there?

(a) Overall Institutional Performance

Overall performance of an institution is assessed taking into account the performance of key variables like (Fig. 6.5):

- Service quality
- Customer satisfaction
- Functional performance
- Employee performance

Key variables are both intra- and inter-dependent. Employee performance leads to functional performance which in turn drives quality and customer satisfaction.

It is evidenced by research that service quality is the customer's judgement of the service which involves a comparison of customer's expectations with customer's perception of the actual service performance. Delivering quality service means conforming to customer's expectation consistently basis. Further empirical scrutiny of service quality can be done using a 22 item scale called 'Service Quality' (SERVQUAL) developed by Parasuraman.

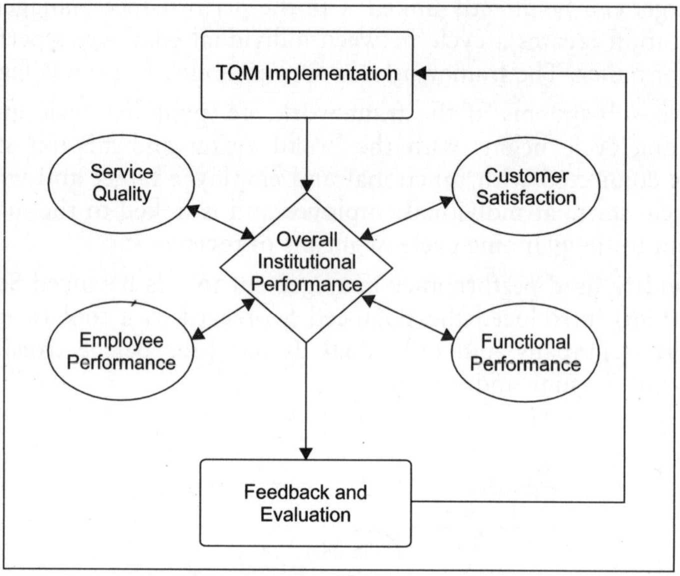

Fig. 6.5: Overall Performance

Information on level of customer satisfaction can help leaders to understand what customers expect of a particular service. It can be done by assessing the gap between the expectations and the service delivered.

Assessment of the key variables leading to overall performance is analysed in detail in later.

Evaluation of customer satisfaction examines the voice of the customer about the desire of the existing and future programmes and services. It also helps in understanding the emerging customer requirements, keeping pace with changing market scenario and delivery of educational services. A variety of voice-of-the-customer strategies is used. Selection depends upon the size of the institution. For example,

- Tracking demographic, economic, societal factors that may bear on customer requirements.
- Holding focus groups with customers.
- Interviewing customers.
- Using critical incidents like customer complaint.

In determining customer satisfaction level, a key aspect is the comparative satisfaction of the customers with competitors delivering similar services. This information can be used for improving delivery mechanism and support services.

This variable examines the level of employee engagement, development and management in an integrated way with strategic objectives and plans at the institutional level. A high performance work is characterised by focus and student achievement, flexibility, innovation, knowledge, communication skills and decision-making skills. The other factors that should be assessed are level of engagement, motivation, compensation and recognition. In addition to these the other indicators include absenteeism, turnover and grievances. Employee development depending on the nature of work and related training are also taken care by the institution for meeting the individual objectives.

(b) Evaluation of TQM Implementation

Evaluation is the process of assessing the outcome. It provides insight for improvement by matching the best practices and performances with the target process and outcome. As TQM is based on the philosophy of continuous improvement, evaluation plays an integral part of the implementation process. Evaluation can be carried out by using the existing standards (ISO, MBNQ, etc.) or by setting one's own institutional standards. To make evaluation a continuous phenomenon, internal procedures are recommended. This process should be carried out continuously and aligned with the other steps of planning and implementation to get the best result. Ideally, it should contain the following steps:

1. Identification of the key parameters
2. Data collection
3. Designing questionnaire
4. Data analysis and interpretation
5. Feedback for improvement

1. Identification of the parameters: This is the first step which determines the ultimate outcome of evaluation. To be effective, the institution should identify the key parameters. The key parameters though similar broadly, varies from institution to institution basing on the environmental factors. In case of DEIs, the key processes include: vision and mission statements; quality policy and plan; leadership; training and development; employee participation;, processes; resources and service quality.

2. Data collection: It is the foundation of any statistical analysis and interpretation. Data can be obtained from primary and secondary sources. The internal data collection is the by-product of routine activities like accounting, finance, personnel, sales, R&D, etc. There are two basic methods of obtaining primary data, namely questionnaire and observation. For evaluation of this kind, primary source for data is recommended. Due consideration should be given to the respondent's profile to represent all levels of employees and stakeholders.

3. Designing questionnaire: Questionnaire is a successful method of collecting information. However, its success depends upon proper designing of the questionnaire. For our purpose, undistinguished questionnaire is recommended. Type of question, content, number of questions and the information desired are relevant issues while designing the questionnaire. The questionnaire should be pre-tested to check its outcome under actual conditions of data collection. A specimen questionnaire is given in Appendix 6, which can be further modified and developed as per the requirement.

4. Data analysis and interpretation: The main objective of data analysis is to arrive at a score for each parameter on a scale. Data can be analysed using statistical tools such as mean, ranking, relative advancement index, correlation, etc. The tools that are to be used should be chosen depending upon the requirement. Statistical analysis should aim at providing meaningful outcomes through the institutional indicators and benefits gained from the TQM implementation process.

5. Feedback for improvement: Based on the survey, the institution would be in a position to identify the strengths and weaknesses of each of the key parameters. The parameters can be ranked on a scale say 1 to 10, where 1 indicates relatively 'advance implementation process' and 10 indicates 'have not begun implementation'. Now the institution should devise strategy for each of these parameters to make TQM implementation a success. The parameters low in the ranking need special attention of the top management for improvement. The goals and objectives including target responsibility of the employees in charge of the parameters need to be revisited, reviewed and reframed. The responsibility, accountability and ownership of the employees be linked with the fresh set of objectives. Reward and recognition of employees can be aligned with the institutional performance based on the key parameters so as to create a competitive environment and create an equity-reward-based performance.

(c) Cost of Quality

The common myth is 'quality is expensive' but the reality is 'quality is free', as the book name of famous TQM guru, Philip Crosby indicates. The critical component of TQM is cost consciousness in terms of quality improvement and management. From this angle, effective resource utilization is very important. Unless qualitative output is achieved, any amount of investment will be futile.

Cost of quality has two important components: cost consciousness and cost management. Cost consciousness implies developing sensitivity about costs and likely returns keeping quality as the focal point and cost management as the natural corollary to cost consciousness, which implies investment decisions.

Barriers to TQM Implementation

In order to implement TQM successfully, it is also necessary to know the reasons why TQM fails. The following is a list of barriers, obstacles, pitfalls, institutions have faced while implementing TQM. Even though this is not an exhaustive list, it does include the frequently faced barriers.

- Lack of top management commitment
- Lack of communication
- Inability to establish a TQM framework
- Insufficient knowledge about TQM
- Lack of institution-wide definition of quality
- Failure in formalising strategy for implementation
- Inability to change institutional culture
- No encouragement for teamwork, empowerment
- Lack of trust

- Belief that TQM costs more
- Lack of motivation
- Lack of training and education
- Improper resource allocation
- Does not believe in customer satisfaction
- View TQM as quick fix

Chapter Overview

This chapter has explained the four stages of strategic framework for implementing TQM in DEIs. The stages are: Where are we now?; Where we want to be?; How we will get there?; and Did we get there? Under each stage, there are few sub-stages which are also discussed. Different questionnaires are given in the appendix that are be used while implementing TQM. At the end of the chapter, barriers to TQM implementation are also enlisted.

Discussion Questions

1. Explain step-wise how TQM can be implemented in a DEI.
2. What are the barriers to TQM implementation in any DEI? Suggest measures to overcome them.

***Appendix* 1**

Quality Culture of the Institute

Directions

Given below is a list of five characteristics. Please put a [x] mark on your choice of alternative in order to indicate your opinion.

Characteristics	That's us all the way (1)	Some is true (3)	We're not like that (5)
1. Our services normally contain waivers, deviations and other indications of their not conforming to requirements.			
2. We have a "fix it" oriented service.			
3. Our employees do not know what management wants from the concerning quality.			
4. Management does not know what the price of non-conformance really is.			
5. Management believes that quality is a problem caused by something other than management action.			

Interpretation

Sl. No.	Range of scores	Status of institution (Crosby)	Crosby's remark
1.	21-25	Critical	Needs intensive care immediately
2.	16-20	Guarded	Needs life support system hook-up
3.	11-15	Resting	Needs medication and attention
4.	6-10	Healing	Needs regular check-up
5.	≤ 5	Whole	Needs counseling

Appendix 2

Customer Satisfaction Survey

Directions

Use the following scale to indicate your answers to the statements below:

1.	2.	3.	4.	5.
Strongly disagree	Disagree	Somewhat agree	Agree	Strongly agree

There is no right or wrong answers. Write the number (1, 2, 3, 4 or 5) that best indicates the extent of your agreement with the statement.

Customer Satisfaction

1. I am aware that customer satisfaction survey is regularly carried out by the institute. ________
2. All employees in the institution give high priority to customer satisfaction. ________
3. The institute promptly acts upon customer complaints. ________
4. Clear cut information about the programmes offered by the institute. ________
5. Get regular assistance in understanding the course. ________
6. Regular and timely advertisement of the programmes offered by the institute. ________
7. Qualitative pre-enrolment counselling is offered. ________
8. The enrolment process is smooth. ________
9. Counselling is done regularly. ________
10. Course material is up-to-date. ________
11. Course material is learner friendly. ________
12. Appropriate media mix. ________
13. Course material is delivered on time. ________
14. Assignments are evaluated on time. ________
15. Assignments are returned with appropriate feedback. ________
16. Result is declared on time. ________
17. Placement service is offered. ________

Interpretation

Sl. No.	Range of scores	Customer satisfaction
1.	75-85	High
2.	36-74	Medium
3.	≤35	Low

***Appendix* 3**

Employee Participation Survey

Directions

Use the following scale to indicate your answers to the statements below:

1.	2.	3.	4.	5.
Strongly disagree	Disagree	Somewhat agree	Agree	Strongly agree

There is no right or wrong answers. Write the number (1, 2, 3, 4 or 5) that best indicates the extent of your agreement with the statement.

Employee Participation

1. The institute has the policy of employee participation. ________
2. Management delegates authority. ________
3. Care for employee's job and career related prospects and problems are given due importance. ________
4. Institute believes in cross functional teamwork. ________
5. Sufficient information is provided to employees by means of regular meetings and other mechanisms. ________
6. Stimulates top-down and bottom-up communication. ________
7. Have effective employee suggestion schemes. ________
8. Provides recognition and reward for employee suggestions. ________
9. Effective policy for job rotation. ________
10. Sound employee management relationship policy exists. ________

Interpretation

Sl. No.	Range of scores	Employee participation
1.	40-50	High
2.	21-39	Medium
3.	≤20	Low

Appendix 4

Institutional Process Climate

Directions

Read each dimension of organization process climate and consider the descriptions at both ends of the scale. Circle the number on the scale that reflects your evaluation of conditions in your institution at this time (1 is the lowest evaluation possible and 20 is the highest evaluation possible)

1. **Reward system:** The degree to which employees, as individuals and as teams, feel they are being recognized and rewarded for good work rather than being ignored, criticized, or punished when something goes wrong.

Rewards are not in line with effort and performance	1. 2. 3. 4. 5.	6. 7. 8. 9. 10.	11. 12. 13. 14. 15.	16. 17. 18. 19. 20.	Employees are recognized and rewarded positively

2. **Standards of performance:** The emphasis placed upon quality performance and achieving results, including the degree to which employees feel meaningful and challenging goals are being set at every level of the institution.

Performance standards are low	1. 2. 3. 4. 5.	6. 7. 8. 9. 10.	11. 12. 13. 14. 15.	16. 17. 18. 19. 20.	Performance standards are High

3. **Warmth and support:** The feeling that friendliness is a valued norm and that employees trust, respect and offer support to one another. The feeling that good human relationships prevail in the day-to-day work of the institution.

There is little warmth and support in the institution	1. 2. 3. 4. 5.	6. 7. 8. 9. 10.	11. 12. 13. 14. 15.	16. 17. 18. 19. 20.	Warmth and support are characteristic of the institution

4. **Leadership:** As needs for leadership arise, people feel free to take leadership roles and are rewarded for shared successful leadership. The organization is not dominated by or dependent upon just one or two individuals.

Leadership not respected or rewarded ; institution dominated by or dependent upon just 1 or 2 individuals	1. 2. 3. 4. 5.	6. 7. 8. 9. 10.	11. 12. 13. 14. 15.	16. 17. 18. 19. 20.	Leadership is accepted and rewarded based on expertise of individuals and teams

5. **Institutional clarity:** The feeling among employees that things are well organized and goals and responsibilities are clearly defined rather than being disorderly, confused, or chaotic.

The institution is disorderly, confused, and chaotic	1. 2. 3. 4. 5.	6. 7. 8. 9. 10.	11. 12. 13. 14. 15.	16. 17. 18. 19. 20.	Institution is well organised, with clearly defined goals and responsibilities

6. **Communications:** Important information is shared quickly and accurately—up, down, and sideways—in the institution.

Information is wrong, censored, or unavailable.	1. 2. 3. 4. 5.	6. 7. 8. 9. 10.	11. 12. 13. 14. 15.	16. 17. 18. 19. 20.	Information is accurate, open and available

7. **Creativity:** New ideas are sought and used in all areas of the institution. Employees creativity is encouraged at every level of responsibility.

The institution is closed and unresponsive to change	1. 2. 3. 4. 5.	6. 7. 8. 9. 10.	11. 12. 13. 14. 15.	16. 17. 18. 19. 20.	The institution is innovative and open to new ideas

8. **Job stress:** Employees are neither overworked nor underworked. Stress levels are appropriate for the job.

Stress levels are harmful	1. 2. 3. 4. 5.	6. 7. 8. 9. 10.	11. 12. 13. 14. 15.	16. 17. 18. 19. 20.	Stress levels are optimum

9. **Ethics:** The emphasis the institution places upon high standards of moral behaviour at all levels of responsibility.

Double standards exist; ethics are low	1. 2. 3. 4. 5.	6. 7. 8. 9. 10.	11. 12. 13. 14. 15.	16. 17. 18. 19. 20.	High standards of conduct are expected at all levels

10. **Tolerance:** The degree of open-mindedness that exists towards different people, ideas and customs in the institution.

Prejudice and discrimination are the norm	1. 2. 3. 4. 5.	6. 7. 8. 9. 10.	11. 12. 13. 14. 15.	16. 17. 18. 19. 20.	Non-prejudice and non-discrimination are the norm

11. **Feedback and controls:** The use of reporting, comparing and correcting procedures such as employee evaluations and financial audits.

Controls are used for policing and punishment					Controls are used to provide guidance and solve problems
	1. 2. 3. 4. 5.	6. 7. 8. 9. 10.	11. 12. 13. 14. 15.	16. 17. 18. 19. 20.	

12. **Resources:** Sufficient financial and physical resources are available to accomplish the job.

Insufficient funds, equipment and supplies					Supplies, equipment, and funds are sufficient
	1. 2. 3. 4. 5.	6. 7. 8. 9. 10.	11. 12. 13. 14. 15.	16. 17. 18. 19. 20.	

13. **Employee growth:** Personal and professional development is emphasized at all levels and in all classifications in the institution.

Employee growth is a low priority in the institution					Employee growth is a high priority in the institution
	1. 2. 3. 4. 5.	6. 7. 8. 9. 10.	11. 12. 13. 14. 15.	16. 17. 18. 19. 20.	

14. **Physical working:** Conditions (lighting, space, heat, washroom facilities, etc.): Safe and comfortable working conditions exist throughout the institution.

Working conditions are poor					Working conditions are good
	1. 2. 3. 4. 5.	6. 7. 8. 9. 10.	11. 12. 13. 14. 15.	16. 17. 18. 19. 20.	

15. **Teamwork:** The amount of understanding and co-operation between different levels and work groups in the institution.

Teamwork is poor					Teamwork is high
	1. 2. 3. 4. 5.	6. 7. 8. 9. 10.	11. 12. 13. 14. 15.	16. 17. 18. 19. 20.	

16. **Employee pride:** The degree of pride that exists—pride of individual workmanship and pride of institution goals and accomplishments.

Pride is low					Pride is high
	1. 2. 3. 4. 5.	6. 7. 8. 9. 10.	11. 12. 13. 14. 15.	16. 17. 18. 19. 20.	

17. **Employee involvement:** Responsibility for decision making is broadly shared in the institution. Employees are involved in decision that affect them.

Low employee participation in decision making	1. 2. 3. 4. 5.	6. 7. 8. 9. 10.	11. 12. 13. 14. 15.	16. 17. 18. 19. 20.	High employee participation in decision making

Interpretation

Sl. No.	Range of scores	Status of institution
1.	1-5.9	Exploitive
2.	6-10.9	Impoverished
3.	11-15.9	Supportive
4.	16-20	Total Quality

Appendix 5

Leadership Quality Analysis

Directions

Use the following scale to indicate your answers to the statements below:

1.	2.	3.	4.	5.
Strongly disagree	Disagree	Somewhat agree	Agree	Strongly agree

There is no right or wrong answers. Write the number (1, 2, 3, 4 or 5) that best indicates the extent of your agreement with the statement.

Leadership Quality

1. Leaders demonstrate constant commitment to vision, mission, quality policy of the institution. ________
2. Participate in TQM implementation and evaluation. ________
3. Desirous of learning, training, and accepting education. ________
4. Believe in empowering employees. ________
5. Have trust in employees and encourage involvement. ________
6. Act as role models and lead by examples. ________
7. Focus on long-term goals and performance. ________
8. Make decision based on fact and make proper use of information. ________

Interpretation

Sl. No.	Range of scores	Quality commitment
1.	35-40	High
2.	17-34	Medium
3.	≤16	Low

Appendix 6

Evaluation of TQM Implementation

Directions

Use the following scale to indicate your answers to the statements below:

1.	2.	3.	4.	5.
Strongly disagree	Disagree	Somewhat agree	Agree	Strongly agree

There is no right or wrong answers. Write the number (1, 2, 3, 4 or 5) that best indicates the extent of your agreement with the statement.

I. Vision and Mission Statement

1. There is an institution-wide awareness of the vision and mission statements. ____________
2. Vision statement is used as a guide to formulate policy and strategies. ____________
3. The vision and mission statements speak for quality. ____________

II. Quality Policy and Plans

1. Employees at all levels are aware of quality policy and plans. ____________
2. The quality policy and plans are regularly updated and reviewed. ____________
3. The policy and plans are implemented in achieving the goals. ____________

III. Leadership

1. Commitment to quality. ____________
2. Empower employees to solve quality issues. ____________
3. Focus on long-term Institutional performance. ____________

IV. Processes

1. Key to the programmes is identified. ____________
2. Systematically managed. ____________
3. Clarity on functional goals and objectives. ____________
4. Reviewed and set target for improvement. ____________
5. Use of CI tools and techniques. ____________

V. Training and Development

1. Carried out as per training calendar. ____________
2. Quality awareness education is part of the training programme. ____________
3. Effectiveness of training is evaluated. ____________

VI. Service Quality

1. Commitment to customer satisfaction. ____________
2. Commitment to help learners achieve their education goal. ____________
3. Learner support on prompt and timely basis. ____________
4. Appropriate to the requirement and level of programme. ____________
5. Course structure is sensible and coherent. ____________

6. Learner course is revised and up-to-date __________
7. Course delivery medium exploited to its' full potential. __________
8. Unbiased approach to student evaluation system. __________
9. Timeliness in evaluation system. __________

VII. Resources

1. Qualitative utilisation of academic resources. __________
2. Optimum utilisation of financial resources. __________
3. Leveraging technological resources. __________

VIII. Employee Involvement

1. Employees agree to target and continuously review performance. __________
2. Employees are involved, empowered and recognised. __________
3. Employee's concern about quality. __________
4. Employees are aware of customer (internal and external) needs. __________

Interpretation

Sl. No.	Range of scores	Status of institution
1.	<33	Uncommitted
2.	34-66	Slow-Movers
3.	67-99	Middle of the Road
4.	100-132	Improvers
5.	133-165	Total Quality

Making Total Quality Management: A Success

7

Chapter Outline

- Foundation of TQM
- Key Success Factors
- Chapter Overview
- Discussion Questions

Chapter Objectives

After completion of this chapter, the reader will be able to:

- Identify the foundations of TQM
- Describe about different key success factors (KSFs) responsible for making TQM a success

Foundation of TQM

TQM as a people-driven management system aims at continual increase in customer satisfaction, by involving all employees across the departments, functions and positions. Involvement of employees is an integral part of quality management as quality is the responsibility of all in everything they do. Quality is quite personal. If employees do not 'buy-into' the quality philosophy, learn the quality tools and techniques, develop the spirit to work together in teams in order to improve business processes and work designs, and use new abilities, skills and knowledge (ASK) in their daily work, then nothing will happen.

The first and most important principle is customer focus. The goal of satisfying customer is fundamental to TQM and is expressed by the institution's attempt to design and deliver products/services to fulfil customer needs. The second principle is continuous improvement, which means commitment to constant examination of technical and administrative processes in search of better methods. Teamwork that is collaboration between managers and non-managers, between functions, and between customers and supplier is the third principle of TQM process (Dean and Bowen, 1994).

Each of these principles, although stated as distinct, is inextricably linked to one another. The ultimate aim is for fulfillment of customer's needs by using the most effective and efficient methods. Customer focus is driven by the desire of an institution to identify customer needs and acquire feedback on his/her satisfaction with the institution's current efforts to meet those needs. Continuous improvement is the next logical step that requires institution to act based on the acquired information. In order to achieve and maintain customer satisfaction, institutions may need to continuously develop better products and services and improve methods of producing and delivering them. Finally, for an institution to experience continuous improvement everyone involved with producing and delivering a good or service must try to identify opportunities for improvement and works together to implement the necessary changes. This requires the collaboration across levels, functions and other institutional boundaries, making teamwork essential.

Other distinctive features of TQM like leadership, process management, individual and institutions learning, internal and external cooperation, employee empowerment and fulfillment (Anderson et al., 1994) are all related to these principles. Visionary leadership, which refers to the ability of management to provide a long-term vision for the institution based on changing customer needs rather than on internal control, is a derivative of the first principle that is customer focus. Top management has to develop and champion a vision for the institution that facilitates the transition to TQM and maintains customer orientation after the transition.

Continuous improvement underlies the shift towards process management and the need to facilitate learning at the individual, group and institutional level. Process management focuses on managing the means rather than the ends. It requires people to understand the institutional processes and seek newer and better ways of their execution. However, employees in a non-TQM environment were not required to examine institutional processes, and often lack the necessary skills to do so. Therefore, process management necessitates the creation of learning environment in the institutions. The learning environment is exemplified by a institution's training, or external and internal educational as well as developmental opportunities that enhance the ability of everyone to participate in process management leading to continuous improvement.

Teamwork leads to internal and external cooperation and the need for employee empowerment and fulfillment. It requires members of the team to indulge in non-competitive activities to achieve better collective goals. If properly implemented, this results in cooperation within an institution and with other institutions with which it interacts. Finally, in order to make teamwork more successful, employees must be provided with decision-making authority and institutional support to make real changes happen to improve the processes. It is also essential to see that they receive monetary and non-monetary rewards for their efforts, leading to initiative and commitment to the institution.

The above discussion clearly elucidates that TQM centers around people. People, if suitably oriented and involved act as the most effective instruments in achieving total quality. By the same token, people who are disinterested or do not share the collective values supportive of a transformation to total quality can be the biggest impediments in the process.

Key Success Factors

There are few key success factors (KSFs) without which the TQM cannot be implemented successfully. These KSFs are discussed below:

I. *Awareness*

Creating awareness among people is an absolute necessity before implementing TQM. People must understand the need for implementing TQM as well as the way it has to be implemented. And moreover, awareness about the programme beforehand would help to reduce their stress level that may develop due to the institutional changes associated with TQM and to encourage them to find out or recommend strategies for its effective implementation.

II. *Vision*

Vision represents a long-term goal that describes 'what' an institution wants to become. A well-articulated vision engages people emotionally to pursue the over-arching purpose of the institution. However, a vision held only by leaders is not enough to create any real change. The management must continuously and creatively articulate the institution's vision and share it with the employees. This can be achieved only through open communication system that facilitates a two-way flow of information. As the institution's alternate goal is to satisfy the customer, therefore, it is imperative that employees must understand what is expected of them as well as their responsibility for achieving results. A well-communicated vision makes the people more innovative. It creates the feeling of delight and encouragement to overcome institutional as well as professional barriers to effective TQM implementation.

The vision of the institution might be originated with the top management, but employees should be involved in the process of shaping the institution's vision to build their commitment and create enthusiasm. The leaders should not only talk about the vision, but also they must enact it. They must 'walk the talk' because employees are the watchers who look for managers' behaviours to symbolize values and expectations. The more consistent these behaviours are with statements, the more employees will believe and follow these statements. Moreover, walking the talk builds trust, thereby making people delighted towards their works. This might in turn encourage them to innovate. Teamwork should be made a part of TQM vision.

III. *Leadership*

Quality is leadership (Kandula, 1997). The top management of the institution is the main driver of TQM. Therefore, the key factor for successful implementation of TQM is his leadership style (Zairi, 1991). TQM requires a particular type of leader and particular style of leadership. A TQM leader should be both transactional and transformational in his approach. Transactional leadership is about 'managing and helping' people to achieve their current objectives more efficiently through practices such as linking job performance to valued rewards, and ensuring that employees have the resources to get their job done, etc. On the contrary, transformational leadership is about 'leading and changing' the institution's strategies and culture so that people have a better fit with the surrounding environment. Transformational leaders are the brokers of dreams. They shape a strategic vision of a realistic and attractive future that bonds employees together and focuses their energy towards a super ordinate institutional goal.

In nutshell, while transactional leadership improves efficiency of people, transformational leadership steers people onto a better course of action. Thus, both the kinds of leadership styles are equally essential to implement TQM more successfully.

IV. *Innovation*

Innovation means junking conventional wisdom, destroying old advantage, violating established norms, re-engineering business practices, and behaving in counter intuitive and indeed unpredictable ways (Mehra, 1999). An innovative institution is one, where people are allowed to do something new and potentially useful without being directly shown or talked (Robinson and Stern, 1977).

Innovation requires a new paradigm and above all people involvement. It has to be constantly fostered and nurtured in the institution. Innovation is fueled by an institution's culture and goals (Dougherty, 1996; and Gundri, Kickul and Prather, 1994); institutional characteristics such as its structure, strategy, technology, resources and rewards (Sternberg and Lubart, 1996; and Woodman, Sawyer and Griffin, 1993); and, the amount of creative behaviours that occur within workgroup as well as the creative behavioural performance of its members (Kreitner and Kinicki, 1998).

Innovation requires an institution culture, where failure is treated not only as a feedback, but also as a badge of honour. It is an anti-thesis of 'doing it right first time'. It encourages mistakes, experimentation and prototyping. This demands trust in the ability of people and instilling in them a sense of ownership. Unless everyone in the institution feels he has a stake in it, the spirit of innovation cannot be unleashed. All this requires entirely new leadership skills. The top management must take the ultimate responsibility for stimulating and nourishing employees' creativity. Achieving total quality through innovation requires them to move away from one-dimensional thinking to paradoxical thinking and learning to balance three kinds of roles: as an architect, network-builder, and juggler. As an architect, leaders must explore the inherent abilities and capabilities of each employee and develop within them an intrinsic belief in his/her own worth. Only then, they will deliver unimagined products/services, thereby delighting their customers. The leader as a network-builder has to build cliques and coalitions in service of innovation and creativity. And finally, the leader as an artist/juggler has to build, integrate and resolve the tensions and contradictions inherent to every organisation.

However, there may be some barriers to innovation which can be overcome by following some strategies (Table 7.1):

Table 7.1: Recommended Strategies to Overcome Barriers to Innovation

Barriers	Strategies to Overcome
• Controlled environment	• Create supportive and open environment. Allow mistakes (up to a permissible limits), experimentation and prototyping as people always learn through mistakes.
• Rigidity in organisational structure and processes	• Provide autonomy, freedom, and flexibility to employees. Avoid excessive discipline.
• Ideation is optional, not compulsory	• Compel each employee to suggest ideas. Do not criticize the erroneous ideas, rather treat them as opportunities for learning.
• Emphasis upon extrinsic, not intrinsic rewards	• Though the present reward and recognition system of the organisation is quite lucrative, yet not sufficient in the sense that it does not provide sufficient intrinsic motivation to employees. Intrinsic motivation can be provided by making the work of people more interesting, challenging, enjoyable and showing appreciation and satisfaction over their work.
• Insufficient opportunity for continuous learning	• Provide people sufficient opportunity for continuous learning. Cultivate creativity through education and training.

V. *Ethics*

Ethics has been defined as the philosophy/science of ethical and moral values. Values often have the character of rules of conduct. Rules of conduct serve partly the objective of realizing a good life for the individual and partly to strengthen and encourage the sense of solidarity. Thus, ethics must have a two-pronged philosophy. On one side, a philosophy about values or rules, and on the other, a philosophy about how these values or rules can be made to be binding. In this latter sense, ethics must become a project for commitment to values, or a project for the development of the community (Floistad, 1995).

Ethics at workplace does play a very crucial role in successful implementation of TQM. Creech (1994) made an extensive study of TQM practices in US based companies and concluded that work ethics, savings ethics and institution loyalty are the major reasons for Japan's success in TQM. People are more involved in the TQM implementation process, when they feel that they are getting fair treatment at the workplace and their institution maintains a high ethical standard.

Ethics involves the study of moral issues and choices. It is concerned with right versus wrong, good versus bad, and the many shades of grey in supposedly black-and-white issues. Since, effective TQM implementation largely depends upon maintenance of ethical standards in the institution; leaders are challenged to make right decisions and to do the right thing that involves morale implications. Therefore, the leaders are advised to make ethical decisions by adhering to the seven general moral principles popularly known as 'The Magnificent Seven' promulgated by Hodgson (1992) (Box 7.1).

Besides, an ethical organisational climate has to be created by managers by developing a meaningful code of ethics for employees, providing training to them to identify and deal with ethical issues, and reinforcing their ethical behaviour. However, it must be remembered by everyone that ethics is an everyday affair, not a one-time announcement of a new ethical code that gets filed away and forgotten.

Box 7.1: The Magnificent Seven: General Moral Principles for Leaders

1. Dignity of human life: The lives of people are to be respected.
2. Autonomy: All persons are intrinsically valuable and have the right to self-determination.
3. Honesty: The truth should be told to those who have a right to know. Honesty is also known as integrity, truth, and honour.
4. Loyalty: Promises, contracts and commitments should be honoured.
5. Fairness: People should be treated justly, fairly, impartially, and equitably.
6. Humaneness: There are two parts: (i) our actions ought to accomplish good; and (ii) we should avoid doing evil. We should do good to others and to ourselves. We should show the concern in form of compassion, giving kindness, serving and caring.
7. The common good: Actions should accomplish the 'greatest good for the greatest number of people'.

VI. *Perception*

Long ago, the Greek philosopher Plato wrote, "we see reality only as shadows reflecting against the rough wall of a cave" (Plato, *The Republic*, Trans. Lee, 1955). In other words, reality is always filtered through an imperfect perceptual process. Perceptual process means receiving information about and making sense of the world around us. It involves deciding which information to notice, how to categorize this information, and how to interpret it within the framework of our existing knowledge.

Perception, specifically social perception (otherwise known as social cognition, or social information processing system) affects each decision and action of an individual. There is a powerful perceptual process called self-fulfilling prophecy (also known as Pygmalion effect) that plays a vital role in causing the action of a person consistent with his expectation.

According to the self-fulfilling prophecy, people first form expectations about the institution, its strategies, culture and processes, etc. and accordingly they direct their work behaviour. Effective coaching, training and communication have a great bearing on their perceptual schemata.

It is assumed that people would be more inclined to get themselves involved in the TQM process depending upon their perception to institutional culture, personal performance, and peer performance. Perception to personal performance depends upon how a person perceives his job, which in turn depends upon what he expects from his job. Thus, expectations of a person always influence his perception to TQM. This fact should be the major consideration while designing the training programmes for TQM.

Involvement of people in the TQM process depends upon their perception to the efficacy of the programme. People's perception to TQM can be developed by using one or more of the following recommendations:

- Formal statements of TQM philosophy, mission, vision, values, and tools to be used. The statements must be clearly communicated and widely reinforced throughout the organisation. The organisational values should give priority to the interest of customers (both internal and external) and suppliers, continuously strivc for quality in every activity, treating people with respect and dignity, promoting teamwork, adopting code of conduct that reflects the highest standards of integrity, and be good citizen.
- Create good work environment.
- Use slogans, language, acronyms and sayings that develop desire among employees to provide excellent customer service. The slogans may be like 'achieve customer satisfaction', or 'whatever it takes', which means employees are encouraged to do whatever it takes to exceed customer expectations.
- Different stories and myths that imbibe the value of doing whatever it takes to saιisfy a customer may be narrated to employees to create enthusiasm.
- Deliberate role modelling, teaching, and coaching by managers and supervisors.
- Leaders' reactions to critical incidents and organisational crises have a significant bearing on employees' perception. Therefore, they should think twice before they act and react.

VII. *Communication*

Effective communication is a critical factor for the success of TQM. The delicate nature of the continuous improvement process, which needs engaging each and every employee personally to focus on improved performance in the job he or she has hired to do, requires an atmosphere of open and honest communications throughout the entire institution. Continuous improvement is impossible without this atmosphere, where mistakes are not made simply because people are afraid to ask. Not are uninformed supervisors who more concerned with office politics than the quality of work manipulating it ever likely to be attained by unhappy employees. For, in fact, quality improvement is not as much about standards as it is about winning the hearts and minds of all the people.

Every institution develops its own communication systems, some formal and rigidly controlled, other informal and uncontrolled. While too much emphasis at either of these extremes might cause problems for an institution, a more important consideration is, whether the communications are open and honest, or restrained and manipulative. Only an open and honest atmosphere has the potential to prevent or overcome serious credibility gaps between the institution and its employees. This kind of honest relation also has the power to release the energies needed to overcome and change the status quo, primarily by driving fear out of the workplace. This will make the employees feel free to become highly creative, and productive. They may even begin to take pleasure in their work.

In order to be effective from an overall institution point of view, communications must take place both horizontally and vertically. Vertical communication usually means there is a network in place to push communications downward but in the spirit of continuous improvement, there must also be a guarantee of an open, honest, and responsive formal system for the upward flow of communications. The horizontal communications take place between peers, especially inter-functional peers. Increased horizontal communication can help employees to understand their jobs better, by helping them to see how their work fits in with the broader operations of the institution.

Besides, management experts also note that effective communication is a cornerstone of ethical work behaviour. Communication by the top executives keeps the firm in its ethical course. The top executives must ensure that the ethical climate is consistent with the institution's overall objectives. Communication is important in providing guidance for ethical standards and activities that provide integration between the functional areas of the business (Ferrell and Fraedrich, 1991).

Before embarking upon a formal TQM programme, an institution has to open up all these positive channels of communication, especially to give all employees the opportunity and encouragement to use the upward channel. The quality policy must be clearly communicated to them and the institution should also gather inputs from them relating to its successful implementation. Because employees represent a reservoir of the most intimate knowledge about how the business really works. Management cannot afford to be without their inputs, if there is to be any hope for its true success. Do not leave communications to chance. Understand its intrinsic value to the achievement of quality improvement and build its effectiveness throughout the institution, right from the beginning (Hagan, 1997).

It is said that management is communication. Every managerial function and activity involves some form of direct or indirect communication. Any managerial decision including the decision for improving quality through TQM would be ineffective, unless it is well understood by those responsible for enacting them. Therefore, in order to make TQM effective, the communication system in the institution must be strengthened. It is suggested that:

- The institution should design an effective communication system. Although it is not possible to demolish the existing one completely, along with that the revised communication system should be more open, honest, and reciprocal.
- Media selection is a key component of effective communication. Therefore, for obtaining and disseminating information about TQM, top management must determine which media is to be used. If an appropriate medium is not used, managerial decisions relating to TQM implementation may be based on inaccurate information and/or important messages may not reach the people who are regarded as the cornerstone of TQM progress.

- In order to encourage people to be more involved in the TQM process, top management should improve their communication competence by trying to be more assertive. An assertive communication style is more expressive and self-enhancing, but does not take advantage of others.
- The top management must communicate with employees at the grass-root level and convince them to enforce ethical standards within the organisation.

VIII. *Mental State (Stress and Delight)*

Mental state of a person plays a pivotal role in regulating his work performance. It is normally assumed that the more a person is delighted with his work; the better would be his work performance and vice-versa. However, life in this competitive era has become hectic and occupational stress is on the rise for several reasons. First, the biggest contributor to work stress revolves around fundamental changes occurring in work institutions. As a result of increasingly competition, people are being asked to deliver a better quality and a greater quantity of work in lesser time with scarce resources. Second, technological advancements make it harder for employees to adapt themselves to new technologies. And, finally, the dynamics of modern life make it difficult to balance the demands between work and home. Research demonstrates that work stress spills over into one's personal life and *vice-versa* (Jones and Fletcher, 1996).

It is believed that a relaxed frame of body and mind is the sine qua non for better quality of work. Stress acts as a major barrier to achieve total quality. It may arise from several sources such as heavy workload, poor job and working conditions, role conflict and role ambiguity, lack of opportunity for career development, poor inter-personal relationship, aggressive behaviour of management, and conflict between work and other roles, etc.

Every leader in the institution must understand the causes and consequences of stress mainly because of two reasons. First, from a quality of work life perspective, employees are more satisfied when they are not under a lot of occupational stress. Second, the morale imperative suggests that managers should attempt to reduce stress as it leads to several negative outcomes such as physiological (increased blood pressure, high cholesterol, heart disease, etc.), cognitive (poor decision making, lack of concentration, forgetfulness, etc.), and behavioural (job dissatisfaction, poor performance, higher rate of absenteeism, turnover, accident, etc.).

In order to reduce the occupational stress, the institution may adopt the following strategies:

- Identify the stressors that cause unnecessary tension and job burnout and remove them. Prepare a well-structured questionnaire and administer the same to all employees to identify the common stressors and receive suggestions for removing them may do this.
- Participative management can reduce occupational stress. Therefore, empower employees so that they will have more control over their work and work environment.
- Administer a well-structured reward and recognition system.
- Managers may also help to reduce the stress level of their employees by: (i) exhibiting supportive behaviour, (ii) showing concern for them, (iii) providing adequate guidance and direction, (iv) focusing on good performance, and (v) providing instrumental support such as financial, material, and other required resources.

- Social support is one of the most effective stress management practices. It refers to a person's inter-personal transactions with others such as co-workers, supervisors, family, friends, and others, who provide emotional or informational support to buffer the stress experience. This calls the need of the company to provide more opportunities to its employees to work through teams, so that they can establish good inter-personal relationship and, thereby obtaining necessary social support. It will help them to reduce their stress level in at least four ways:
  - (i) Esteem support: Employees will feel that they are valued and worthy. This in turn will increase their self-esteem and perceived ability to cope with the stressor.
  - (ii) Informational support: The peers will provide information to interpret, comprehend, and probably to remove the stressors.
  - (iii) Emotional support: People seek out and benefit from the emotional support of others, when they face threatening situations.
  - (iv) Social companionship: It will provide opportunity to people to fulfil their need for appreciation and belongingness.

IX. *Rewards and Recognition*

Equitable rewards and recognition for accomplishment play a vital role in stimulating positive work performance. Recognition is the heart of quality improvement programme. Recognition that is honest, deserving, and sincere forms the base of good management and provides management with a tool that truly integrates people into the quality improvement system. Once quality measurements are in place and specific improvements are verified, then formal recognition should be accorded to individuals and groups in a manner that they can appreciate and their associates can understand. This is one of the best methods for sustaining personal interest and individual effort for continued quality progress. Spontaneous recognition from supervisors and managers to employees is the most effective and inexpensive type available, especially if done in front of as many employees' peers as possible. Their bosses as well as peers for doing a good job have pointed out many quality surveys that a primary desire of most employees is to be recognised. Failure to take advantage of this tactics by the management is a business blender of the first order (Hagan, 1997). Reward and recognition for accomplishment delight the people, and motivate them to be more involved in the TQM process as well as to be more innovative and creative.

X. *Maturity and Breadth*

Maturity and breadth represents the social, moral and emotional maturity of people and their broad range of interest in different activities. Maturity level influences the degree of involvement of people in TQM implementation. It largely determines whether people demonstrate cooperative behaviour, treat others fairly and respectfully at the work place, etc. It is assumed that the higher the social/moral maturity level of people, the more they do believe that their work is important to the success of the institution and accordingly they share responsibility for its success or failure. Such people also demonstrate high ethical work behaviour and they are likely to be more creative than others.

Social/moral maturity levels of people play a key role in perceiving others' behaviour as well as maintaining and adhering to ethical principles at workplace. The maturity level of people is exhibited in how they treat others, whether do they really demonstrate cooperative behaviour at the workplace, and the interest they show in different activities.

In this context, it is recommended that people must be trained and motivated in order to develop cooperative spirit, to treat others fairly and respectively, and to live up to high ethical standard in the organisation.

XI. *Attitude and Morale*

Attitude is defined as "a learned pre-dispositions to respond in a consistently favourable or unfavourable manner with respect to a given object" (Fishbein and Ajzen, 1975). TQM needs an institution-wide adherence to new values and principles. It indicates that the starting point for TQM has to be the creation of a new collective paradigm or mindset, and development of positive attitude in all the members of the institution, so that all in concert makes the movement to the point where the institution has to be.

Quality comes mainly from people as a result of attitudes and values, not by technology alone. Unless the TQM drive aims at attitudinal change, divorcing stereotype beliefs, it may not be feasible to introduce it (Singh, 1991; and Chakraborti, 1997). Thus, changing attitude that is supportive to total quality is an absolute necessity for its effective implementation. There are many tactics to change and develop employees' attitudes towards TQM. Some of these tactics include: clear and credible communication, creating total quality institutional climate, etc. Although attitudes often are resistant to change, they can be influenced through proper education and training that may help to change underline beliefs. Regular employee – attitude surveys can also let managers know, if their ideas and changes go with or against the grain of popular sentiment.

Attitude of a person always affects his work performance. Work attitudes of people are reflected in their job satisfaction and moral as well as commitment to institution. Satisfaction of employees and their morale are always associated with customer satisfaction which is the ultimate goal of TQM. Satisfied employees provided better customer satisfaction for two reasons. First, job satisfaction affects the general mood of people. People who are in good mood are likely to communicate friendliness and positive feelings which customers appreciate. Second, satisfied employees are less likely to derelict their jobs. This allows the institution to have employees with more experience and better skills to serve the customers. Therefore, in order to provide more job satisfaction to employees and uplift their morale level the institution must ensure for:

- Providing equity and fairness in treatment.
- Building institutional comprehension. Affective commitment is likely to be strengthened when employees have a solid comprehension of the activities of their institution. Employees should be regularly informed about various organisational activities and allowed personally experience the organisational crisis. People often develop apathetic attitude and feel themselves disconnected, when they do not know what is going on in the institution.
- Providing more opportunities for employee involvement. People develop positive attitude when they feel that they are part and parcel of the organisation, and their action and decision guide the future of their institution.

- Trusting employees. Put faith upon your employees. However, it is a reciprocal activity. To receive trust, the leaders/managers must demonstrate trust. Employees identify with and feel obliged to render quality work for their institution, only when only when they trust their leaders/managers.
- Administering a good quality of work/life programme.

XII. *Customer Satisfaction Sensitivity*

TQM is a customer-centered management approach. It recognizes that continuously satisfying the customers is the root to the success in the market place (Thiagarajan and Zairi, 1997). The ultimate goal of TQM is to delight the customers. Therefore, at the outset, the institution must enhance the quality of customer services. Two important issues need to be addressed by the institution while setting goals for obtaining customer satisfaction. First, it must bear in mind that customers are the sole judge of the quality of its services, which they assess by comparing the service they receive with the services they truly desire. Second, institutions tend to ignore service quality, when competitors start vying for their business. Therefore, the institution must clearly state its customer service goal in terms of the following five criteria:

- Reliability: Improving the ability to perform the promised service accurately.
- Tangibles: Providing better physical facilities, tools, equipments, personnel, and communication materials.
- Responsiveness: Developing more willingness to help customers and provide them prompt services.
- Assurance: Improving the knowledge and courtesy of employees and their ability to convey trust and confidence.
- Empathy: Making the provision of caring and individualised attention to customers. Develop the abilities of employees through proper training to understand customer's feeling and desires.

XIII. *Resources*

The old saying that 'he who has the gold makes the rules' sums up the idea that resources are power. There must be proper allocation and utilisation of resources such as man, money, equipments, materials, etc. in order to ensure effective implementation of TQM in the institution. Proper allocation of resources plays a major role in the successful implementation of any programme. Therefore, allocation of resources (both monetary and other resources) to the TQM programme became a crucial decision for the top management. If the institution expects each of functional unit to implement TQM based on normal resources budgeted to it, then the implementation of the programme will definitely suffer. Low budgetary allocation will also lead to little or no formal training on TQM related issues. This is quite imperative for the employees in the institution to get themselves acquainted with various tools used in the TQM programme. They need to be taught how to design and implement quality improvement projects as well as quality circles. Proper allocation of resources such as supply of right tools, equipments, and materials also facilitate performance of people.

XIV. *System Feedback Coordination*

TQM experts say, in order to improve quality of work one has to work smarter, not harder. In order to work smarter, needless to say one needs not only sound education and appropriate skill training, but also constant instructive and supportive feedback. Feedback exerts a powerful influence on work behaviour and job performance by improving role perceptions, ability and motivation. A well-administered feedback system improves employee ability by frequently providing information to correct performance problems. It also let people know what behaviours are appropriate or necessary in a particular situation. Besides, feedback is also a great source of motivation. Positive feedback fulfils personal needs and makes people more confident that they are able to accomplish certain tasks. Employees receive objective feedback from various sources such as superiors, subordinates, peers, and outsiders (customers). Another major source of feedback is oneself.

Feedback improves role perceptions, ability, and motivation of people. Therefore, the company must carefully devise/redesign the present feedback mechanism.

Top management should keep the following tips in mind while providing feedback to employees:

- Devise a value-based (value in terms of achieving excellence and competence) and objective feedback system for the institution.
- Break away from the strict superior-to-subordinate feedback.
- Provide feedback to employees from multiple sources.
- Relate feedback to existing performance goals and clear expectations.
- Provide feedback in explicit terms.
- Channel feedback to key result areas.
- Give feedback as soon as possible.
- Focus feedback on quality of performance, not personalities.
- Give both positive and negative feedback: positive feedback for encouragement, not just final results; and negative feedback for improvement, not criticism.
- Base feedback on accurate and credible information.

XV. *Empowerment*

"Empowerment is moving decision-making down to the lowest level, where a competent decision can be made" (Hodgetts, 1996). The highest degree of empowerment is delegation, the process of granting decision-making authority to lower-level employees, which amounts to power distribution. As it has been rightly pointed out by Covey (1989) that "Management must empower its people in the deepest sense and remove the barriers and obstacles it has created that crush and defeat the inherent commitment, creativity, and quality service that people are otherwise prepared to offer. To receive joy and pride in one's work is the right of all and it is the management practices that prevent it. To achieve total quality, managers must become leaders, drawing from their people their greatest capacity to contribute ideas, creativity, innovative thinking, attention to detail and analysis of process and product to the workplace. In other words, management must become empowering leaders".

The keys to 'empowerment' are sharing information with employees, building institutional structure that will provide more freedom of action to people, and involving people in the decision-making process. These may be easy to understand, but are really hard to implement. It requires tremendous courage of the institution to share sensitive information. It takes real growth to allow teams to take over the management decision-making processes. And above all, it takes perseverance to complete the empowerment process (Rahdolph, 1995).

XVI. *Training*

Training is a process of updating the knowledge, developing skills, bringing attitudinal and behavioural changes, and improving the trainees' ability to perform efficiently and effectively. Every institution has a basic responsibility to educate and train its employees and this responsibility is magnified when quality management programme is launched in the institution. Whether TQM is a new system or a newly renovated old system for a institution, it is essential that all participants, i.e. all employees must have knowledge of its principles, values, objectives, tools and techniques and the institution's plan for its implementation. This implies that employees must be educated why TQM is being done and trained how well it has to be done. Besides, when employees learn new role patterns essential for TQM implementation through training, they are likely to experience less stress and feel more comfortable with breaking previous routines. This is evident from the Japanese experience. One of the significant facts responsible for the present world leadership in quality attained by Japan is its emphasis laid upon training of personnel in Quality Control.

TQM is an institution-wide activity. Adoption of TQM needs to focus on the continuous improvement (CI) tools and techniques which must be disseminated among employees through proper training and education. As training is an effective medium of measuring communication competence, developing managerial and technical competence, and generating enthusiasm for implementing TQM effectively, the institution must devise a better, well thought-out and properly organized training programme with a thrust on the aspects:

- Making effective use of various TQM tools.
- Multiple-skill development.
- Team building and group-centered activities.
- Providing and receiving constructive feedback relating to the quality of performance.
- Stress management
- Managing communication competence: improving the ability to use all the modes of transmitting, understanding, and receiving ideas, thoughts, and feelings (verbal, listening, non-verbal, written, electronic and the like) for accurate transmission and exchange of information and emotions.

XVII. *Quality Policy and Guidance*

Quality policy of an institution is a documented outcome of the process of strategic quality planning. It serves to provide internal consistency between the goals and the procedures of a institution, by aligning each member, division, and element of the institution towards its long-term objectives. In order to be effective, such policy documents have to posses the following characteristics: the statements has to be clear, brief and unambiguous; it must be widely circulated; it must focus on a meaningful and attainable specifics, rather than vague generalities; the policy must communicate the values and beliefs on the basis of which the overall plan has been framed, while simultaneously specifying the approaches that are to be used in the attainment of goals; and, it must be signed by the CEO, and/or his team, and then faithfully adhered to by them, all others in the institution too must abide by it (Wakhlu, 1994).

XVIII. *Organisational Structure and Processes*

Organisational structure refers to the division of labour as well as the patterns of coordination, communication, workflow, and formal power that direct institutional activities. An institution with a narrow span of control and high degree of formalization and centralization is called a mechanic institution. On the contrary, an institution with a wide span of control, little formalization, and highly decentralized decision-making is called an organic institution. Whether an institution will adopt an organic or mechanic structure, it largely depends upon its quality policy.

A TQM institution needs a leaner and more organic structure that can accommodate strategic balancing act between cost, quality, and speed. Therefore, the institution has to restructure itself so as to become more customer-focused, dedicated to continuous improvement and learning, which hopefully would enable it to mimic the speed and flexibility of a TQ institution. In this context, some strategies are recommended which are enlisted in Table 7.2.

Table 7.2: The Desired Shape of an Institute to Achieve TQM

Sl. No.	Characteristics	Present	Desired
1.	Design of the institution	To meet customers' requirements	To satisfy and delight the customer
2.	Task definition and knowledge required	Narrow, technical	Broad, general
3.	Task flexibility	Relatively rigid and routine	Flexible and varied
4.	Degree of hierarchical control	High	Low (more emphasis on self-control)
5.	Linkage between individual's contribution and institution's objectives	Vague, indirect	Clear, direct
6.	Specifications of techniques, obligations, and rights	Specific	General
7.	Primary communication pattern	Hierarchical and vertical	Lateral and multi-directional
8.	Primary decision making style	High authoritarian and less participative	Less authoritarian and more participative
9.	Emphasis on obedience and loyalty	High	Low
10.	Nature of work	More individual-oriented	More team-oriented and less individual centered
11.	Information hoarding	Less sharing	Information rich and more sharing
12.	Reward and recognition	Time, effort and rank	Skill, contribution and result
13.	Feedback system	Single source from top to bottom, and rarely from peers and subordinates	Multiple sources

Chapter Overview

In this chapter, three foundation stones of TQM have been identified: *customer focus, continuous improvement* and *teamwork*. All the three are necessary for implementing and surviving TQM in an institution, if any one is missed then TQM will get destabilized. Apart from these 18 KSFs have been identified for making TQM a success in any institution. The KSFs are:

1. Awareness
2. Vision
3. Leadership
4. Innovation
5. Ethics
6. Perception
7. Communication
8. Mental State (Stress and Delight)
9. Reward and Recognition
10. Maturity and Breadth
11. Attitude and Morale
12. Customer satisfaction sensitivity
13. Resources
14. System feedback coordination
15. Empowerment
16. Training
17. Quality Policy and Guidance
18. Organisational Structure and Processes

Discussion Questions

1. Describe the foundation of TQM citing suitable examples.
2. What are the key success factors (KSFs) of TQM? In your opinion, which is the most important one and why?

Quality Accreditation

8

Chapter Outline

- Meaning of Accreditation
- Accreditation Process
- Institutional Considerations
- Benefits of Accreditation
- The Challenges DEIs Pose for Accreditation
- Chapter Overview
- Discussion Questions
- Appendix 1: ISO 9000:2000 Model
- Appendix 2: Baldrige National Quality Award (BNQA)
- Appendix 3: European Foundation for Quality Management (EFQM)
- Appendix 4: European Standards for Quality Assurance

Chapter Objectives

After completion of this chapter, the reader will be able to:

- Discuss the concept of accreditation
- Explain the process of accreditation
- Outline the benefits and challenges of accreditation
- Describe different quality standard and assessment models

Meaning of Accreditation

Accreditation is a system for recognizing educational institutions and professional programmes affiliated with those institutions for a set level of performance, integrity and quality, which entitles them to confidence of the educational community, and public they serve. In addition to internal quality management of institutions/providers, external quality assurance and accreditation systems have been adopted in more than 60 countries (UNESCO, 2005). Quality assurance (QA) and accreditation bodies are responsible for assessing the quality of higher education provision. The existing systems of quality assurance and accreditation often vary from country to country and sometimes within the country itself.

Some have governmental bodies for quality assurance and accreditation, and others have non-governmental bodies. Furthermore, some differences exist in the terminologies used, the definition of "quality", the purpose and function of the system including its link to the funding of students, institutions or programmes, the methodologies used in quality assurance and accreditation, the scope and function of the responsible body or unit, and the voluntary or compulsory nature of participation.

Accreditation is defined as a process of self-study and external quality review used in higher education to scrutinize colleges, universities and higher education programs for quality assurance and quality improvement. The process is designed to determine whether or not an institution has met or exceeded national published standards for accreditation and is achieving its mission and stated purpose. The process usually includes a self-evaluation, peer reviews and site visits. The process results in accreditation if the institution or program is successful (Hayward, 2006).

Accreditation certifies the credibility, integrity and achievements of educational institutions to students, public, government, and funding agencies on national and international levels (Kilfoil, 2007). Accreditation allows perspective students to know that their credentials will be widely accepted (Leventhal, 2005). Stella (2004) defines accreditation as "an evaluation of whether an institution (or progamme) in terms of recognition as an institution of higher learning or approval for offering degree granting programmes or public funding. It typically results in a certification that is valid for a fixed period". Howell et al. (2007) in their comparative analysis of six different regional distance education accreditation agencies have observed that "accreditation is one (and perhaps the primary) means of quality control that can help providers of distance education (DE) realise their potential in helping students maximize the benefits generated by this mode of delivery and learning".

Accreditation Process

Accreditation aims at assessment, improvement and accountability. Kilfoil (2007) has identified internationally, accreditation best practice involves some or all of the following:

- Transparent criteria communicated in advance, usually developed with stakeholder involvement.
- A widely published application procedure, including costs that might be involved.
- A briefing meeting between the accrediting body and the institution.
- Capacity building (training of evaluators and/or institution staff).
- A self-study produced by wide participation in the institution, based on the pre-determined accreditation standards, including student surveys.
- Materials evaluation and a pre-evaluation readiness visit by peer reviewers.
- Analysis of self-study and a site visit by peer reviewers (usually senior people).
- A peer report, with an opportunity for the institution to respond before it is sent to the accrediting commission/agency, an appeals procedure.
- An improvement cycle.

Accreditation can be done at institutional or programme level. *Institutional accreditation* focus on the institution as a whole as the primary focus of the assessment process. In *program accreditation* the primary focus is individual academic and professional programs.

There are different types of accrediting options and agencies. Each considers accreditation differently as per their set standards. The following paragraphs explain types of accreditation agencies (more specifically for DEIs) and their functioning styles.

A. **Regional Accreditation:** As such there are no regulatory bodies for higher education or for DE and training. An European project on accreditation aimed at ensuring transparency of degrees and promoting mobility at European and international levels was developed under EU auspices (Sursock, 2001). However, in Europe there are only six regional accrediting agencies that evaluate and accredit the institution as a whole but do not accredit its individuals and programmes. In order to develop a common frame of reference regarding online or distance education offerings, the regional accrediting organizations collaborated to develop the "Best Practice for Electronically Offered Degree and Certificate Programmes" (Robinson, 2004). According to van Damme (2001), further progress in Europe on accreditation is likely to be slow. In the US, the Council for Higher Education Accreditation (CHEA), which represents over 3,000 institutions, has fostered regional accreditation while acknowledging the problems of decentralised educational systems and national isolation (Petersen, 1999). Countries in the South Asian Region are considering mutual recognition of degrees (Hawkridge, 2003). For example, in India IGNOU being the apex body of accreditation and mutually recognizing the degrees provided in distance mode by other DEIs.

B. **National Accreditation:** In general as the World Bank (2002) notes, rich countries have established or begun to establish accreditation. National accreditation usually focuses on an entire institution that has a narrowly focused mission or delivery model rather than institutions with a large variety of different programmes (Robinson, 2004). According to the CHEA website, there are currently six recognized national accrediting agencies within the USA only. While, UK has a QA agency that performs audits of teaching and research in universities and colleges, including distance education institutions such as UKOU. In India, IGNOU is the national accrediting agency for DEIs, NAAC for conventional universities and colleges.

C. **Specialised/Professional Accreditation:** These accrediting agencies evaluate individual programmes within an institution such as law, medicine, pharmacy, business management, etc. which may or may not have received regional accreditation for the entire institution. One basic difference between a specialised accreditation agency and a regional agency is the use of competency standards or outcomes by specialised accrediting agencies. These agencies evaluate programmes that are focused on a relatively narrow window of knowledge, skills and attitudes. In USA, Accreditation Council on Pharmacy Education (ACPE) is the accrediting agency for pharmacy institutions. In India, National Board of Accreditation (NBA) is the accrediting agency for technical and some other professional education. Specialised accrediting agencies are also attempting to improve their own ability to evaluate the quality of programmes using distance learning by reviewing and revising their standards. The crucial dimension of quality in specialised accreditation is the adequacy of the educational programme as it relates to professional expectations and requirements for entry and practice in the field.

D. **International Accreditation:** There is no agreed international quality framework for higher education and accreditation and QA systems very widely (Larsen, Martin and Morris, 2002). UNESCO fosters debate in this field through its Global Forum on International QA, Accreditation and Recognition of qualification. In a contribution to this debate, Van Damme (2001) suggests that an international initiative is essential in this field. Some observers while noting the danger of massive bureaucracy are in favour of international QA systems, at least for higher education. Most existing schemes are national and do not cover foreign providers, whether a bricks-and-mortar campus or operating through distance education or online. A more recent trend seen is DEIs obtaining accreditation from outside the country. It implies that DEIs want to gain confidence of current students and prospective students around the globe in their DE programmes and services by meeting rigorous international QA standards (Jung, 2005). For example, Monash has obtained ISO 9001 certification for its services; OUM has also obtained ISO 9001 certification and USQ too. UT is also in the process of selling international accreditation and quality certification from ICDE. In the rapidly changing and evolving field of DE, international accreditation will certainly contribute to support capacity building efforts of an DEI and gaining international confidence in its courses and services. Some of the widely used international quality standard and assessment models are given in Appendices 1 to 4.

Institutional Considerations

Regardless of the sector in which DE is working, the accrediting agencies have independently developed standards, policies or processes for QA of DE. Some of these take the form of new standards, while others are adding to existing standards (CHEA, 2002). The following seven fundamental features compiled from variety of sources briefly present institutional considerations while seeking accreditation (Padhi, 2007):

1. **Institutional mission:** In the DE environment, accrediting organizations focus on the relevance of the distance learning programmes and courses to the institution's mission. The accrediting organizations consider the following sub-criteria.
   - Is the mission of the institution consistent with its intent to provide educational programming at a distance?
   - Why is the institution interested in distance education programs?
2. **Institutional organizational structure:** Accreditor generally provide institutions with considerable flexibility in establishing structures that meet an institution's particular needs when developing distance learning initiatives. All require effective planning and evaluation systems and appropriate administrative structures that allow the institution to achieve its distance learning goals. Institutional structures for distance learning may vary significantly based on interest in sub-contracting or entering into other arrangements for delivery of distance learning rather than the institution itself providing distance learning. The sub-criteria can be:

- Is the institution committed to allocating resources to a distance education initiative and is that commitment in terms of personnel, finances, etc.?

3. **Institutional resources:** Accrediting organizations also address an institution's financial capacity to provide an educational program that meets generally accepted norms for quality. The sub-criteria can be:
   - Is the institution committed to allocating resources to a distance education initiative and is that commitment in terms of personnel, finances, etc.?
4. **Curriculum and instruction:** Accrediting organization standards related to curriculum and instruction vary considerably because of the different types of institutions they accredit and the diverse credentials (degree or certificate) the institutions award. However, certain common features do prevail. The standards address the content of the curriculum, the structure of the credential awarded, and the institution's process for reviewing and updating the curriculum. This includes appropriate academic support for the educational programs of the institution, including library and learning resources. The appropriateness of the subject matter for delivery at a distance is also a focus of accreditation attention. Academic support that is essential to the distance learning environment is also addressed accreditation review. This includes the technology and methodology the institution uses to deliver the instruction. Sub-criteria can be:
   - Does the institution have the appropriate courses matched with the appropriate outcomes, how is it ensuring that outcomes are being met, is the technology being appropriately used, etc.?
5. **Faculty support:** In a distance learning environment, faculty support includes technological support for delivery of distance learning offerings. Appropriate training for faculty in technology is also important. Faculty capacity to teach in a distance learning environment is essential as well. Sub-criteria can be:
   - Is the institution providing resources that help develop the faculty to provide online instruction and has it given appropriate consideration to the issues of faculty load, content ownership, copyright, intellectual property, etc.?
6. **Student support:** Accrediting organizations require adequate and appropriate support for the students served by the institution in a distance learning environment. This includes a major emphasis on technical support. Student interaction with faculty is central to the quality of distance learning. This includes developing a sense of community in the distance learning environment. Sub-criteria can be:
   - Does the institution provide distance learners with access to advisors, facilities, learning resources, counseling, and accommodation of students with learning disabilities, etc.?
7. **Assessment and evaluation:** One of the most significant changes in accreditation in the last few years has been the increased attention accrediting organizations have been giving to student learning outcomes. Where once accreditation focused almost exclusively on educational resources and processes such as course syllabi, faculty qualifications, library holdings and physical plant, central to accreditation reviews

today is evidence of student achievement. Institutional accreditor requires institutions to sustain a comprehensive system for the evaluation of the institution's educational effectiveness in relation to student learning. More important, however, is the accreditor requirement that institutions must document, as a result of their evaluation of their effectiveness, that they are in fact meeting their educational mission and goals and that their student outcomes are at an acceptable level. This is true in the distance learning environment as well as campus-based learning. Sub-criteria can be:

- How the program's effectiveness is being evaluated, are the outcomes being reviewed for clarity, what is being done to compare learner performance to intended learning outcome, etc.?

Benefits of Accreditation

Kilfoil (2007) has identified some benefits of accreditation as follows:

- Helps institutions identify strengths and weaknesses through standards-based self-evaluation and external peer review, and to effect continuous improvement.
- Provides triangulated data on performance and educational effectiveness (self-evaluation, peer review, student surveys).
- Institution-wide involvement in this reflective process can provide a new sense of purpose and identity.
- Provides individuals, employers and governments with reliable information on the quality of education, which is important, both to the nation and for recognition in the global knowledge economy.
- Peer-driven accreditation can positively affect education quality because the training reviewers receive builds capacity in the system and they observe or recommend good practices across the system.
- Institutions that take the process seriously and involve as many people on campus as possible in the self study can use the results of the accreditation to improve the institution.

The Challenges DEIs Pose for Accreditation

DEIs challenge accreditation in a number of ways:

- Many of the measures used in traditional accreditation reviews do not apply to online institutions, among these are the institution's full-time faculty, the number of volumes in the research library, and the amount of time that students are in class (Wellman, 2000).
- How can it be determined if a course offered online is equivalent to a traditional classroom-based course?
- Who will accredit a university that does not have a physical campus? Regional accreditation, as its name suggests, is based on the physical location of the institution. Western Governors Univerity, a collaboration of 18 states and Guam, has its administrative headquarters in Utah (located within the Northwest Association of Schools and Colleges accreditation region) and its academic headquarters in Colorado

(located within the North Central Association of Colleges and Schools accreditation region).

- Even for those institutions that do have a physical campus, what happens when the student is in another region and never sets foot on the physical campus? (www.distancelearningnet.org/reports)

Chapter Overview

Accreditation is a process of recognition by an external quality assurance agency. It benefits the stakeholders of the institute in judging the quality of service that they are going to provide. As DEIs are treated as second grade HEIs it is very much essential for them to prove their quality of services and accreditation is a means for that. Basically, there are four types of accreditation agencies and some international quality standard and assessment models like ISO, MBNQ, etc. Accreditation can be done at institutional and programme level. There are number of benefits of accreditation and also few challenges associated with it. However, with proper leadership and considering the cost effectiveness methodologies, accreditation can be of great help to the DEIs.

Discussion Questions

1. Define accreditation and outline the process of accreditation.
2. Outline the benefits and challenges of accreditation of DEIs.

***Appendix* 1**

ISO 9000:2000 Model

ISO 9000 is an internationally recognized Quality Standard which provides a comprehensive Quality Management System. The main objective of ISO 9000 is to promote development of standards world wide to improve operating efficiency and productivity and reduce costs. The ISO 9000 Quality System is a model that provides a unique framework for any organization to establish a customer-oriented (customers here include both internal and external customers) quality system that is internationally recognized and can be independently assessed and certified.

This model emphasizes on the following:

- The importance of identifying and understanding the needs and expectations of customers as well as other concerned parties to ensure that their requirements are being met.
- The commitment of top management to support the implementation of the quality management system and to continually improve the system.
- The effective utilization of organizational resources in implementing the quality management system.
- The control of the product and/or service realization processes to ensure all requirements are being met consistently.
- The measurements of quality management system processes to determine the effectiveness of the system and improvement opportunities.

Steps that are required to follow for ISO 9000: 2000 are as follows:

ISO 9000:2000 (4) Quality Management System

1. Develop a quality system and a manual that describes it.
2. Develop and implant quality system procedures.
3. Develop quality plans for products, processes and projects and customer contracts.

ISO 9000:2000 (5) Management Responsibility

1. Appointment of committed senior personnel to manage quality systems and give necessary authority.
2. Develop a quality policy which describe organisation's attitude toward quality.
3. Develop customer focussed quality objectives.
4. Define quality system responsibilities; give quality system personnel the authority to carry out these responsibilities.
5. Define a procedure that senior personnel can use to review the effectiveness of the quality system.
6. Develop a quality record keeping system and develop procedures.

ISO 9000:2000 (6) Resource Management

1. Define a clear-cut record on the provision of resources.
2. Develop a system for assignment of personnel to those jobs, which suits their skill sets.
3. Develop training procedures for all personnel in the organisation.

ISO 9000:2000 (7) Product Realisation

1. Develop document procedure to identify customer requirements, review the existing products and medium of communication with customer.
2. Develop document procedures to control design and/or development planning, inputs, outputs, review, verification, validation and changes.
3. Develop document procedures to identify and track products/services from start to finish.
4. Develop packing, packaging and marking methods and procedures to protect and control quality of products/services and packaging materials.
5. Develop methods and procedures to protect and preserve product/service quality prior to delivery and while the product is still under control.
6. Develop procedures to protect products/services after final testing and during product delivery.

ISO 9000:2000 (8) Measurement, Analysis and Improvement

1. Develop methods and procedures to obtain optimal customer satisfaction.
2. Develop internal quality audit procedures which determine whether quality activities and results comply with written quality plans, procedures and programmes. Also to evaluate the performance of quality system and to verify effectiveness of corrective actions.
3. Select statistical technique to measure and monitor product conformity and develop process to control non-conformity.

Appendix 2

Baldrige National Quality Award (BNQA)

BNQA is an organizational excellence award that is administered by US Commerce Department and the award process is overseen by the National Institute for Standards and Technology (NIST). It has been established since 1987 to recognize performance excellence in the US organizations. Education category has been added in BNQA since 1999. This award is based on an organizational performance excellence model. The BNQA Excellence Model for Education provides for a quality management system having seven categories (called Baldrige performance excellence criteria) which provide a framework for improving overall performance in an institution.

Using BNQA Model for Education, colleges and universities can take steps to improve the following areas of their institutions, thereby achieving organizational objectives and improving performance results:

1. Leadership—Evaluate how senior leaders guide the institution.
2. Strategic Planning—Examine how the institution sets strategic directions and how it determines key action plans.
3. Students/Stakeholders and Market Focus—Review how the institution determines student/stakeholders and market-driven requirements and expectations; and how it builds relationships with and acquires, satisfies and retains students.
4. Measurement, Analysis and Knowledge Management—Evaluate the use of analysis and improvement of data and information to support key organizational processes and the institution's performance management system.
5. Faculty/Staff Focus—Review how the organization empowers faculty/staff to develop to their full potential, and how human resource policies and procedures are aligned with the institution's objectives.
6. Process Management—Examine aspects of student learning and support processes, and see how they are designed, managed and improved.
7. Organizational Performance Results—Evaluate performance and improvement for student satisfaction, financial and marketplace performance, human resources, supplier and partner performance, operational performance, and governance and social responsibility. This category also examines how the institution performs relative to competitors (benchmarking).

***Appendix* 3**

European Foundation for Quality Management (EFQM)

EFQM has been originally developed jointly by practitioners and scientists having its first publication in 1991. Since then, it has been continuously reviewed and improved. The model is consistently reviewed to improve it. The main features of EFQM Model are following:

- EFQM Excellence Model is a non-prescriptive and the most 'value-added' quality management framework in the world. This 'value-addition' is mainly due to one of its very important features that this model recognizes society as one of the major stakeholders for an excellent organization. This feature makes this model very suitable for special types of organizations like universities, colleges and other institutions of higher learning.
- The EFQM Excellence Model is based on nine major criteria. There are thirty-two sub-criteria of this model, distributed under nine major ones. The thirty-two sub-criteria of the EFQM model actually explain the depth and breadth of the nine major criteria of the model. The grids in the EFQM model explain the linkages among the 9 major criteria and 32 sub-criteria.

Appendix 4

European Standards for Quality Assurance

The standards are in three parts covering internal quality assurance of higher education institutions, external quality assurance of higher education, and quality assurance of external quality assurance agencies.

Part 1: European standards and guidelines for internal quality assurance within higher education institutions

1.1 *Policy and procedures for quality assurance*

Institutions should have a policy and associated procedures for the assurance of the quality and standards of their programmes and awards. They should also commit themselves explicitly to the development of a culture which recognises the importance of quality, and quality assurance, in their work. To achieve this, institutions should develop and implement a strategy for the continuous enhancement of quality. The strategy, policy and procedures should have a formal status and be publicly available. They should also include a role for students and other stakeholders.

1.2 *Approval, monitoring and periodic review of programmes and awards*

Institutions should have formal mechanisms for the approval, periodic review and monitoring of their programmes and awards.

1.3 *Assessment of students*

Students should be assessed using published criteria, regulations and procedures which are applied consistently.

1.4 *Quality assurance of teaching staff*

Institutions should have ways of satisfying themselves that staff involved with the teaching of students are qualified and competent to do so. They should be available to those undertaking external reviews, and commented upon in reports.

1.5 *Learning resources and student support*

Institutions should ensure that the resources available for the support of student learning are adequate and appropriate for each programme offered.

1.6 *Information systems*

Institutions should ensure that they collect, analyse and use relevant information for the effective management of their programmes of study and other activities.

1.7 *Public information*

Institutions should regularly publish up to date, impartial and objective information, both quantitative and qualitative, about the programmes and awards they are offering.

Part 2: European standards for the external quality assurance of higher education

2.1 *Use of internal quality assurance procedures*

External quality assurance procedures should take into account the effectiveness of the internal quality assurance processes described in Part 1 of the European Standards and Guidelines.

2.2 *Development of external quality assurance processes*

The aims and objectives of quality assurance processes should be determined before the processes themselves are developed, by all those responsible (including higher education institutions) and should be published with a description of the procedures to be used.

2.3 *Criteria for decisions*

Any formal decisions made as a result of an external quality assurance activity should be based on explicit published criteria that are applied consistently.

2.4 *Processes fit for purpose*

All external quality assurance processes should be designed specifically to ensure their fitness to achieve the aims and objectives set for them.

2.5 *Reporting*

Reports should be published and should be written in a style, which is clear and readily accessible to its intended readership. Any decisions, commendations or recommendations contained in reports should be easy for a reader to find.

2.6 *Follow-up procedures*

Quality assurance processes which contain recommendations for action or which require a subsequent action plan, should have a pre-determined follow-up procedure which is implemented consistently.

2.7 *Periodic reviews*

External quality assurance of institutions and/or programmes should be undertaken on a cyclical basis. The length of the cycle and the review procedures to be used should be clearly defined and published in advance.

2.8 *System-wide analyses*

Quality assurance agencies should produce from time to time summary reports describing and analysing the general findings of their reviews, evaluations, assessments, etc.

Part 3: European standards for external quality assurance agencies

3.1 *Use of external quality assurance procedures for higher education*

The external quality assurance of agencies should take into account the presence and effectiveness of the external quality assurance processes described in Part 2 of the European Standards and Guidelines.

3.2 *Official status*

Agencies should be formally recognised by competent public authorities in the European Higher Education Area as agencies with responsibilities for external quality assurance and should have an established legal basis. They should comply with any requirements of the legislative jurisdictions within which they operate.

3.3 *Activities*

Agencies should undertake external quality assurance activities (at institutional or programme level) on a regular basis.

3.4 *Resources*

Agencies should have adequate and proportional resources, both human and financial, to enable them to organise and run their external quality assurance process(es) in an effective and efficient manner, with appropriate provision for the development of their processes and procedures.

3.5 *Mission statement*

Agencies should have clear and explicit goals and objectives for their work, contained in a publicly available statement.

3.6 *Independence*

Agencies should be independent to the extent both that they have autonomous responsibility for their operations and that the conclusions and recommendations made in their reports cannot be influenced by third parties such as higher education institutions, ministries or other stakeholders.

3.7 *External quality assurance criteria and processes used by the agencies*

The processes, criteria and procedures used by agencies should be pre-defined and publicly available. These processes will normally be expected to include:

- a self-assessment or equivalent procedure by the subject of the quality assurance process;
- an external assessment by a group of experts, including, as appropriate, (a) student member(s), and site visits as decided by the agency;
- publication of a report, including any decisions, recommendations or other formal outcomes;
- a follow-up procedure to review actions taken by the subject of the quality assurance process in the light of any recommendations contained in the report.

3.8 *Accountability procedures*

Agencies should have in place procedures for their own accountability.

PART B

GLOBAL PRACTICES AND EXPERIENCES

Quality Practices at Open Universities Australia

9

—*Ann Deden*

Introduction

What makes for quality in the online learning experience? Adherence to theory-based standards for interactivity and meaningfulness? Positive feedback from students? Excellent marks? Return on investment when online learning becomes a business venture? Each factor can carry different weight depending on the goals and perspective of the university, commercial service provider or student. Years ago, Juran simply defined quality as 'fit for purpose'. Clarity about purpose and about the range of purposes a product or service must fulfill is crucial. Certainly, the notion of quality as some sort of equivalence with on-campus courses bears questioning. Too often, academics take such guidance literally, and produce recorded or transcribed lectures—in effect reproducing, even exaggerating the shortcomings to which face-to-face teaching is susceptible. Surely, we want to take advantage of the technologies, the use of today's team approach integrating academics with instructional designers, programmers and other specialists to create a fresh-start opportunity to excel.

Open Universities Australia (OUA)'s student customers can use our offerings for a range of purposes including making up classes they failed on campus, demonstrating their ability to handle university work so they can be admitted to an on-campus program, finishing a degree started elsewhere, improving their learning skills, or completing an entire academic degree. The evolving experience highlights both the challenges and the possibilities of defining, achieving and managing quality in online higher education.

Open Universities Australia (OUA)

OUA is a non-profit organisation. Originally funded by the federal government, it has been self-supporting for several years, and operates on a healthy financial footing. Since the company is non-profit, shareholders cannot receive dividends. Instead they and non-shareholders alike receive payment for units and programs offered as well as product development grants and professional development services. Each shareholder has a seat on the OUA Board.

At the same time, because it is a business, OUA is particularly focused on customer satisfaction and its effect on the company's financial bottom line. Therefore, its working criteria for quality materials, tutorial services and support services include measures of impact on per student return on investment. OUA makes significant investments in marketing, product development, and service provision. The return on these investments is constantly scrutinized. Indicators monitored include:

- Enrolment—total and analysed by age, location, subject area and sales channel
- Retention in the form of repeat business (sales of units per student)
- Customer satisfaction
- Price sensitivity in target market segments
- Cost-effectiveness of quality improvements—the scale of improvement created and the effect of the cost and outcomes on funds available to pay product and service providers as well as to fund continuous, across-the-board quality improvement.

OUA functions as the core organizer and brokerage for units of study and degree programs from seven shareholder Australian public universities as well as several non-shareholders. OUA provides open access to undergraduate study, regardless of the individual's academic background, and controls the cost of undergraduate units to ensure affordability for those most in need of access to tertiary learning. Postgraduate study is available to qualified individuals. All degree programs are online, with 85 per cent of units online or in an appropriate mixture of modalities including the web. A few programs require short, intensive face-to-face attendance and/or supervised field internships.

In the quality arena, OUA has been taking on increasing levels of responsibility and leadership with regard to academic materials and course design, tutorial support, and student support services. In 2006, OUA and its provider universities served 19,500 students taking an average of 2.6 subjects per year, spread across four undergraduate study periods and three postgraduate sessions. Upwards of 700 academics teach subjects offered through our organisation. The majority of our students are domestic, although we are exploring limited offshore service expansion.

Quality in Academic Materials and Course Design

OUA has so far established three processes for assuring the quality of unit resources and of the structure, design and content of learning activities. A fourth process, analysis of student progression data is beginning to contribute to quality improvement.

1. Unit Surveys

One process is the implementation of end-of-unit student satisfaction surveys. These are conducted on a sample of our units every study period, and reported to the respective universities for inclusion in regular review and improvement cycles. Group information and trends are also reported to the Academic Programs Committee of OUA and to the Board.

The survey investigates satisfaction with unit materials, contents, learning activities, and related administrative services. Initially, evaluation of the unit tutor was not included, as this was considered the exclusive domain of the universities' own survey instruments. However, starting in 2006, tutor performance as an online learning facilitator is also queried. The universities now routinely incorporate the results of OUA's Unit Surveys in their unit and academics' reviews. Each unit is surveyed once per year, with units participating in pilot quality projects evaluated every study period in which they are offered. OUA schedules its surveys to complement, rather than compete with the university's surveys of the same subjects.

We analyse survey results by university and by item/theme across the universities. This process has enabled us to discriminate between factors that are going well such as materials delivery and library support, and those that need additional work such as the level of tutor support or the meaningfulness of learning activities. Units with poor learning activities evaluations are referred to the quality manager for review and engagement in an improvement process that follows the new product development quality assurance process outlined below.

2. Product Development Milestone Reviews

The second quality assurance process is the review of unit materials by OUA's quality manager. A set of criteria, adapted from one developed at Edith Cowan University, Perth, Western Australia, provides an objective basis for feedback (Herrington et al., 2001).

OUA provides significant funding to assist provider universities in developing meaningful, effective online and mixed-mode learning resources. Each development project is based on a proposal that becomes, in effect, a performance contract, with features and milestones defined. At each milestone, OUA's quality manager reviews the work against the above quality standards, and gives corrective advice as needed, along with praise for the standards achieved. Academics' and instructional developers' responses to this constructive feedback have been positive. Incremental funding is only released once any requested improvements have been made.

3. Program Reviews

Each year, a few existing programs are selected for quality review against the agreed standards in Exhibit 1. This provides another opportunity to update older programs or programs with low enrolments. Again, development support is available based on proposed upgrades.

Exhibit 1: OUA Unit Quality Standards

Learning pedagogy

- *Authentic tasks*

  The learning activities involve tasks and contexts that reflect the way in which the knowledge will be used in real life settings.
- *Opportunities for collaboration*

  The environment encourages and requires students to collaborate, thereby encouraging problem solving and critical thinking.
- *Learner-centered environments*

  There is a focus on activities that provide degrees of freedom, decision making, reflection and self-regulation.
- *Engaging*

  The learning activities challenge learners and provide some form of encouragement and motivation to support their engagement.
- *Meaningful assessments*

  Authentic and integrated assessment is used to evaluate student achievement.

- *Competencies*

  Competencies are scuffled well, with no big gaps—so that incremental tasks lead to final assessment tasks on exam.

Learning resources

- *Accessibility*

  The learning resources are organized in ways that make them easy to locate and access.

- *Currency and richness*

  The learning resources are appropriate and reflect a rich variety of perspectives.

- *Strong use of media*

  The materials use the various media in appropriate ways.

- *Inclusivity*

  The materials demonstrate cultural and gender inclusivity.

Delivery strategy

- *Clear goals, directions and learning plans*

  Unit information and expectation of student roles are clear.

- *Communication*

  The unit provides opportunities and encourages dialogue between students and lecturers/tutors and students.

- *Equity and access*

The unit materials and activities are accessible and available to all students enrolled in the unit.

4. Performance Data Analysis

In addition to these two routine academic product quality assurance processes, OUA also examines academic outcomes data. Information on withdrawals, completions, passing marks and failing marks is used to highlight units or programs that may be in need of improvement. Further analysis is generally required to determine what combination of solutions could be most useful: improved advising, so that students do not take a subject before they are ready to do so, improved subject sequencing and prerequisite structures, and/or improved teaching and learning resources and processes. Appropriate interventions are then initiated with the provider, often with funding for product redevelopment or tutor training.

An Example

The typical OUA student is an adult between the ages of 20 and 45, employed full time and/or with significant home and family responsibilities. Their lives are already intensely busy. Sixty per cent of our students are female. Most have no prior university experience. Very few have ever attempted the level of academic self-management that online distance learning requires.

In 2004, OUA conducted a needs survey as part of a market analysis. Table 9.1 displays potential students' ratings of their concerns about distance learning—issues that might keep them from enrolling or contribute to failure.

Table 9.1: OUA Survey: Student Concerns and Projects Addressing Each

Student concern	%	Issue (literature)	OUA projects
Staying motivated	50%	Isolation/engagement	Online tutor training
Insufficient tutor support	47%	Isolation/engagement	Online tutor training
Isolation of distance education	39%	Isolation/engagement	Online tutor training
Insufficient study time	28%	Study management	Quick skills modules
Access to research materials	26%	Learning skills	Library
Figuring out what to study	17%	Study management	Quick skills modules
Ability to write a university essay	18%	Learning skills	Gateway
Fear of exams	16%	Learning skills	Quick skills modules

Source: Marshall (2006)

In addition to setting the agenda for much of our work on quality improvement, this information was used in consultation with Dr. Lorraine Marshall of Murdoch University (an OUA program provider) to develop specifications for a series of Quick Skills Modules that could support students in addressing some of their key concerns.

At this point, OUA had already contracted with Murdoch and other providers to create and deliver a variety of foundation skills units. Some, but not all, degree programs required completion of one of these units. However, it was agreed that OUA's first-time students, new to self-managed learning, also needed to develop essential skills akin to project management in order to keep themselves on track. And they needed help when they were studying—not when the topic might come up in a unit of study.

As a result, OUA funded Murdoch's development of a series of Quick Skills Modules which students could purchase for a nominal fee and use for a prolonged period. Totally self-instructional, each module would have clearly defined learning outcomes, interactive learning activities that could be tailored to the individual's goals and needs, ways of planning and evaluating plans based on rubrics and guidelines, and is capable of completion in about two hours.

The quality of the modules was assessed in terms of (1) student retention after completion of their initial unit(s) of study and (2) pass rates in the units being studied when the modules were accessed. There was no way to determine how or to what extent students used the modules after purchasing them.

In 2005, 47.2% of beginning OUA students who had not done the modules passed the units they attempted, whereas 51.7% of Quick Skills students passed their units. Thus, there was a 4.5% improvement in academic outcomes for the Quick Skills cohort.

Equally important, Marshall (2006) found that:

> Quick Skills students enroll for more study periods than other students. Thus, the modules [met] their objective of increasing the re-enrolment rate of students. The data shows that 80% of Quick Skills students enroll beyond one study period compared

with 46.4% of other students. Or put another way, the attrition rate after one study period is 20% for Quick Skills students and 53.6% for other students. Similarly, 57.9% of students who registered in the modules enrolled in three or more study periods compared with 23.1% of those students who did not take the modules. Thus, students who take the Quick Skills modules are more likely to continue to enroll over more study periods than other commencing students.

Table 9.2: Student Retention (8 Study Periods)

	Number of 13 week OUA study periods							
2005 cohort	1	2	3	4	5	6	7	8
Quick Skills students	80.0%	57.9%	26.6%	14.5%	5.3%	2.4%	1.6%	0.8%
Other students	46.4%	23.1%	11.2%	5.1%	2.1%	1.4%	0.7%	0.3%

As a result of this focus on needs-responsive academic product design quality planning and measurement, Murdoch University won the national 2006 Carrick Institute of Higher Education award in the category of Flexible Teaching and Learning for the creation of the Quick Skills Modules. OUA and its commitment to access and equity featured prominently and OUA was officially recognized as project sponsor.

Tutorial Support Quality

On Australian university campuses, the term "tutor" refers to someone who conducts small group workshops and discussions in between lectures delivered by the unit academic. Hired on short-term contracts, tutors are often postgraduate students, teachers from other sectors who hold postgraduate qualifications, or retired academics. However, in the online environment, many regular academics (lecturers or above) also serve as tutors.

A question of balance: The most significant continuing quality issue has been the effort to balance low cost for students, sufficient payment to providers, and quality education delivery. Low cost was adopted as part of the mission of the organization, to ensure that OUA represents the most affordable access to higher education. While this is still the case, OUA has raised its prices as enrolments and regular university fees have risen. Along with higher prices come higher customer expectations regarding product, teaching and service quality.

Provider payments: Clearly, payments to providers can directly impact the quality of students' learning experiences. For example, some providers tightly restrict the service each student receives, in an effort to control costs. This kind of approach can actually make it hard for students to contact their tutors, as lower-paid support personnel intervene in the first instance, to keep costs down.

The need for quality management: Through OUA, a student may take units from a variety of providers, all contributing to a degree offered by the university that structured the program and that offers the bulk of core required units. Thus, a student might have one unit in which the tutor provided excellent online discussion facilitation, another with no tutor interaction at all, and another where the tutor was very available, but only by phone or email.

With variation in how unit delivery is staffed and technically supported, there can be substantial variation in the quality of tutorial support provided. OUA sees quality tutorial support—especially in first year units—as crucial to achieving improvements in student retention. In addition, "more tutor interaction, please" is the one theme most often repeated in the open-ended feedback section of OUA's unit quality questionnaires. Achieving this without threatening the business model is a key challenge.

Each OUA course is supported by one or more online tutors, depending on enrolment. As an external broker, OUA has had a very limited ability to affect lecturer or tutor behavior or tutor management practices, which have sometimes varied dramatically. In some instances, tutors have done nothing but mark assignments—often giving little or no corrective feedback. At the other end of the scale, some tutors have spent endless hours responding to individual students' e-mails and phone calls.

Neither approach was satisfactory. With the marking-only tutors, students complained vigorously and were often discouraged from continuing their studies through OUA. Their evaluations of their experience, as expressed in both objective and open-ended unit survey questions, were predominantly negative.

When high levels of individual student support were the norm, tutor burnout was high. Crucially, these tutors—typically the only tutors for their units—were unable to respond to rapid growth in student numbers. Neither group of tutors felt they had time to facilitate online discussion groups, which tended to be unmanaged and therefore elicited negative comments from students. Thus, an important tool for building motivational online learning communities, teaching critical thinking and reflection, and leveraging tutors' subject knowledge was going unused.

Student feedback indicated strongly that those who experience effective discussion facilitation had little patience with tutors who did not provide this support. Without it, many student customers felt cheated of value.

Since August 2004, OUA has engaged in a series of pilot projects that have gradually increased the amount of tutor training OUA is providing to its universities. The consortium has conducted trials of three separate approaches to improving the effectiveness of online tutoring in terms of achieving improved student outcomes, satisfaction and retention rates. The first was simply to pay for more tutor hours. The second was to provide some training in online teaching, and also pay for more hours.

In the pilot studies, tutors have been trained in specific techniques, than required to provide more and particular types of tutorial support at key times in a study period, and to document the process and its outcomes. OUA has then looked at student marks, completions and retention, in addition to the logs, to determine the effect. The goal has been to discover a pattern and level of tutorial support that produces consistently improved results in these three areas. If that can be achieved, the consortium will modify its business model in order to implement the approach more systemically.

Neither of the first two approaches provided significant or consistent results. The third trial, running in 2006-07, involved providing two days of intensive training in a defined method for facilitating group work, called Student Centered Discussion. An additional half day was focused on how to adapt this method to the effective use of class discussion boards. Additional tutor hours were also purchased, strictly to cover the cost of preparing these discussions and keeping logs required for the pilot.

Tutors of first-year subjects trained in online Student Centered Discussion (SCD) spent their extra paid hours for one study period adapting their units to this technique and their second study period beginning to implement it. Tutor logs indicate a high level of compliance and follow-through. This has been a significant improvement over the previous attempt to encourage changed online tutor behavior. Significantly, it demonstrated that tutors can be willing to be accountable for their performance in defined tasks and roles.

Initial results indicate improved student results and satisfaction. All units included in the SCD Online trial showed improved student outcomes, with very substantial improvements in half.

Additionally, unit surveys reflected the following improvements in student satisfaction (Table 9.3).

Table 9.3: Unit Evaluation Comparisons

Survey item	Overall % positive responses	SCD units % positive responses
10. The learning activities kept me engaged.	79.8	82.5
14. My lecturer/tutors use of online discussion groups helped me to learn.	62.12	71.5
18. Rate your overall satisfaction with the unit.	54.05	61.9

SCD student comments with regard to these items included:

Item 10:

- I found the learning of study skills and the learning logs to be extremely insightful. A very useful unit.
- This unit prepared me for my future studies. I have gained a lot more confidence by doing this unit. I am now more aware of my weaknesses and strengths and can now acquire the skills I have learnt from doing this unit.
- The best feature of this unit was the discussion board. When fellow students actively participated I felt that the sharing of ideas and questions helped with the learning process.

Item 14:

- The tutors were positive and encouraging.
- The clear and precise instructions provided by the tutor.
- The tutor was excellent and very quick in responding to queries on the discussion board.

Item 18:

- The online component was good. It enhances the learning experience to share ideas with other students. The weekly study activities were creatively structured to extend study, so that history topics were looked at from broader perspective.
- The help of the tutors was excellent.
- The use of the discussion board by other students and especially by the tutor. The self tests were also invaluable. The variety and amount of practice questions with solutions were really helpful. The tutor was prompt in replying to queries.

Thus, early indications are that Online SCD may offer a powerful toolset for OUA tutors going forward. The items on which the SCD units outscored the others are precisely those areas in which improvement is most needed. Training, data collection and evaluation are continuing. Training is being refined to emphasize the online experience and reduce delivery costs and time.

However, this is not the end of the quest for manageable, reliable quality assurance of tutorial support. As illustrated by the initial phase of the online SCD trial, management engagement and expectations play a crucial role in what happens in online unit delivery. OUA is soon to embark upon a trial of a unified approach to the management of tutorial services based on training and a single set of quality standards. Again, business criteria for cost-effectiveness as well as tutor acceptance plus student outcomes, retention and satisfaction will be the quality measures imposed.

Quality Student Services

One of the biggest challenges facing online distance education is the provision of student services equivalent to those available on campuses. In the area of student advising, the challenge is particularly great when open access and unit-based, rather than program-based enrolment is the norm, as it is with OUA.

Life Support Services

In some service areas, we seek to exceed, rather than match the service quality universities provide on-campus students. As previously discussed, the Quick Skills Modules are available around the clock. The same is true for support in times of personal crisis. Financial exigencies force most Australian universities to offer counseling support services during limited daytime hours and only in face-to-face mode. We needed to do better than that.

Every year, we have a few students who find themselves in emotional crises related to their study workloads and outcomes. Our member universities are not required or able to support these students, who may live thousands of miles away from the institution(s) with which they are studying. Calls or e-mails from students in crisis often exceed our enrolment advisors' skills, and can create significant distress within both OUA and university work groups.

To address this situation, OUA has contracted with Crisis Support Services (CSS) in Melbourne, Victoria, to provide 24x7 phone support through a toll-free number. Unlike a community crisis service, this organisation's experienced professional psychologists have been familiarized with our advising and administrative processes and with the way students study and interact with their universities through OUA. Also, our advisors have been trained in the basics of handling distressed callers and referring them to CSS. We have also agreed the type of aggregate data analyses CSS will perform and report to OUA, so that we can better understand and, hopefully, minimize study-related causes of distress. This constitutes a planned continuous quality improvement endeavor. It may also be the first such service offered by an online tertiary education provider.

Career Management Services

Another new venture into service quality improvement at OUA has been the initiation of a relationship with a provider of online as well as face-to-face or phone career management advice. Upon inspection, we found that most career services and events at universities were focused on young people new to the job market. In contrast, OUA's students are mature adults, most with considerable work experience. Many are studying because they have hit an employment ceiling or dead-end, and want new ways to get ahead and to grow as professionals.

EPR, another Melbourne-based firm but with offices around Australia, has adapted an American online career self-analysis, planning, and resume' writing package to the Australian context. OUA has begun offering this as a free resource for its students. Usage analysis, including any purchases of additional individual fee-based services plus user feedback will tell us how well we have understood and met our customers' needs, and give us guidance for future service improvements.

Conclusion

The Quick Skills Modules, Tutor Support Management pilot project, crisis support and career management services are all examples of OUA's application of TQM principles to the delivery of online higher education. This approach is pervasive throughout the organisation, and could just as well have been illustrated by:

- The Computer Systems Integration project, pulling together all administrative processes and records to facilitate more satisfactory customer service, linkage with universities' systems, and data analysis for outcomes measurement and future planning.
- The systematic, needs-based development of increased relationship selling, product knowledge and provider awareness amongst our advisors. This has improved sales and, as further developed, should produce advice and problem-solving that is increasingly well-matched to students' individual needs.
- Pilot relationships with other academic service providers aimed at further improving tutorial support.

It is important to bear in mind that none of these quality assurance roles were automatically granted to OUA. It was vital to win the universities' trust through collegiality, fair dealing, transparency, participatory decision-making, and demonstrated interest in helping each university prosper from their involvement in OUA. OUA never forgets that it exists to serve both students and the universities. Neglect of either constituency would undermine the foundations of collaboration upon which OUA was built. Honoring those commitments has made a focus on quality an obvious and shared value. The outcomes of our quality efforts and investments are visible in the work produced and in the enthusiasm and pride with which participating academics and university leaders view their OUA association.

Quality Management at Open University of Hong Kong

10

—*Todd C.Y. Ng* and *Danny S.N. Wong*

Introduction

To many traditional higher educational institutions, Distance Learning (DL) is always different and difficult. It challenges the traditional face-to-face educational model in many ways. In DL, teachers and learners are often separated from each other in the learning process. Technical media, prints, audios, videos, and computers transmit the contents of the course instead of the teacher. Students study anywhere other than on campus, and are encouraged to learn rather than being taught. Consequently, DL also presents a huge challenge to the traditional notion of Quality Assurance (QA) in higher education. Before the advent of DL, many traditional institutions could think of QA as "a tenured full-time faculty member with a PhD teaching the course", "courses and degree programs offered by and on a residential campus", or "students learning by sitting in the same room with a professor" (Twigg, 2001). All these notions were not applicable to DL, and consequently skepticism on the validity of DL as a credible pedagogical method arose. As a result, DL pioneers and practitioners had to devise elaborate mechanisms and processes to assure the quality of DL, with a view to establishing the proper status of DL in the higher educational world. QA thus became a critical facet of any DL institutions.

Established as a pure distance learning institution, the Open University of Hong Kong has more reasons than many others to develop and maintain an intricate and effective Quality Assurance system.

The Open University of Hong Kong

The Open University of Hong Kong (OUHK), previously known as the Open Learning Institute of Hong Kong (OLI), was established by the Hong Kong Government in 1989. Its primary mission is to provide sub-degree, degree and postgraduate study opportunities to working adults through distance education. It has a unique mandate among public universities in that it was required by the government to operate on a self-financing basis, starting from its fourth year of operation. Despite the financial constraint and its short history, it has established a strong reputation in the field of open and distance education. In 1999, it was conferred two major international awards for its achievement in open and distance education by the Commonwealth of Learning and the International Council for Open and Distance Education. In 2006, it had about 15,000 students studying its 150 DL programmes. It operates on a credit system. Students take *courses* of 5, 10 or 20 credits to complete a *programme* at sub-degree, degree or postgraduate level. One credit is equivalent to about 30 study hours. 40 credits a year is equivalent to the study load of a full-time student. Students accumulate 120 credits to get an ordinary Bachelor's degree, 160 credits for a Bachelor's Honours degree, and 60 graduates for a Master's degree. The University keeps a small core of full-time academic staff for course development and course coordination works (generally referred to as course coordinators, or CCs). A large number of part-time tutors are hired to conduct optional tutorials for students to discuss any problems they have with their study.

Factors Affecting the Development of the Quality Assurance System of the OUHK

Since its early days, the OUHK has long been renowned for having an intricate and elaborate quality assurance system. The OUHK's QA system is characterized by its layers of committees and advisory groups, substantial presence of external scrutiny, and individual and collective initiatives. These characteristics are prevalent in all major aspects of the university's operation, including programme and course development, delivery, and student assessment. The system's complexity is necessary because of the nature of distance learning as well as circumstances peculiar to the university.

Distance Learning

Just for the reason of practicing distance learning alone, the university needs a vigorous QA system. DL, as the late comer and unorthodox alterative to face-to-face classroom instruction, was seen as a marginal addition deserving little attention in most traditional higher educational institutions. It was considered more as a profit-generating side-track rather than a genuine educational activity with respectable pedagogical values. These perceptions arose mainly because of the challenges presented by DL to the traditional face-to-face teaching. In her paper, "Distributed Education: Challenges, Choices, and a New Environment", Dr Judith S. Eaton, President of the Council for Higher Education Accreditation in the US, outlined how DL redefined the fundamental facets of higher education. Specifically, with DL,

- The meaning of a "higher education institution" is altered, as virtual media like the Web, chat rooms, and even the telephone replace the physical classrooms as the medium of content delivery. "An 'institution' no longer needs to be anchored in physical space and time; it can exist anywhere, anytime..." (Eaton, 2001).
- The meaning of a "university degree" is altered, as students can study in two, three or four institutions either serially or simultaneously to get a degree qualification. The university degree, instead of being a "culmination of a distinctively institutionally based experience", becomes "an idiosyncratic amalgam of educational experiences" (Eaton, 2001) taken up by the students at different institutions with a mixture of study methods.
- The role of the faculty is altered, as curriculum design and curriculum delivery become separate tasks, and standardized course materials replace the individualistic curricula designed by the faculty; and, as a result of the above.

- The task of accreditation is altered, as the traditional site-based tasks adopted by external accreditors such as visiting campuses, examining classrooms and touring facilities, are of limited applicability for DL institutions. The accreditors and hence the Government may not find it so immediately appropriate to extend to DL institutions the principle of self-regulation prevalent in traditional institutions. External scrutiny may have to take on a more exacting and rigorous dimension.

If the accreditors are skeptical about DL, the perception of the general public may then be ten times worse. In Hong Kong, this problem of perceived poor quality of DL was exacerbated by the history of unscrupulous institutions claimed to be practicing DL in Hong Kong. On top of that, the OUHK/OLI as a brand new standalone DL institution when established in 1989 faced an even "trickier assignment" (Eaton, 2001) because of its short history and the need to build reputations for quality over time.

The nature of DL per se, the historical background, and the youthful nature of the institute are sufficient motivations for the OUHK/OLI to establish a strong and sturdy QA system.

Open Entry and Mass Education

Like many DL institutions, the OUHK adopts the policy of open entry for most of its degree and sub-degree programmes. During the early 1990's, people in Hong Kong were uncertain about what would happen after Hong Kong was handed over from UK back to China on 1 July 1997. Many well-educated people chose to immigrate to other countries looking for the insurance of a stable life. In view of the depletion of quality human resources, the Hong Kong Government decided to expand the provision of tertiary education opportunities in order to produce more degree graduates. The OLI was a result of this policy initiative.

The notion of open entry to university-level study, however, was unheard of in Hong Kong. The situation was compounded when, driven by the long pent-up desire to pursue higher education, more than 60,000 people applied to study at the institute when it opened its door in 1989, with a view of getting a degree. The institute was then perceived to be offering education for the masses indiscriminatingly, and, as Frazer (1994) put it, "mass higher education brought about concerns first for standards and then quality". The combination of open entry and mass education made potential students and employers alike highly skeptical of the quality of the institute's "input", i.e. the students entering the institution, and the "output", i.e. the graduates. To remove this skepticism, a potent QA system is again imperative.

Self-accreditation and University Status

The OUHK started off not as a *university*, but as "The Open Learning Institute of Hong Kong" in 1989. At that time, it did not possess self-accreditation status, let alone the university title. Soon after its establishment, the institute set the target of attaining self-accreditation status in the earliest realistic timeframe in order to boost its academic reputation and student recruitment ability. To achieve this target, a solid QA system would be the cornerstone, and external recognition would be the requisite means. Between the eight years starting from 1989 to 1996, the institute was subject to no less than four institutional reviews conducted by external accreditation bodies:

- A working party from the British Council for National Academic Awards (CNAA) visited the institute in May 1989 to give advice on its academic and administrative structure and processes in its infant year. The advice provided the foundation for the institute's QA system at all major levels of activities, including programme and course development, course presentation, and student assessment.
- The Hong Kong Council for Academic Accreditation (HKCAA) visited the institute in December, 1990 for a comprehensive institutional review. The recommendations and responses arisen from the visit included: seeking external programme validation shortly, devolving responsibility for academic and financial decision making, broadening the subject disciplines, seeking a site for a permanent campus, and, crucially, planning for self-accreditation status.
- Following one of the recommendations made in the 1990 visit, the HKCAA visited the institute in 1992 to validate mainly the self-developed programmes. In addition to the successful validation of the programmes, the HKCAA also made more detailed recommendations on the institute's operation such as the need for an overall academic strategy for programme planning, the course development process, student counseling and support, advanced standing policies, staff scholarship and research, etc.
- The HKCAA paid a critical visit to the institute in June, 1995 to assess whether the institute had in place the appropriate QA system that justified it being granted the self-accreditation status. The verdict was generally positive. The HKCAA concluded that self-accreditation status could be granted to the institute on the condition that, within one year, the institute had to make some modifications to its QA system that would compensate for the lack of external academic input into programme validation when it became a self-accrediting institution. The most significant modification made then was the creation of the post of External Programme Assessor, who offered expert academic advice on programmes being proposed and revalidated, in effect playing the role of the external accreditors in programme validation. Other changes included the creation of the post of Vice President (Academic) to act as the focal point of the QA processes, the preparation of course reports for each course delivered, etc.

A year after the fourth visit, in 1996, the self-accreditation status was granted. Another year later, in 1997, the university status was attained and the institute changed its name to the Open University of Hong Kong. Central to all these progressions and achievements is the QA system adopted and evolved at the institute.

Self-financing

The OUHK was required to operate on a self-financing basis starting from its fourth year of operation in 1993/94. Except for one-off grants for capital projects such as campus development, the university has to rely on mostly the tuition fee paid by its students to maintain its recurrent expenditure, including salaries, premises maintenance, tutorial room rentals, etc. In Hong Kong, private tertiary institution was a rarity, and, until recently, they had never been able to receive government blessing for its quality. As a result, "self-financing" was perceived to be synonymous with "poor quality", to the point where more than half of the Hong Kong public did not think that the university was actually established by the government as a bona fide tertiary institution. Should this misconception prolong, the university would have serious difficulties doing things as basic as establishing a good reputation and recruiting students. Therefore, the university worked hard to create a vigorous quality assurance system that would go a long way towards establishing the university as a institution and removing the misconception of being second-rate.

Besides skepticism about quality, the self-financing mandate also brought about the unwanted facet of cost pressure. To successfully operate on a self-financing basis, the university naturally has to exert stringent cost control. That, however, may strangle the objective of maintaining a elaborate quality assurance system. For instance, to show that the courses can stand up to external scrutiny, external course assessors are hired to review the course content and assess its comparability with other similar courses in the market. A Course Team of at least three staffs is needed to develop a course, which helps to ensure the quality of the course materials, but also adds considerably to the staffing costs. To obtain approval for their courses and programmes, the academic staffs have to prepare and amend lots of proposals and reports to get through several levels of committees, which takes time and manpower. A sound QA system, however, is critical to the ultimate survival of the university, and therefore the university has never wavered in its commitment towards creating and implementing a full-bodied QA system despite the costs involved.

Quality Assurance System of the OUHK

It is against this background of being a self-financing, pure distance learning institution seeking self-accreditation and university status that the QA system at the OUHK was designed and developed. It has stood several formal tests of serious external scrutiny, and has forever been evolving for the last eighteen years. It has been a robust system from day one, and a persistent recommendation that it has received over the years has been how to simplify it rather than amplifying it.

The OUHK QA system can indeed measure very well against established guidelines on quality assurance of distance learning such as the six guidelines and 23 precepts developed by the Quality Assurance Agency (QAA), UK and the 24 benchmarks for Internet-based distance learning developed by the Institute for Higher Education Policy (IHEP), Washington DC, USA. Using a framework based on the six QAA guidelines, the OUHK's QA system is described in detail below:

1. *Integrated Distance Learning System Design*

QAA Guideline 1 advises DL institutions to adopt "an integrated approach" in designing a DL system. Broadly speaking, the integrated approach suggests that the institution should adhere to fundamental academic values as well as maintain a sound financial ground. This is especially relevant for the OUHK as a higher education institution operating on a self-financing basis.

1.1. Academic Values

Since its opening in 1989, the OUHK has offered sub-degree, degree, and postgraduate level of education opportunities through DL to nearly 140,000 working adults in Hong Kong. It now offers more than 150 DL programmes and 200 DL courses each semester, with a breadth of subjects ranging from Arts, Social Sciences, Business, and Languages, Education to Computing, Engineering, and Nursing. The language of instruction of about 60% of the DL courses offered are English, with about 40% in Chinese to cater for students with different language preferences. Most of the sub-degree and degree level programmes are open to anyone above the age of 17 without any requirement on educational background. The programmes and the QA system had gone through several rounds of external scrutiny, and the institution had achieved self-accreditation and university status by 1997. Amid all the teaching activities, the university has also taken care to allocate manpower and financial resources to carry out academic researches, principally on Open and Distance Learning. By the end of 2006, it had produced more than 30,000 graduates. It has indeed made education available to all, and with a quality that can withstand regular external examinations.

1.2. Self-financing

While placing great importance on achieving the academic values expected by the academic community, the university also has to grapple with the self-financing mandate imposed by the Hong Kong Government. As a result, financial prudence has always been an embedded value within all facets of the university's operation. Examples include:

- **New programme proposal**: All new programme proposals have to describe in details the expected tuition fee income and the costs required to deliver the programme in the first five years. Market surveys have to be conducted to ascertain the market potential of the programme.
- **Programme revalidation**: When going through revalidation, the enrollment performance of the programme must be reviewed, and it is a key factor in determining the continued offering of the programme.
- **Staff costs**: Staff costs, including those of the full-time staff as well as the part-time tutors, account for over 80% of the university's operating expenditure. Therefore, they are constantly being reviewed with regard to the market rates and the institution's affordability. The pay packages of full-time staff including the academic staff are reviewed periodically. The rates paid out to part-time tutors on attending tutorials, marking assignments, etc. are reviewed and approved every year.
- **Planning and budgeting**: Similar to all prudent organizations, the university devises strategic plans laying out its long-term objectives every few years, and carries out a budgeting exercise every year. Through these processes, all staffs are made aware of the institutional direction and operating priorities of the university.

With a combination of a strong market sense and cost consciousness, the university has been able to balance its budget in nearly every one of its 17 years of existence.

1.3. Compliance with QAA Guideline 1

The OUHK's mission statement concisely reflects the values placed by the university on open access and academic rigor on the one hand and sound financials on the other.

- The mission statement states that it commits to "make education available to adults, principally through of a system of open access and distance education".
- One of its stated key values is to make higher education "available to all those aspiring to it, regardless of previous qualification, gender, or race".

- It pledges to provide "sustainable and affordable high-quality programmes and courses across disciplines and at a variety of levels to meet the needs of lifelong learners".
- It also commits itself to "excellence in teaching, scholarship, research and public service".

These core values represent OUHK's integrated and balanced approach in developing itself as a proper distance learning institution.

2. *Programme Development, Approval, Review, and Revalidation Process*

The QAA Guideline 2 calls for "the establishment of academic standards and quality in programme design, approval and review procedures". At the OUHK, these academic standards and quality are upheld by two similar but separate sets of procedure: one for developing and approving new programmes, and the other for reviewing and revalidating existing programmes.

2.1. New Programmes

New programme proposals are initiated by the schools. A Programme Team consisting of two or three academic staffs within the same school proposes new programmes based on institutional strategic direction, academic considerations, and market demand. The initial proposal is presented in a brief report called Outline Programme Proposal (OPP). The OPP contains general statements on the programme aims and objectives, programme structure, market need, etc. It will first have to be reviewed by other academics within the same school and approved by the school Board. Then it has to receive approval in the Senate in order for it to go to the second stage of programme development—Detailed Programme Proposal (DPP).

The DPP contains detailed explanations of the programme's aims, structure and content. It describes in details the course syllabi, course delivery schedule, and assessment methods of each course. Additional resource commitments for developing and delivering the programme such as new course development, laboratory facilities, library collections, staffing, etc. must be mentioned. In preparing the DPP, the Programme Team is expected to seek the advice of the Advisory Peer Group (APG). The APG consists of four to six representatives of local business, professional, or academic communities with expertise on the subject area of the programme being proposed. The APG members may comment on the relevance of the proposal in the local context, suitability of the course materials, assessment method, etc. The Programme Team is expected to incorporate their comments where appropriate into their proposal.

The draft DPP will then be reviewed by the Internal Validation Committee (IVC). The IVC is chaired by the Vice President (Academic) and comprising the school Deans and Registrar. It reviews and offers feedback on the draft DPP from the perspectives of academic units other than the school proposing the programme. The Programme Team then revises the DPP where appropriate in order to proceed to the final programme approval stage.

The final programme approval stage consists of two key external elements. Firstly, the DPP needs to receive written support from the External Programme Assessor (EPA). The EPA is usually a reputable academic in the relevant field of study. His role is to comment on the programme proposal with respect to local relevance, comparison of the programme with other local programmes, the suitability of the curriculum, and the expected standard of graduates.

The EPA summarizes his comment in the EPA Report, which, along with the DPP, will then be submitted for review and recommendation for approval by the second external element—the Programme Review and Validation Committee (PRVC). The PRVC is chaired by the President of the university. It includes four external members who are distinguished academics from other local institutions. Not necessarily possessing expertise in the field of study of the proposed programme, they serve as detached yet knowledgeable observers of the proposal, lending valuable comments and advice. The PRVC determines whether to give a recommendation for approval by the Senate for each programme proposal. Having received a positive recommendation, the programme proposals may then proceed to seek final approval by the Senate for presentation to the students.

2.2. Existing Programmes

All existing programmes of the OUHK at Bachelor's and Master's degree level have to go through periodic revalidation. The revalidation helps to ensure that a programme continues to uphold the standards of quality. It allows the academic staffs to review the programme's suitability for continuation and to propose changes to the courses and the programme in the context of societal developments.

The revalidation process is very similar to the review process of new programme proposals beginning from the DPP stage. The Programme Team prepares a revalidation submission, which includes a thorough review of the programmes' implementation, course development, student performance, and a plan for continued development. The submission should include essential supporting documents such as course syllabi, qualifications of programme staff and tutors, sample reports from External Examiners of the courses, course evaluation reports based on student survey results, and graduate survey reports on their career progress and satisfaction with the programme. Similar to the DPP, the revalidation submission is reviewed by the Advisory Peer Group, the Internal Validation Committee, the External Programme Assessor, and the Programme Review and Validation Committee. The Senate is responsible for final approval of the revalidation and continued presentation of the programme.

All programmes of 120 credits or less are revalidated every five years, while full Honours programmes of 160 credits are revalidated every six years. The period of revalidation was determined based on the average duration that a student takes to complete a full 120-credit or 160-credit degree qualification. The programmes are revalidated as a suite, with all sub-degree and degree programmes in the same subject reviewed at the same time in a single document.

2.3. Compliance with QAA Guideline 2

The OUHK's programme review and approval process complies with QAA Guideline 2 in the following ways:

- There is a detailed and documented process for programme review and approval. In fact, official external accreditors have often found the OUHK process too elaborate and suggested ways to simplify it. Seasoned external academics and visitors have often expressed amazement at the seriousness the OUHK takes for its programme review and QA process in general.
- The OUHK's QA process includes a substantial element of external scrutiny. The OUHK's programmes are examined by external academics through three formal

means: the Advisory Peer Group, External Programme Assessor, and the Programme Review and Validation Committee.

- The programmes are monitored, reviewed and subject to regular revalidation. The learning materials are verified, modified and updated regularly.
- When developing new programme proposals, the academic staffs thoroughly consider the academic standards, course delivery, assessment methods and quality control processes to ensure the quality of the programmes.

3. *Course Development, Delivery and Review*

3.1. Course Development

Once a programme receives final approval by the Senate, it can be offered to applicants and students. An OUHK programme comprises a number of courses. For new DL courses, a Course Team has to be formed to develop the course materials with the help of an internal or external Course Developer. A typical Course Team consists of two academic staffs with the necessary subject expertise, a Course Designer, and the Course Developer. In the initial stage, the team develops (i) the Blueprint, which consists of a detailed course syllabus, a set of learning activities and outcomes, a course plan, and the assessment strategy; (ii) a Course Guide, which briefly describes what the course is about, what it contains, and some information about tutorials and assessment; and (iii) the first 12 weeks of study units for review by the Internal Validation Committee and then approval by Senate for presentation. The 12 weeks of study units form the first batch of course materials for the students, who will pick them up on campus or at an offsite distribution centre. The Course Team will then continue to develop the remaining course materials, which will be mailed to the students in time for them to complete the course as scheduled.

A key external element to the course development process is the External Course Assessor (ECA). The ECA is usually a seasoned academic with the relevant subject expertise. He acts as an independent reviewer of the course's academic content, giving comments on various aspects such as the level of difficulty of the materials, the suitability of assessment items, and the comparability of the course syllabus with similar courses offered elsewhere. Any new DL course or existing DL course undergoing major revision will need the appointment of an ECA. A favorable ECA Report on the completed course is an essential element for gaining Senate's approval for perpetual presentation of the course.

3.2. Course Delivery

OUHK courses are classified mainly into five levels: Foundation, Middle, Higher, Honours, and Postgraduate courses. Most if not all courses carry 5, 10 or 20 credits. Completion of 120 credits of courses will earn an ordinary Bachelor' degree. Completion of 160 credits will earn a Bachelor's Honours degree. Multiple exit points exist at Certificate (30 credits), Diploma (60 credits), Associate Degree (80 credits) and Higher Diploma (80 credits) level. Master's degree programmes require 60 credits of postgraduate level courses. Students can accumulate the credits without any time limit, but they do have to fulfill the programme requirement on the distribution of levels of credits earned, and satisfactory completion of the compulsory courses and elective courses. In addition, for Honours-level qualifications, the level of Honours classification must be determined. The classification uses a formula based on the results earned in courses at and above Middle-level, with a heavier weight towards the results attained at Higher or Honours level.

A typical OUHK DL course consists of a set of study materials, usually print-based and sometimes in multi-media. Textbooks and/or reference readings may be included. Besides studying the course materials, the students may also attend several two- or three-hour tutorials on an optional basis to meet with the part-time tutors of the course and discuss any difficulties with studying the course contents. Laboratories, special seminars and day schools are also provided to the students. Further details of the OUHK's student support mechanism are provided in section 4.

3.3. Compliance with QAA Guideline 3

QAA Guideline 3 touches on "the assurance of quality and standards in the management of programme delivery". At the OUHK, the programmes are delivered through the courses, and the quality and standards of course delivery are assured in the following ways:

- Engaging a Course Team and an External Course Assessor to ensure that the course materials developed are up to the required standards.
- Allowing students to complete a programme with no time limit, in keeping with the philosophy of Open and Distance Learning.
- Appointing part-time tutors to ensure that the students receive appropriate tutorial support in addition to studying the course materials by themselves.

4. *Student Support*

4.1. Student Support Mechanism

The OUHK's student support mechanism consists of the following facets: tutors and tutorials, online learning support, and library facilities.

The tutors are a critical element of the OUHK's DL system. They are responsible for holding the tutorials with a normal group size of 35 students, answering the students' enquiries on telephone, online or through e-mail, counseling the students on their study progress, and marking the students' assignments and examinations. Most of them are professionals and/or academics in their field, usually with a second degree. In order to ensure that they will perform their roles effectively, all of them go through a tutor training programme that introduces background information of the OUHK, the university's DL method, and their role as OUHK's part-time tutors. They study a set of Tutor Orientation Training course material by themselves, much like the way their students learn. They will also attend face-to-face meetings and workshops that aim at improving their tutoring skills, and professional development seminars that aim at long-term development of the tutors. In addition to holding tutorials, they will also make time available to answer students' questions through telephone and e-mails.

Besides the tutors, online learning support has been growing in importance over the last few years. The Online Learning Environment (OLE) offers online support to students irrespective of whether the courses they are studying requires its use or not. Utilizing the WebCT courseware system, the OLE offers three interactive tools: an e-mail facility, an online Discussion Board for asynchronous, peer-to-peer and tutor/CC-moderated discussions, and a Chat-Room for asynchronous discussions. The students also make extensive use of online assignment submission in many courses. As of the 2006/07 academic year, all OUHK courses can boast some kinds of online elements supporting the students' learning.

Student support also comes in the form of physical facilities in addition to virtual ones. The OUHK's 20,000 sqm main campus houses 21 tutorial rooms, a library, a computer laboratory, four science laboratories, a multimedia laboratory, an audio-visual centre, a language laboratory, a lecture theatre, and a disabled students' resource centre. Besides the main campus, the university also owns a regional learning centre that provides another 13 tutorial rooms, a lecture theatre, a student lounge, and a computer laboratory. In addition to self-owned facilities, the university also has to rent outside premises for holding tutorials, providing self-study centres for its large contingent of DL students.

Inside the main campus is the OUHK Library. It occupies two out of 12 floors of the OUHK main campus. Its physical collection includes over 110,000 printed and multi-media items, and 1,000 printed serials. In addition, the Electronic Library was launched in 1997 to provide online access to library resources for the students. At that time, it was the largest of its kind in Asia. For its technological achievement and impact, it won the prestigious international Stockholm Challenge Award in 2000. As of 2006, over 15,000 electronic books and 15,000 electronic serials were stored in the Electronic Library.

Inside the Library is a Disabled Students Centre. The Centre includes four multi-media stations for students with impaired sight or hearing to study specially adapted versions of the course materials. Equipments such as specially configured notebook computers are available on loan to students with disabilities. Besides the Disabled Students Centre, the university also makes other efforts to help disabled students such as allocation to accessible facilities for tutorials and exams, specially prepared exam papers and other materials, car parking arrangements, etc. All facilities on the main campus and in the regional learning centre are accessible to students in wheelchairs. Besides disabled students, the university also caters to the need of the inmate students studying OUHK courses in correctional facilities. Special administrations of course exams are made for them. They can also access the university's collections electronically or through a representative.

4.2. Compliance with QAA Guideline 4

The QAA Guideline 4 calls for the promotion of "autonomous learning with realistic aims and practical methods". With the support mechanism mentioned above, the OUHK has worked hard towards enabling students to learn independently. The quality of these support services is evaluated regularly through student surveys. In particular, students can rate and comment on the performance of tutors on completion of every course every semester. The CCs and then the school will study the course evaluation reports and take appropriate action to improve the tutors' performance or decide on their suitability for re-appointment.

5. *Student Communication*

5.1. Communicating with Students—Means and Contents

For all its education philosophy, programme and course delivery systems, and student support mechanisms, the university has to communicate all these information to the students. This is done primarily through three means: hardcopies, e-mails, and its website.

Hardcopy information mainly consists of publications mailed to or picked up by students. These publications primarily include:

- **Prospectus:** Consisting of general information of study at the university updated every year.
- **Courses Supplement:** Including information on the courses being offered for the upcoming semester.
- **Student Handbook:** Covering all the rules and regulations that the students have to adhere to during his study. It is updated every year.
- **Open Link:** A quarterly newsletter publishing the latest news and events of the university.

In addition, all students are given a CD-ROM containing the Student Handbook, Library Handbook, general OUHK information and some remote access softwares.

Before 2004, the university often mailed one-off short notices such as change of tutorial venues, examination venues, etc. to students. Since October 2004, the university has adopted the policy of communicating with students through e-mail, and hardcopies will not be mailed as far as practicable. Besides information mailed by the university, the students can also use the e-mail system to make enquiries to the tutors, submit and receive assignments, etc. To better prepare the students in using the e-mail system, a booklet on the use of the university's e-mail system is sent to all new students every semester. The students can also call at a technical support hotline if they have problems using the system.

Internet technology enables the creation of modern websites that can at once be informative and interactive. The OUHK Student Intranet is one of five intranets housed under the OUHK Portal. It conveys information such as:

- General OUHK information, including OUHK's history and structure, reports and publications, student experiences and activities, services for students with disabilities, etc.
- Study-related information, including programmes and courses, programme regulations, student records, financial support, credit exemptions, tutors, assignment submission, timetabling, examinations, graduation, career services, etc.
- Student support information and services such as online registration, updating of student records, tutorial group selection, course material delivery schedule, library services, assessment results enquiry, graduation application, Online Learning Environment, TV schedule of OUHK programmes, etc.
- Announcement of news and events, and various channels of sending feedbacks to the university such as making enquiries through the Information Centre, completing a short questionnaire indicating the areas of study interest not being offered by the university, etc.

5.2. Compliance with QAA Guideline 5

QAA Guideline 5, "Student communication and representation", is a straight-forward description of an institution's obligation to communicate to the students all necessary study-related information. Section 5.1 demonstrates that the university has communicated such information to students thoroughly through efficient and effective means.

6. *Student Assessment and Course Review*

6.1. Student Assessment

For course assessment, most OUHK courses utilize two forms of assessment: (i) continuous assessment, and (ii) a final examination. Continuous assessment typically consists of a number of Tutor-Marked Assignments (TMAs) and sometimes Computer-Marked Assignments (CMAs). Usually a course gives a choice of TMAs to the students on the philosophy of giving some rooms to the DL students, who are usually working adults, to get used to the DL way of study. However, there is also the counter-argument that giving students a choice of assignments will encourage them not to do one or two assignments, which may play against the philosophy of continuous assessment for DL courses. Therefore, the university has recently adopted a more liberal stance towards this issue, and the schools may propose a choice or no choice of TMAs for their courses as long as the assessment strategy is still considered pedagogically sound by the school and the External Course Assessor.

The marking of the TMAs are monitored by a full-time academic staff responsible for the course, called Course Coordinator (CC). The CC reviews a number of assignments scripts for each tutor and check the quality and consistency of his markings. Through this monitoring, the CC can also find out whether the assignments are at the right level of difficulties and whether the learning objectives are being achieved. The CC also monitors how quickly the tutors return the assignments back to the students.

The second part of the assessment mechanism is examination. Most OUHK courses consist of a final written examination held in a conventional, face-to-face setting. The CC prepares the examination script and the tutors mark them. An External Examiner (EE), usually an experienced academic in the field of study, is appointed to monitor the examination as an external, independent party. He comments on the exam paper before it is printed, and reviews a sample of marked exam scripts before the marks and awards are confirmed. On completion of the course, he makes a report to the university on his observations of various aspects of the examination, including the students' performance in comparison with that of other institutions. An EE can be appointed for up to six courses.

A student's overall performance in the course is reflected by an Overall Course Score, which is a combination of the assignment and examination scores. The scores and awards for each individual student are determined in a Standardization and Award (S&A) meeting, usually attended by the CC, an internal academic staff of the same school, and an administrator of the meeting. The S&A meeting can help to identify and adjust for anomalies such as tutors whose markings are too severe or lenient, students with marginal scores, absence of students for the exam due to illness, etc. It also determines the awards for outstanding students. The S&A meeting helps to ensure that the scores and awards given to students are fair and not subject to prejudice or whims of individual tutors. The scores and awards of the students of each course are then passed onto the school's Course Results Group for final approval.

6.2. Course Review

The OUHK's course review process consists of two parts: course evaluation and course report. On completion of every DL course every semester, the students are asked to complete a course evaluation questionnaire online. The questionnaire consists of (i) about 20 statements about the course for the students to indicate how much they agree or disagree with them on a five-point Likert-scale; and (ii) two qualitative questions asking the students to express their views about the course. The results of the course evaluation, along with other data, are used by the CCs to produce a comprehensive Course Report on the overall delivery of the course and the performance of the students. The Course Report is reviewed by the School Board and summarized observations are presented to the Academic Standards Review Group for discussion and suggestions on ways of improvement. Key issues are presented to the Senate for further discussion and resolution.

6.3. Compliance with QAA Guideline 6

QAA Guideline 6 touches on "student assessment", and calls for the use of appropriate assessment method and summative and formative assessments. The OUHK meets this guideline in the following ways:

- Assessing students through continuous assessment and examination to ensure that the students have really learned what they are supposed to, and have reached a satisfactory level of academic knowledge.
- Having the Course Coordinators and the External Examiners to review the standard of the examination scripts and monitoring the marking of the assignments and the examination.
- Determining the scores and awards achieved by each individual student through a group discussion in the Standardization and Award meeting to ensure the fairness of the course scores for the students.
- Evaluating the delivery and student performance of every course every semester.

Institutional Awards

A vigorous QA system has been central to the academic quality of the OUHK, which in turn is critical to the development of the university as a whole. Besides attaining self-accreditation and university status, the university has earned widespread international respect as a centre of excellence in open and distance learning. In 1999, the university received two major institutional awards from international organizations of distance educators, including:

- Award of Excellence for Institutional Achievement in Distance Education conferred by the Commonwealth of Learning (COL).
- Prize of Excellence for Institutions awarded by the International Council for Distance Education (ICDE).

In addition to awards, the university hosted several international gatherings of distance educators such as the 12th Annual Conference of the Asian Association of Open Universities (AAOU) in 1998, and the Conferences on Research in Distance and Adult Learning in Asia (CRIDALA) in 2000, 2002 and 2005.

These international awards and activities are a testament to the university's development as a distance learning institution, for which the QA system is the backbone.

Conclusion and Future Development

By mid-2007, the Open University of Hong Kong has existed for 18 years. The QA system has withstood the test of time, and is constantly evolving in response to new challenges arising for the university. In particular, the university is currently facing three issues that have important impact and ramifications on the QA system.

The first issue is the university's expansion of face-to-face programmes. Since 2001, in response to government's policy initiative, the OUHK piloted several traditional full-time face-to-face sub-degree programmes for fresh secondary school leavers. By 2007, the number of students had grown to over 2,000. The university has been adopting basically the same QA system for DL programmes and courses for the face-to-face counterparts with minor adaptations in some areas (e.g. no ECA is needed for face-to-face courses with DL counterparts). As face-to-face programmes are likely to expand in scope and size, the QA system may have to be refined considerably in order to take care of the different nature of face-to-face teaching, e.g. the more important role played by the academic staff in the teaching process, the reduced need for a set of formal course materials, etc.

The second issue concerns pure online courses. Since the late 1990's, the university has been developing online elements such as quizzes, hypermedia materials, streaming audio and video clips, etc. for inclusion in its courses. Today, all OUHK courses feature some kind of online elements. In late 2007, the university is going to pilot a Master's degree programme featuring purely online courses to test the local as well as Mainland China market. This again poses the challenge of how the university should adapt its QA system for the online courses with their special characteristics, e.g. online course materials, online lectures, online assessments, etc.

The third issue is the continual obligation to be subject to external institutional review. Despite the attainment of self-accreditation and university status ten years ago, the university is still required to go through an institutional review by the Hong Kong Council for Academic Accreditation about every five years. The university is entitled to think that there is already an ample presence of external elements in the QA system, e.g. the External Programme Assessors, External Course Assessors, External Examiners, Advisory Peer Groups, and external members in the Programme Review and Validation Committee, etc. to assure the academic quality of the university. The added value provided by formal, periodic external institutional reviews may now be reduced.

Amid all the focus on external scrutiny, ultimately any sound QA system should largely be the work of the internal academics. They are the initiator, implementer, and evaluator of all the courses and programmes that go through the entire QA mechanism. Through years of hands-on experience, the university's academic staffs have already developed a quality culture of self-evaluation that would remain intact even without substantial external input. As Lindop (1985) put it, "...the most reliable safeguard of standards is not external validation or any other outside control; it is the growth of the teaching institution as a self critical community". After eighteen years of experience, the OUHK believes it has developed a QA system that would safeguard the academic integrity and vigor of its offerings—in the past, present and future.

Quality Management in Course Development and Delivery at the University of the West Indies Distance Education Centre

11

—*Dianne Thurab-Nkhosi* and *Stewart Marshall*

Introduction

With globalization there has been increasing pressure on tertiary education institutions in the Caribbean region to move towards the use of new Information and Communication Technologies (ICTs) to widen access to their programmes. In 2004, the University of the West Indies Distance Education Centre (UWIDEC) began using a blended approach to course delivery, which involved online courses as part of the course delivery mix. Between 2004 and 2007 UWIDEC converted thirty-four of its courses to the blended format. With the move to blended learning, there is recognition of the need to ensure the quality of the programme offerings. While UWIDEC currently has a set of quality assurance procedures for the development of its print materials, these procedures do not provide for quality in the use of the new ICTs, including web-based tools. This chapter explores the quality assurance processes being adopted by UWIDEC to meet the challenges faced in course development and delivery as UWIDEC expands its online courses.

The University of the West Indies

The University of the West Indies (UWI) is a regional university, which serves sixteen English-speaking territories of the West Indies. The university began teaching in 1948 as a University College affiliated with the University of London, and became an independent University in 1962. UWI now has campuses at Cave Hill in Barbados, St. Augustine in Trinidad and Tobago and Mona in Jamaica. The total student strength was approximately 36,700 in 2005-06.

UWIDEC and Distance Education in the Region

UWI is now a dual mode institution offering teaching by distance education as well as face-to-face. In addition to the three main campuses, the university has centers in all of its non-campus Caribbean countries as well as in the rural areas of Jamaica and Trinidad & Tobago, which form part of a network making up the UWIDEC.

UWIDEC was established in 1996 to expand the university's initiatives in distance education. This was in recognition of the fact that transition rates to tertiary and university education are much lower than expected (Kambon and Busby, 2000) and this may be due to a lack of access particularly for those prospective students living under less privileged circumstances. Kambon and Busby (2000) point out that Caribbean countries have made significant progress in the education sector with regard to the provision of equal access to primary school and overall literacy rates. They point out that in the English-speaking Caribbean, a larger share of national income is allocated to education than in any other region of the developing world, averaging around 5.5% compared to 3.4% for Latin America and 4.2% for Africa (IADB, 1999). While this is the case, expenditure on education is more focused on primary and secondary education. UWI as a regional institution, therefore, recognized the need to widen access to programmes by providing distance education options.

Currently, UWI offers degree and diploma level programmes at its thirty centres located throughout the English-speaking Caribbean. These programmes are offered using a combination of synchronous (real time) and asynchronous (delayed time) interaction. The synchronous interaction is facilitated through the audio-conferencing system of UWIDEC and face-to-face tutorials, while print materials and some computer-based activities and resources comprise the asynchronous elements.

Incorporation of ICT

Prior to the setting up of UWIDEC in 1996, the university's initiatives of distance teaching were implemented through UWIDEC's forerunner, the University of the West Indies Distance Teaching Experiment (UWIDITE). The core technology used by UWIDITE was audio-conferencing, which linked several remote sites across the region to facilitate the synchronous delivery of selected courses and programmes (Kuboni, Thurab-Nkhosi and Chen, 2002b). UWIDEC now employs a mix of media in the delivery of the university's distance programmes, with pre-packaged print materials being the core component supported by face-to-face tutorials, audio-conferencing and some online elements. Increasingly, ICT (especially the Internet) is being used in distance education to create learning environments in which learners, tutors and learning resources can all be networked (Frydenberg, 2002; Marshall and Gregor, 2002). However, adoption of the Internet in the Caribbean significantly lags that in the United States and other developed countries.

The UWIDEC Blended Learning Project

The thirteen courses to be converted were selected as pilot courses based on the willingness and skills of lecturers/course developers at the Mona, Cave Hill and St. Augustine campuses. The course developers were content specialists for the respective courses and each worked with a course development team comprising a curriculum specialist, editor, web designer/multi-media specialist and technician.

The Minimal Package

Based on the timeframe within which the pilots were to be ready for delivery, a minimal blended learning package was decided on which included:

- Printed resources that UWIDEC traditionally provided.
- A website comprising course outline, course administration details, e-mail, discussion forums, links to resources.
- A CD-ROM comprising lectures (Power Point slides with audio and/or video), for 10 of the 13 pilot courses.

Changes to the Course Development Process: Incorporating CDs and Online Elements

Traditionally, UWIDEC has followed four phases of course development.

Phase 1: Concept development.

Phase 2: Pre-production—Preparation of elements.

Phase 3: Production—Authoring or sign off of all creative/educational/editorial input.

Phase 4: Post-production—Review and Evaluation.

Vaughan (1998) and England and Finney (1999) identify a number of stages in the multi-media production process. Generally, out of the many steps identified by these theorists, one can identify seven steps generally used in multi-media (Thurab-Nkhosi and Seecharan 2005).

1. Brainstorm—Concept development.
2. Treatment—How the idea will be expressed in an educational and a multi-media context.
3. Storyboard/Mock Up—Visuals and text put together in a series of Key Frames.
4. Storyboard to Script—A more detailed treatment including narrative, visuals and directions.
5. Pre-production—Preparation of elements including text, stills, audio and visuals.
6. Production—Authoring or sign off of all creative/educational/editorial input.
7. Post-production—Review and Evaluation.

Stages 2 to 4 identified by Vaughan (1998) and England and Finney (1999) were not necessary in a largely print-based environment. With the move to blended learning however and the incorporation of both online learning and CD development, UWIDEC was required to expand the course development team and adjust the course development process to facilitate the new developments.

The course development process adopted during the blended learning pilot project was as follows:

1. During the concept development phase the course developer/content specialist met with the course development team to conceptualize the content and format of the online courses and in the case of 10 of the 13 courses, the CD.
2. Following this initial meeting/brainstorming session, the course developer was required to formalize the concept, following which a series of meetings were held with the web developer/multi-media specialist to ensure that the content and concept were appropriate for multi-media production.
3. A production workshop was later held on the Cave Hill campus, with all course developers, curriculum specialists and web administrators from each of the three UWI

campuses. This workshop was intended to bring together all the pre-production work and finalize production of the CDs. Following this workshop, UWIDEC staff and course developers were expected to complete the CDs.

4. Simultaneously with the development of the CDs, the web administrators, editors and curriculum specialists worked with the content specialists to conceptualize and produce the course websites.

The seemingly condensed version of the multi-media process adopted by UWIDEC largely arose due to time constraints brought on by the need to meet grant conditions for the CDs. In 2005, CDs were completed for 10 pilot courses, distributed to students and reviewed. In September 2005, nine online course websites were developed and launched for students. While maintaining the commitment of academics was a difficult undertaking, the vision of a more flexible learning package for students, motivated staff to continue on the project. In January 2006, six online sites were added. By January 2007 a total of thirty-four courses had been converted for online delivery. While there has been some success with regard to the development of online courses and CDs, it is to be noted that there were challenges also.

Quality Management at UWI

In August 1996, the UWI Board for Undergraduate Studies (BUS) began its duties, with one of its responsibilities being to plan and direct a system of quality audit and quality assurance for the UWI (OBUS, 1997). As stated by Leo-Rhynie (2006),

> It [quality] has been viewed in terms of excellence, of consistency, of meeting certain standards, as transformation of students, as value for money and as meeting market demand.

The definition of quality adopted by the BUS for its work at UWI is one of "fitness for purpose" (OBUS, 2000). However, as noted by former Director of UWIDEC, although there is an official UWI policy on quality, the institution has not documented a clear position on "the issues of standards and/or quality assurance in the case of distance education" (Koul, 2003). In the absence of specific guidelines for distance education within the quality management framework of UWI, UWIDEC has been planning and directing the evolution of such a framework specific to its evolving blended approach by developing tools to ensure internal processes meet objectives.

Defining a Quality Management Framework for UWIDEC

The term quality assurance in education is "used in a general sense to include audit, evaluation, accreditation and other review processes and elements" (Knight, 2003 quoted in Gift, Leo-Rhynie and Moniquette, 2006). The BUS identifies two variations of the quality assurance process at UWI, namely an internal and an external process. The internal process is concerned with the quality of the learning experience of the student while the external relates to the outcomes of the teaching/learning process. At UWI, when a particular discipline has been selected for review, the process is as follows:

1. A member of staff of the quality assurance unit meets with the member of staff teaching the discipline to orient the staff member to the purposes of the review.
2. A Quality Assurance Review Team is appointed. This review team comprises 3 or 4 members, with representation from the same discipline on another campus and 2 or 3

independent members. The independent members are 1 or 2 senior academics from outside the Caribbean and at least 1 person from the Caribbean with professional expertise in the discipline but not employed at the UWI.

3. Prior to the visit of the Quality Assurance Review Team academic staff undertake a self-assessment to examine the stated aims and objectives of the discipline. The self-assessment also identifies the issues having an impact on the learning experience of the students.
4. The Review Team uses the self-assessment report as a guide to investigate the extent to which aims and objectives are being realized. The team visits the campus for 4 or 5 days and tests the validity of the self-assessment report.
5. The Review Team submits a written report, which is distributed by the Quality Assurance Unit. A year after the review, the department reports to the Board of Undergraduate Studies and the Board for Graduate Studies and Research (Beckles, and Whitely, 2002).

Quality Management Process at UWIDEC

At UWIDEC, internal and to some extent external quality assurance processes and procedures have been implemented for aspects of the institution's operations. Most of these processes while existing in written form in various policy documents, have not been documented as part of a comprehensive quality assurance policy. Moreover, there are gaps in the existing processes, which have been identified by Whitely (2000) and Koul (2003). Using the IHEP (2000) quality indicators to provide a framework, Table 11.1 outlines the current UWIDEC processes for quality assurance.

Table 11.1: Existing UWIDEC Processes for Quality Assurance

Quality Indicator	UWIDEC Process/Procedure	Whether Documented
Institutional Support	• Fees paid to academic staff as an incentive for course development • UWIDEC courses recognized for assessment and promotions • Support staff providing course administration assistance and facilitating communication with non-campus sites for course coordinators	• UWIDEC Statement of Policies and Principles
Course Development	• Team Approach • Standards for ideal course development process documented and agreed to by all three course development teams • Standards for when the ideal course development process breaks down • Writer and editor procedures	• Curriculum Development Handbook: Quality Assurance Process and Procedures
Course Structure/Design	• Clear instructional design process • Use of graphics, photos and Illustrations • Professional page composition • Built-in student exercises and practice opportunities • Professional printing and binding	• Course Plan Forms Style Guides Templates
Teaching/Learning Process & Student Support	• Local tutor support • Audio-conferencing • Student Support Officer	
Faculty Support	• Course development training	
Evaluation and Assessment	• Course evaluation • Research Officer	

It is clear that existing quality assurance processes and procedures are no longer adequate, particularly as UWIDEC has moved into online/blended learning.

Quality Management Tools for Online Learning

The challenges identified earlier all impact on UWIDEC's ability to deliver quality online programmes. It was therefore recognized that in addition to addressing the challenges through relevant policy and administrative changes, it was necessary at the level of teaching and learning, for the organization to devise some way of ensuring that quality standards were met at every stage of the course planning, development and delivery process. To this end the curriculum teams on each of the three campuses have developed a series of quality management tools and mechanisms to guide the planning, development, and the delivery of online courses in particular. The tools and mechanisms outlined below cover course development, staff and student orientation, and evaluation. At the moment, these tools and mechanisms do not form part of any formal procedure for quality assurance but are used in day-to-day operations for quality management.

Course Development Benchmarking Tool

The curriculum teams recognized that benchmarking (McKinnon, Walker and Davis, 2000) and other quality assurance tools were gaining popularity as universities realized the importance of quality assurance in tertiary education (Inglis, 2005). The curriculum teams therefore took a decision to use an existing quality assurance tool, which had been tried and tested in a university facing similar challenges to UWIDEC, as a basis for the development of a draft UWIDEC tool. The tool selected was a benchmarking rubric developed by a research team at the University of Botswana (UB). This tool was selected because one member of UWIDEC St. Augustine's curriculum development team had been involved in the development of the UB Benchmarking Rubric and saw the similarities in the challenges faced by both institutions operating in developing contexts, with limited resources (Lee, Thurab-Nkhosi and Giannini-Gachago, 2005).

In April 2003 the UB's e-Learning Quality Rubric was tested on four Southern African Development Corporation (SADC) environmental courses that were developed through a regional development project. The review was conducted prior to the courses being delivered. The quality reviewers that utilized the draft e-Learning Quality Rubric for evaluation of the e-Learning courses found a number of benefits and weaknesses through this "pilot" test of the instrument. Findings from this "pilot" test were used to (a) modify and improve the rubric for use in the e-Learning Pilot projects and (b) to assist in determining guidelines for quality and best practice models for e-Learning courses at the University of Botswana (Lee, Thurab-Nkhosi and Giannini-Gachago, 2005).

The curriculum development teams at St. Augustine, Mona and Cave Hill with permission from the team leader of the UB research group reviewed the UB's Benchmarking Rubric and arrived at a format and specific criteria to be covered in a quality assurance tool for UWIDEC. While the UB Benchmarking Rubric was essentially an evaluation tool to be used at the end of course development, it was felt that UWIDEC should develop a quality assurance tool to be used throughout the course development and delivery process. The criteria used by UWIDEC were informed by international criteria established for measuring quality in distance education (ADEC, 2002; IHEP, 2000; Michigan Virtual University, 2002).

Based on the criteria, and UB Benchmarking Rubric, the UWIDEC quality assurance tool was designed to be used during three stages of course development, namely pre-production, production and evaluation. A series of teleconferences were held to arrive at the draft quality assurance tool (Appendix 1). It was decided that this tool would be used on a pilot basis as new online courses were developed so that revisions to the tool could be based on practical experience.

Orientations for Staff and Students

Recognizing the need to prepare course coordinators, tutors and students for the move to asynchronous delivery, UWIDEC conducted a series of training and orientation sessions.

Training e-Tutors

Three training workshops catering to 150 tutors from throughout the region were conducted in January 2005. Coordinators of the various UWIDEC Centres were asked to nominate from among existing tutors of the 13 pilot courses, those who demonstrated commitment and would be willing to function as e-Tutors.

Training Students

In order to prepare students for the online experience, an orientation course entitled "Improving Your Study Skills" was mounted from July 18-August 24, 2005. The course was intended to provide students with the opportunity to improve their capability in using web-based or online learning as well as their critical reading skills. A total of 834 students participated in the six-week course, which covered the following topics:

- Preparing for online learning;
- Study Strategies;
- Understanding the Reading Process;
- Taking Notes and Writing Summaries.

163 students completed evaluations of the course, which indicated that less than half (36.3%) agreed that a face-to-face orientation was essential. Many of the students (48%) agreed that they were able to navigate the course easily however 38% agreed that they were able to access the online resources easily. While 42% of the students agreed that tutors were well-prepared, 33.1% felt that feedback from tutors was not timely and that not enough student-student and tutor-to-tutor interaction took place.

This course has been revised and offered each year since its first offering in 2005.

Guidelines for Course Coordinators, e-Tutors and Students

Recognising the challenge faced by course coordinators, tutors and students as UWIDEC continues to develop its online learning capacity, the course development team has prepared the following guidelines and documents:

- Lists of duties and responsibilities for tutors and course coordinators outlining the expected tasks of all e-Tutors and course coordinators.
- Guidelines for the UWIDEC Tutor—This identifies the personal qualities, responsibilities, reporting relationships and duties of the e-Tutor as well as strategies for successful e-Tutoring.

- E-tutoring tasks for the blended learning course, update for Semester 2, 2006-07.
- Course coordinator tasks for the blended learning course—Semester 2, 2006-07.

Evaluation

Monitoring Mechanisms by Course Managers and Production Assistants

To ensure that e-Tutors, course coordinators and students remain active in the courses, staff members of the course development unit of UWIDEC have been assigned to monitor activity in the course and queries in the student-tutor discussion forum. These members of staff make weekly contact with course participants who are not interacting or are not active in the course.

Student Course Evaluations (Student Satisfaction Approach)

While UWIDEC has not formally adopted the student satisfaction approach suggested by Harvey, feedback from students has played and continues to play an important role in quality assurance and programme improvement. Thus far this has largely been done through student evaluations of the online/blended experience. Two weeks before the end of the semester students were asked to complete a course evaluation developed by the coordinator of the blended learning project. The evaluation comprised forty-two close-ended and three open-ended questions and required students to give feedback on various aspects of their online experience using a Likert scale

e-Tutor Evaluations

As is the case with the student evaluations, e-Tutors have been asked to complete an evaluation of the e-Tutoring experience. The evaluation for e-Tutors comprises four sections of closed items and one section with four open-ended questions. The evaluation asks about the e-Tutors' satisfaction with administrative arrangements for the course and effectiveness of the course elements as well as their views on their confidence performing specific tasks in the online environment and the online experience in general.

Conclusion

In order to provide online distance education that is "fit for purpose", an organization must ensure: institutional support; effective course development; learner-centered interactive delivery; support for students; support for faculty; and a system of evaluation.

This chapter has discussed some of the ways in which UWIDEC seeks to improve the quality of its distance education operation in the new online environment. The tools and mechanisms outlined cover the very important aspects of course development, staff and student orientation, and evaluation.

Just as the quality of course development and delivery can always be improved, so too the management tools used determine this quality can themselves be improved. Thus, the tools and mechanisms used by UWIDEC are continually being refined.

Appendix 1

UWIDEC Quality Assurance Tool

Sl. No.	Activity	Person(s) Responsible	Timeframe	Assumptions	Measurable Output	Remarks	Score
1	An e-Learning course development checklist has been completed	Course developer and instructional designer	Will be set when course writer's contract is being signed	A separate, comprehensive tool that identifies the elements in a course plan exists	A course concept outlining choice and combination of media, content areas, assessment		
2	Clear student learning objectives have been developed	Course developer and instructional designer			Student learning objectives stated clearly in the course plan		
3	Clear performance criteria set	Course developer and instructional designer			Assignments, rubrics for students		
4	The course plan includes active learning, i.e. case study, problem based, anchored learning	Course developer and instructional designer					
5	The plan includes opportunity for student to student interaction	Course developer and instructional designer					
6	The plan includes opportunity for student to instructor interaction	Course developer and instructional designer					
7	The plan includes the use of further resources, e.g. links, presentations, audio, video files	Course developer and instructional designer					
8	The plan includes the appropriate use of technology tools for the objectives	Course developer and instructional designer					
9	Draft course content has been prepared in manageable segments based on the course concept	Course developer and instructional designer					
10	Draft content and course concept have been reviewed	Instructional designer					
11	Draft content has been edited	Editor					
12	Relevant copyright information has been requested	Editor					

Sl. No.	Activity	Person(s) Responsible	Timeframe	Assumptions	Measurable Output	Remarks	Score
13	A consistent, visually appealing course design has been developed	Graphic designer					
14	Website structure has been defined, i.e. areas for course, pages in these areas	Web designer					
15	HTML pages have been developed and uploaded	Web designer					
16	The homepage not only provides information and guidance, but also it is engaging	Web designer and graphic designer					
17	The course outline provides all information required of the student in the course	Course developer and instructional designer					
18	Course schedule contains all information on assignments and assessment dates	Course developer and instructional designer					
19	Consistent guidance available for student and easy to access	Web designer					
20	Easy to navigate through course components	Web designer					
21	Easy to navigate through the content	Course developer and instructional designer					
22	All segments have manageable amounts of information	Course developer and instructional designer					
23	Learning activities are part of the course content delivery	Course developer and instructional designer					
24	A consistent, visually appealing course design has been developed	Graphic designer					
25	Accessibility issues are addressed	Web designer					
26	Course orientation designed	Team					
27	Tutors assigned for the course						

Sl. No.	Activity	Person(s) Responsible	Timeframe	Assumptions	Measurable Output	Remarks	Score
28	Communication tools developed for the course	Team					
29	Response time for communication decided on	Team					
30	Learning styles are considered throughout the material	Course developer and instructional designer					
31	All chats and discussions will be moderated	Course developer					
32	Assignments developed to encourage critical thinking	Course developer and instructional designer					
33	Self assessment activities have been developed	Course developer and instructional designer					
34	Opportunities for student input into assessment criteria	Course developer and instructional designer					
35	Course evaluation	Team					

Quality Practices and the UK Open University

12

—Richard Lewis

Introduction

The UK Open University (OU) is widely acknowledged to be one of the world's most successful distance learning universities, not that it really likes to describe itself as such. It much prefers to say that the mode of education provided by the Open University is that of *Supported Open Learning*. It enrolled its first students in 1971 and has now well over 200,000 students.

At its foundation the OU was both revolutionary and traditional. It was revolutionary in that it did not impose entry qualifications or select its students. It was the students who selected the university. It was traditional in that academic research has always been an important part of its portfolio and it has always striven to ensure that the standards of its qualifications were comparable with of the UK university system as a whole.

Its revolutionary entry policy meant that it has always placed considerable importance on demonstrating the quality of its operations and on the rigour of its assessment of students.

How the OU Works

In order to understand the OU's quality practices it is necessary to understand how the university works. The following describes what might be termed the "basic undergraduate model" on which there are many variations. The postgraduate model, especially in relation to taught masters' degrees is not fundamentally different; perhaps the most significant differences are that the shorter duration of the postgraduate awards and the point that most of them have traditional entry qualifications.

OU undergraduate awards are based on the accumulation of credits. Students enrol on courses (or modules) that generally run from February to October. Each course has a number of credits attached to it, usually 30 or 60, and a level 1, 2 or 3. In order to obtain an honours degree a student must have at least 360 points of which at least 240 must be above Level 1 and of which at least 120 must be at Level 3. Students who want an unnamed "open degree" have a very wide range of choice and there are virtually no constraints on their chosen pathway, for example a student can take his or her first course at Level 3, the highest level. The OU has a very well-developed system for recognising the credits by other institutions and many thousands of students each year are given credit in respect of successful study at other institutions.

In addition to the open degree, the OU has designed over 40 named degrees. In order to obtain a named degree a student would have to follow a specified pathway, although they might have a good degree of choice on that pathway.

The OU is aware that not all things that can be taught at a distance, for example advanced laboratory work, and it therefore provides a number of residential schools. These are usually held on the campus of another university in the long (summer) vacation. The residential requirement affects only a minority of students.

The modular structure of the OU's programme meant that for the first 30 or so years of its life its quality processes were very much focussed at the course level but, as will be explained later, it is now moving its focus to the programmes that lead to the relatively recently introduced named degrees.

The Desegregation of the Academic Function

As will also be explained later many of the quality assurance practices that apply to the Open University are exactly the same that found in "conventional" universities. In fact, in terms of quality assurance, the main distinguishing feature of the OU, which it shares with a number of other so-called "mega universities,"[1] is its size and in particular the very large number of students in a course, some courses have over 5,000 students. The consequence of this is that the OU has to adopt a practice rather inelegantly described as "the desegregation of the academic function". In other words, the staff members who produce the course material cannot, as they would under the traditional academic model, also teach the students. This situation is not unique to distance education and may be found in large campus universities with high population courses where the courses may be designed by the faculty but where the bulk of the face-to-face teaching is done by graduate assistants or part-time staff. Equally, the desegregation of the academic function is not an inevitable feature of distance education, there are in the United States, for example, many instances of small population distance learning courses where only one academic is involved.

All students on a course are allocated to a tutorial group of between 20 and 30 students to which is allocated an Associate Lecturer (AL). ALs are part-time members of staff but many of them hold a full-time post in a university, including the Open University, or other educational institutions. The allocation is done on a geographical basis. In the UK, in high population courses, rooms are hired in many locations across the country so that ALs can meet their students on a regular but, from the point of view of the students, on an optional basis. Nowadays physical contact of this type is steadily being complemented by electronic contact.

Open entry was a revolutionary development in its day so the OU has always made sure that it had in place rigorous student assessment procedures. The typical model, although there are an increasing number of exceptions, is that in order to obtain a credit the student must both pass an unseen invigilated examination taken at the end of the course[2] and gain a passing grade on the basis of a number of Tutor Marked Assignments (TMAs).[3]

The TMAs are marked by the Associate Lecturer (in the earlier part of the OU's history Associate Lecturers were called Tutors) to whose tutorial group the student has been allocated. But the TMAs are much more than a form of continuous assessment. The university sets considerable store on the comments made by the ALs. These should far beyond confirming whether the student got the answer right or wrong. The comments are regarded as an important part of the teaching process.

In the UK, England is divided into ten regions while there are national offices in Northern Ireland, Scotland and Wales. The regional and national offices serve four main functions:

- They are the base for members of the full-time academic staff (sometimes referred to as regional academic staff) who act as the academic line managers of the ALs based in that region. In addition regional academic staff may undertake research and/or work with their colleagues based at the university's headquarters at Milton Keynes on course production.
- They provide administration services that are best undertaken locally such as the hiring of rooms to be used for tutorials and examinations.
- The regional and national offices provide advice and assistance (together with their colleagues in Milton Keynes) related to non-course specific issues.
- The staff, especially the Regional and National Directors, represent the OU in the area.

Equivalent arrangements are made in respect of students based outside the UK.

The academically related functions, that in the traditional model may be carried out by one individual are, in the OU, divided as follows:

- Designing the course and producing the course material—central and regional academic staff together with others such as editors and interactive media developers.
- Regularly updating the course material and designing examination papers and other means of assessment—the Course Maintenance Team which is largely made up of full-time academic staff.
- Directly supporting the students on course related matters—the Associate Lecturers. In the past it was the ALs who provided virtually all the direct student support at the course level. While the role of the AL is still central to the OU model the advent of new technologies which allow for online support and computer conferencing means that members of the central course teams are now playing a larger part in direct student support.
- The provision of academic support not directly related to the course, for example, careers advice—regional and central administrative and academically related staff.
- Teaching at residential schools (where appropriate)—specially recruited staff but under the supervision of members of the full-time academic staff.
- Marking the final examination papers—in some courses the marking is done by members of the full-time staff while in others it is undertaken by specially recruited staff (who are usually already acting as ALs) but under the supervision of members of the full-time academic staff.

This breaking down of the function does present problems from the quality management point of view. For example, great care must be taken with student feedback as the people responsible for producing, maintaining and updating the course material may not, other than on an isolated basis, meet the students who are taking their courses.

But the problems caused by the desegregation of the academic role is more than compensated by the benefits that it brings to quality assurance. In the "bad old days" what went on in the lecture theatre and tutorial room was a very private matter between the teacher and his or her students. So if the teaching was bad, or the content of the course unsuitable, it was only the students who were in a position to be aware of the weaknesses but their lack of knowledge often meant that they were unaware of the weakness or, if their were so aware, their lack of status meant they could not do very much about it.

In contrast, in a university such as the OU the teaching process is not a private operation and people other than the course teacher and the students have far greater knowledge upon which they can form a view on the appropriateness of the course materials and the quality of support given to students.

National Arrangements for Quality Assurance

The Open University is, like every other university and higher education institution in the UK, subject to the national quality assurance arrangements.[4] The UK system is outlined below:

The Quality Assurance Agency (QAA)

All universities are subject to QAA. The QAA's style of operations has developed over the years. Under its present model it conducts an *Institutional Audit* on a peer group basis, i.e. it is largely undertaken by academics from other universities, and is, to a major extent, focussed on assessing the effectiveness of the university's internal quality assurance procedures. The audits take place every five or six years.

The QAA has, in consultation with HEIs and others produced what it refers to as an *Academic Infrastructure* which is described by the QAA as "...a means of describing academic standards in UK higher education. It allows for diversity and innovation within academic programmes offered by higher education."[5]

In other words, the academic infrastructure does not, on the whole, present a set of rules that should be slavishly followed but a number of benchmarks against which universities are required to demonstrate that they took into consideration when designing their own programmes.[6]

The Academic Infrastructure is Made Up of the Following Elements

- *The Framework for Qualifications in Higher Education.* This provides guidance on the titles and structures of awards which may be offered in the UK higher education system. It provides descriptions of the generic competences required to be demonstrated for the award of a qualification at the different levels including certificate, honours level baccalaureate degree, masters and doctoral degrees.
- *Subject benchmark statements.* These set out expectations about standards of degrees in a range of subject areas. They describe what gives a discipline its coherence and identity, and define what can be expected of a graduate in terms of the techniques and skills needed to develop understanding in the subject. At the time of writing the QAA had issued honours degree benchmark statements covering 46 subjects.
- *Code of practice for the assurance of academic quality and standards in higher education.* It provides guidance on maintaining quality and standards for universities and colleges subscribing to the QAA. It is made up of ten sections covering such topics as postgraduate research programmes, students with disabilities and the assessment of students.

- *Programme specifications.* A programme specification is a concise description of the intended outcomes of learning from a higher education programme, and the means by which these outcomes are achieved and demonstrated.

External Examiners

The system of external examining is well established in the UK dating back to 1832 with the foundation of the University of Durham (Silver, 1994). External examiners mainly come from other universities, but might also, in vocational areas, be practitioners. External examiners are appointed to all examination boards that are responsible for the award of qualifications. Their two main traditional tasks are:

(i) to ensure that degrees awarded in similar subjects are comparable in standard across higher education institutions,[7] and

(ii) to ensure that students are dealt with fairly in the system of assessment and classification (Silver, Stennant and Williams, 1995).

In the main the external examiners carry out these responsibilities by approving the examination paper and checking the marking of the scripts.

While their traditional roles remain basically unchanged, the ways in which they are discharged has been subject to quite substantial change over the last two decades or so because of such things as the introduction of continuous assessment and the very large increases in student numbers not matched by a corresponding increase in the numbers of external examiners (Lewis, 2005).

Because of the way OU degrees are earned through the accumulation of credits earned from individual courses, much of the work of the external examiners takes place at course level although there is now an increasing involvement at programme level.

Teaching Quality Information (TQI) Website[8] and the National Satisfaction Survey

These are relatively new innovations that were introduced with the strong encouragement of the government following the ending of the system whereby the QAA undertook programme reviews in addition to Institutional Audits.

One of the main purposes of the TQI website is to supply information to students when deciding to which universities to apply but there has been a lack of agreement about the type of information that students would find helpful. In its earliest manifestation, the website included not only quantitative information about such things as graduation and employment rates but also qualitative information including summaries of external examiners' reports and the reports of internal programme reviews. However, following a review—the "Burslem" review (HEFCE, 2006) carried out on behalf of the Higher Education Funding Council for England (HEFCE), Universities UK and Guild UK[9] it has now been decided that the web site will only include quantitative data.

The tqi website also gives the results of the *National Students Survey* (NSS). This is a survey of final year students who are asked to report on their level of satisfaction with various aspects of their academic experience, namely teaching, assessment and feedback, academic support, organisation and management, learning resources and personal development. The students are also asked to rate their satisfaction with their overall experience.[10] The NSS has survived the Burslem review and it results will continue to be carried by the tqi site.

A Quality Culture or a Bureaucratic Culture

Much is made these days of the need to develop a "quality culture" whereby all members of the university whether academic or administrative staff or students are fully seized with the need for quality and seek to achieve high standards through every action they take. This is of course an ideal, but the fundamental notion underpinning the concept of a quality culture is that it is the day-to-day actions of individuals that are important; far more important than the drafting of documents however erudite or the ruminations of a committee however eminent its members.

This line of thinking sometimes results in a suspicion of complex systems and extensive committee systems on the grounds that they are too "bureaucratic" and get in the way of the "real work".

I tend to think like that and am inherently suspicious of what appear to be over complex systems but I am also aware that it is too easy to jump to conclusions without fully understanding the situation.

In this context my fear is that some will find the OU systems that I will describe as being over complex and bureaucratic. I do not think it does suffer from these sins. There are a number of reasons why the OU does need to operate what might appear to be an over elaborate system. One factor is its very large size and the wide geographical dispersion of its activities. The other is that I believe, for good reasons, the OU is very risk averse.

One of the reasons is that many of its students are also taking risks in that they have not entered a university possessing the conventional array of comfort blankets in the form of entry qualifications. Many of its students take great risks because they have not, so far, found success in any educational sector or because they are moving entirely new fields of study. The OU must ensure that the risks of things which are under the control of the university going wrong are minimised.

A related issue is that for the reasons described above the OU relies on many different groups working together in harmony and if one of the parties messes up the consequences will be felt throughout the system.

How the OU Ensures Quality

In Course Production

The OU believes that the course materials are the most important learning resource. They are specially designed to take the place of lectures, seminars and library-based study which students would undertake at conventional universities. The core component of the study materials is normally a series of specially written course texts. These are augmented by some or all of a range of other learning resources: study guides; videotapes; audio-cassettes; textbooks and specially commissioned collections of articles; resource files; specialist software (on CD-ROM, DVD or as web downloads), and password protected on-line services such as computer conferencing and library facilities.

Throughout its life the OU has had access to the BBC and broadcast programmes that were specifically related to its courses. It was only in 2006 that it decided that, in the light of the other means of conveying information that are now available, these were no longer necessary. It still does produce programmes for transmission on the BBC but these are now not course specific but are of a more general educational interest.

Course production is not, as is still the case in many universities, the responsibility of a single individual. The course team is a very important feature of the OU. The core of the team are full-time academic members of staff but it also includes academic reading members (including, in many cases, Associate Lecturers), an editor and designer to assist with the presentation of the final printed texts, media and IT specialists who will produce the specific software and a course manager responsible for administrative arrangements of the operation of the course. The exact mix depends upon the requirements of the individual course.

The fact that the course material is not at risk of being subject to individual idiosyncrasies is itself a powerful tool for helping ensure quality, but OU practice goes much further than that.

All course teams are required to nominate an External Course Assessor who is appointed by the university. Only persons of sufficient seniority, experience and academic reputation are eligible for appointment. The External Assessor assesses the structure, balance, coverage and level of the overall content of the course, the effectiveness of its teaching material, its approach to teaching of any practical components, and its treatment of issues relating to gender and minorities. The External Assessor also gives feedback to the course team throughout the course's development and provides an interim and final report. The reports may be made available as public documents, so contributing to the university's openness about academic standards, and transparency of the process by which they are achieved.

There are, as described above, many safeguards built into the system to ensure the quality of the course material but should, for some reason, they all fail there is one very important backstop. That is the fact that OU course material is in the public domain, in fact many universities draw on OU teaching material for their own courses. If there are problems with the course materials then the wider academic community would, in one way or other, soon bring them to the university's attention.

In Course Presentation

The Monitoring of TMAs

Reference has already been made to the importance of the TMAs and in particular on the emphasis placed on the AL's comments which is held to be an extremely important part of the learning process.

In a conventional institution it is unusual for a member of staff's teaching, whether it be in the lecture theatre or seminar room, to be observed and when this does take place it is usually regarded as being a very special occasion. In the OU in contrast this process of "observation" or rather "observation and comment" is a regular part of the process.

In the university's own words "The monitoring of assignment marking is central to the University's quality assurance procedures."[11]

The monitoring, which is usually undertaken by a member of the central or regional academic staff, has the following objectives:

- To ensure grades given by different ALs are consistent with each other and with the intentions of the course's Examinations and Assessment Board.

- To ensure that each AL's correspondence teaching is appropriate in both quality and quantity.
- To provide staff development for ALs and to share good practice in correspondence tuition.
- To enable the Examinations and Assessment Board, including the External Examiner, to see the way in which the course and its assessment has been received by students and ALs.

The numbers of TMAs that are subject to monitoring varies depending on such factors as the experience of the AL, the credit rating of the course and whether it is in its first presentation but it is university policy to ensure that every AL is monitored.

The selection of the TMAs for monitoring is done after they have been marked so, unlike the lecturer who can see that he or she is being observed, the OU ALs does not know when their teaching is to be monitored.

In addition to the monitoring carried out by the OU's own staff, external examiners are also sent a sample of each of the TMAs for the course with which they are associated.

The Examinable Component

As discussed earlier the OU's has a two-pronged assessments procedure—the TMAs (and occasionally CMAs) and what is elegantly described as the "examinable component". The examinable component is usually an examination but it might take the form of a dissertation or project.

Because of the large population of many of the OU courses it would be impossible in most cases for an individual, or a small team of individuals, to mark all the examination scripts. The OU is acutely aware of the need to ensure consistency of grading and takes great to ensure that this is achieved.

It is university policy that marking schemes must be produced for all examination papers, and moderated by the external examiner.

Before marking begins all markers participate in a co-ordination exercise where a representative sample of scripts is considered and the marking standards are set. A minimum of 15% or 15 pieces of work from each member are monitored, that is second marked by members of the Examination and Assessment Board or by experienced Associate Lecturers acting on behalf of the Board. The scores given by markers who are found to be lenient or severe can be adjusted at the Standardisation meeting. Where markers are found to be inconsistent, remarking of all scripts from that marker will take place.

A Standardisation meeting takes place for each course to report on the monitoring of the sample scripts from each member of the marking teams. The Examination and Assessment Board considers how the examination paper has been answered by the cohort as a whole, and whether the marking has been completed to the standards expected. Where this is not the case, procedures exist for corrective action, e.g. the adjustment of examination scores at marker level, question level or overall examination level, or remarking of scripts.

The Monitoring and Regular Review of Courses and Programmes

In 2007, the OU is introducing a new system for the monitoring and review of its courses and programmes. The most significant change is that courses will not be reviewed on an annual basis but generally at the end of its first presentation and mid-way through its life. At the time of writing this chapter not all aspects of the new system have been put into place so in order to be able to provide a comprehensive picture the system that was in use up to 2006 will be described.

This has presented some difficulties in deciding what tense to use. In some cases, the past tense would be appropriate but for other aspects of the system the present tense would be more appropriate as the feature being described is not being changed. To avoid some clumsy constructs the present tense will be used throughout this section.

Course Review

All courses are subject to annual monitoring. The annual report combines an overview of quantitative information about student registrations, progress and completion rates, with qualitative information about the feedback received and the action taken by the course team, significant changes to the course or the performance of students, etc.

Summaries of the reports are considered by academic units, i.e. the faculties and schools of the university. They confirm that annual reports have been completed, drawing out issues for attention at unit level, and in particular, identifying high- and low-performing courses (or those which have changed from year-to-year in these respects) in relation to student feedback and student performance. Outcomes of the annual course report process are considered at institutional level.

In addition to annual monitoring courses are subject to a more intensive review process at up to three stages during their life.

- after the course's first presentation
- at its mid-life
- in advance of a decision to extend the life of the course or to remake it

Academic units are responsible for carrying out a review at the end of first presentation. All new courses are routinely included in the annual courses survey and course teams are expected to use this feedback, together with feedback from Associate Lecturers, Regional Academic Staff, etc. to review whether the course has achieved its aims and objectives, and to identify and rectify any problems.

Mid-life course reviews usually take place in the sixth year of presentation of courses which have a standard life of eight years or an indefinite life, and every four years after that. The review panel includes an external member if the life of the course is likely to exceed ten years. Approval of the panel's recommendation is the responsibility of the academic unit board, acting on behalf of the Senate.

The process for extending the life of a course starts with a notification of the intention in the academic unit's annual unit plan. A course life review panel is convened by the unit administering the course. The panel includes members of the unit familiar with both the course materials and the presentation of the course. If it is considering a course life of more than ten years, the panel includes in addition a member from outside the unit and someone from outside the university.

The course life review panel considers how the course is presented, the printed and other teaching material, statistical information on student numbers and progress and issues related to resources.

The panel prepares a report which includes its assessment of the academic health of the course, any essential or desirable alterations that it believes should be made to the course and a specific proposal for any extension or shortening of the agreed course life.

Programme Review

The above described monitoring and review at the course level but the OU also undertakes annual monitoring and regular reviews at the award level. It has set up a number of Programme Committees which carry responsibility for one or more awards. For each award the committees on an annual basis receive information on:

- Student registrations for each award and its compulsory and core courses.
- The number of students claiming awards.
- Result profiles of courses within those awards.
- Classes of degree awarded.

Programme Committees also receive an annual report from one or more External Advisors covering:

- The appropriateness of the courses within each award and the structure of the award.
- The objectives of the award and how these are achieved through the individual courses within the award.
- The validity of the awards in comparison with comparable awards made by other institutions with reference to any benchmarks and professional requirements (where applicable).
- The classification profiles of students who have achieved the award.

In addition the Programme Committee receives reports from the Course Teams for the core courses in the relevant award on:

- How the progression/pass rates compare with previous year.
- The main messages from the feedback available.
- The external examiner(s) report, and response made/action taken.
- What was done last year in the light of the previous review and whether it was effective.
- Whether the tuition and assessment strategies continue to be appropriate and effective.
- Comments on the role of the course in relevant awards.
- What is planned in the light of profile/pass rates and feedback in the coming year.

The university undertakes a programme for periodic review of all its awards. The review process is being carried out over a six year cycle, with all taught provision on the same subject areas being reviewed at the same time. The process is described as being an internal review but the panel does include at least one university appointed external member.

The aims and objectives of the review process are to:

- Address the requirements of the QAA external review framework.
- Focus on student satisfaction, performance and achievement in programmes/awards (as distinct from courses).
- Review the curriculum including the interdisciplinary elements.

- Lead to quality enhancement through an independent critical evaluation of the curriculum and so make a positive contribution to quality assurance within the university.
- Demonstrate the effective and ongoing management of the quality and standards of programmes/awards, and the reliability of information.

Summaries of the reviews were at one stage made publicly available through their inclusion on the Teaching Quality Information Website (www.tqi.ac.uk) but as explained earlier this is no longer to be the case. Institutions of higher education are, however, being urged to find ways of making such information available.

Box 12.1, which is the introduction to the periodic report on programmes leading to degrees in Mathematics at the OU, and which is to be found on the tqi website, provides a flavour of the reports.

Box 12.1: Periodic Review Report

The Faculty of Mathematics and Computing programmes in the area of Mathematics and Statistics were subject to internal review in September 2005. The review considered the MSc in Mathematics, BSc (Hons) Mathematics, BSc (Hons) Mathematics and Statistics, BSc (Hons) Computing and Statistics, BSc (Hons) Computing and Mathematical Sciences, BSc (Hons) Economics and Mathematical Sciences and the Undergraduate Diplomas in Mathematics and Statistics. The purpose of internal periodic programme review at the Open University (OU) is to: Strengthen the internal focus on students satisfaction with, and performance and achievement in, awards, as distinct from courses (modules); Provide an opportunity for reviewing areas of the curriculum which may involve inter-disciplinary and inter-faculty discussion for which there is no other forum; Offer informed yet independent critical evaluation of the provision, and promote discussion within the subject area which is likely to lead to quality enhancement; Demonstrate to the university's Academic Board and stakeholders (including staff, students and funding bodies) that the institution possesses rigorous mechanisms for the management of the quality of its programmes and the standards of its awards and is using these effectively and consistently. Also that the institution has the capacity to, and is very likely to continue to, secure and maintain quality and standards in the future and that the publicly available information it provides is complete, accurate and reliable. Provide a focus for information and review at programme/award level which will help the university to address the requirements of the Quality Assurance Agency external review framework.

Source: http://www1.tqi.ac.uk/sites/tqi/index.cfm?section=data_tabs&gtab=periodic&id=76056&hei=126&typ=2&crs=&area=12&subj=G100,G200,G300,G990,G910,G000,G900

The report has the following sections:

- Conduct of review.
- Evidence base.
- External peer contributions to process.
- Overview of the main characteristics of the programmes covered by the review.
- Conclusions on innovation and good practice.
- Conclusions on quality and standards.
- Conclusions on whether the programmes remain current and valid in the light of developing knowledge in the discipline, practice in its application and developments in teaching and learning.
- Forward-looking recommendations for actions to remedy any identified shortcomings, and for future enhancement of quality and standards. This section also lists points for commendation.
- Actions taken by the institution in response to the review.

The Student Input to Quality Processes

The OU has a very well-organised and effective Students' Association which is organised on a regional basis. Students are represented on virtually all committees and boards of the university including the Council, the Senate and Faculty Boards. It is probably the case that because the vast majority of OU students are experienced adults they make a more effective contribution to the working of the university's committees than is the case in other universities.

The main instruments used to monitor and evaluate the students' opinions relating to the courses, the learning outcomes and the services offered to students are the *End of Course Surveys*. The surveys provide feedback at different levels:

- High-level general university feedback for institutional performance indicators, which is used as trend data to identify where students are becoming more or less satisfied and therefore areas which may need to be investigates in more depth.
- Course-specific feedback that can be used by course teams to establish and record areas of excellence and areas of weakness that may need to be addressed.

Reports on the findings are considered at university-level, regional and academic unit level. Award Surveys are carried out to coincide with an internal periodic programme review of a specific subject area, see the earlier section on programme reviews.

There is a regular programme of surveys on issues such as student withdrawals, characteristics of new students, studies of students' careers while other topics may be the subject of special surveys. Recent examples of the special surveys include the cost of OU study and issues surrounding access to technology.

Review of Research Degree Programmes

This chapter has been largely been concerned with the OU's undergraduate programme but brief mention should be made of the quality processes associated with its research programmes. The OU has over 18,000 graduate students including nearly 500 full-time research students.

Research degree standards are subject to rigorous approval processes at initial registration, degree registration and examination.

The Research Degrees Committee monitors the quality and standards of provision.

These arrangements include a requirement for:

- A first year report for full-time research students.
- A probation report for all part-time research students.
- An annual progress report for all other current students.

The responsibility for ensuring that the process is satisfactorily completed rests with the Head of Discipline/Department. The review processes are designed to identify issues which may be causing problems for the student, the supervisors and the discipline as well as assuring that a satisfactory standard of progress is being achieved.

Conclusion

The UK Open University has in place an extensive system of quality procedures. The main distinguishing features being the extensive use of academic experts from outside the university whose role in the OU goes far beyond the conventional role of the external examiners and the team approach that is applied to course production in particular, but also to many other aspects of the university's life. The fact that the OU's material is in the public domain and the sheer size of the OU's student body also means that it when things go wrong, and even in the OU things do go wrong occasionally, it is very difficult to hide the problem from public gaze.

Perhaps inevitably this chapter has concentrated on procedures but the importance of the internal quality culture must not be ignored. If I can end on a personal note I would say that in my experience I have never come across a university where the desire to help its students is so strong. But there is more to it than that. During my period as pro-vice-chancellor I chaired a meeting in one of the regional offices that involved 15 members of the OU staff. Of those 15, 13 were either current students of the OU or had been students in the last one or two years. So if things should go wrong in terms of the services the OU provides to its students you would probably first learn about the problem from your colleague at the next desk.

Notes

1. UNESCO have identified 20 mega universities, i.e. is universities with more than 100,000 students *Source*: http://portal.unesco.org/education/en/ev.php-URL_ID=42857&URL_DO=DO_TOPIC&URL_SECTION=201.html
2. The OU has a large number of examination centres in the UK and a much smaller number overseas and students can choose which centre to attend. Otherwise the student can pay a fee to be examined elsewhere so long as the university is assured of the adequacy of the invigilation arrangements.
3. Some courses have Computer Marked Assignments (CMAs) which, as the name suggests, are marked automatically by the computer.
4. In terms of UK institutions, there is one exception to this, the University of Buckingham., the only wholly privately funded university in the UK. However, the University of Buckingham does participate on a voluntary basis.
5. http://www.qaa.ac.uk/academicinfrastructure/default.asp
6. While the QAA is careful to avoid words like rules and regulations there are certain parts of the academic infrastructure departures from which might be difficult or even impossible to justify, for example aspects of the *Framework for Qualifications in Higher Education.*
7. The system is not as effective in ensuring that standards are comparable across subjects.
8. www.tqi.ac.uk
9. Universities UK and Guild UK are the organisations representing the heads of universities and other institutions of higher education.
10. In the two surveys held so far the OU came top in both years for overall satisfaction.
11. Quality and Standards in the Open University, Fact sheet 4, Assessment and Awards, http://www.open.ac.uk/foi-docs/d15903.doc

Quality Assurance and Assessment System in Distance Education: Stepwise Actions and Pragmatic Experience of Universitas Terbuka, Indonesia

13

—*Aminudin Zuhairi, Dewi Padmo, Kristanti A. Puspitasari* and *Agung S. Putra*

Introduction

Universitas Terbuka (UT) is an open university, established in 1984 as the 45th state university to provide opportunity and access to university education, for in-service teachers, working adults and recent high school graduates. UT was founded as a part of the government's national strategies to improve participation in higher education. In 2006, UT enrols more than 320,000 students, residing in different parts of the country, with over 95% of whom are working adults. UT has major roles to play in developing high-calibre human resources needed for the nation's sustainable development. Since its foundation, UT has enrolled over 1.2 million students and has produced over 600,000 alumni, working in various fields of the profession.

UT students learn from the course materials delivered by the institution and from other learning resources accessible from other institutions. UT has developed multi-media learning packages for its students, with the printed materials as the major media supplemented with audio cassettes, video programs, computer-assisted instruction, web-based materials and online tutorials. Learner support is provided to facilitate student learning activities in the forms of tutorials, counseling, study groups as well as administrative services. Students' needs for tutorials are provided and facilitated by regional offices. A number of tutorial methods have been implemented, namely face-to-face, correspondence, broadcast, and online tutorials. Currently, UT has four Faculties (Teacher Training and Educational Science; Mathematics and Natural Sciences; Economics; Social and Political Sciences), with 35 Programs of Studies. Additionally, it has a Graduate School offering three Masters programs in Public Administration, Management, and Fishery Management. UT media resources for learning include 117 courses with radio tutorials, 377 courses with online tutorials, and 1002 televised tutorial programs.

The major challenge for UT is to provide quality university education at a distance accessible by students with different level of economic capacity, access to ICT facilities and limited ICT literacy. Since 2002, UT has launched *UT Online* services, aiming at introducing web-based academic and administrative services for students. The web-based academic services consist of online courses and online tutorials while the web-based administrative services includes online counselling and online information dissemination. An online examination system has also been introduced for some courses to facilitate students' flexibility in taking semester examinations. The availability of communication infrastructure is one of the critical aspects in providing online learning services along with the technical skill of the students in using online services. UT has conducted socialisation and training in online learning services to improve ICT literacy of students.

UT Approaches to Quality

Quality improvement has become imperative and served as a vital management and competitive strategy for distance education institutions to meet increasing demand for customer satisfaction. Pressures for quality improvement have emerged internally and externally. Internally, distance education institutions are challenged to undertake continuous improvement. Externally, stakeholders have persistently questioned the quality, accountability, effectiveness and efficiency of educational endeavour, in which they make greater contributions as users. To respond to pressures from the stakeholders, governments have set up independent quality and accreditation agencies as part of the effort to improve the quality of education, and institutions have started to put a lot of effort to address the challenge for improving the quality of their educational practice. For many institutions, there have been growing trends that funding from the government and student enrolments depend significantly on the quality and performance of the institutions. For distance education, the news has been encouraging, in which a recent account has confirmed that there is no reason in principle that large-scale distance education system cannot achieve high quality services (Daniel, 1996, 1999).

Quality in distance education covers a number of aspects, including products, processes, production and delivery system, and philosophy (COL, 1997). Quality of products includes such things as course materials, number of graduates, examination pass rates, and admission in further studies. Quality of processes covers areas such as learning and teaching processes, advising students, coordinating external course and test item writers, networking with regional offices, managing student record system. Quality of production and delivery system includes course production, print and multi-media production, test item production, scheduling, warehousing and stock control, getting materials to students, and transmission of broadcast. Quality of philosophy covers such things as vision, mission and policy statement, institutional culture, governance, corporate culture, and public image (COL, 1997). Quality assurance (QA) is based on the assumption that quality can be improved continuously. Policies, systems and procedures that are developed must ensure that staff can critically question the quality of distance education products, processes, services, and philosophies, and they attempt to improve it continuously. The UT QA system is a systematic and comprehensive effort to improve quality.

Effort to improve the quality of distance education provision at UT has started since as long as the UT was established in 1984. In fact, the UT itself has from the beginning served as an agent of change for quality improvement of national human resources, including in-service teachers, working adults, and recent graduates of senior high schools. The UT approach to quality management is distinctive and unique. The UT quality management system has been modelled on existing framework, i.e. the *Asian Association of Open Universities* (AAOU) *Quality Assurance Framework* which is then adopted, modified and contextualised to suit the specific needs of UT for the Indonesian context. The UT effort to implement the quality management system has been rooted in its Strategic Plan and Operational Plan. Back in 2001, the UT Operational Plan 2001-05 clearly states that the UT development programs focus on three areas, i.e. academic quality, student participation, and internal management (UT, 2001). Then more recent institutional planning documents have been published, i.e. Strategic Plan 2005-20 and Operational Plan 2005-10 (UT, 2004; 2004a).

Then, an actual step to put quality management approach into action was through the establishment of a Quality Assurance System Committee in 2001 to work thoroughly on the design, development, implementation, and evaluation of QA system. The Committee worked with people from various units across the university to develop QA policy manual and QA work manuals. When ideas about QA have been more widely accepted, a Quality Assurance Centre was founded in 2003 to plan, organise, coordinate and facilitate the quality assurance mechanism and continuous improvement effort of the institution's distance education services.

Developing QA policy was a significant initial step to do and it was no easy task, even when there was a well-defined source of reference. Adopting the draft of the Asian Association of Open Universities (AAOU) QA Framework was a pragmatic way, as it did not need to invent a new wheel. Modification and contextualisation of the adopted framework to suit institutional needs took a great deal of time, effort, and energy. Then it has to be followed with intensive socialisation as part of internalisation effort to enhance the staff understanding of QA meaning and values. A document called "Quality Assurance System for Universitas Terbuka" was produced in 2002 after numerous consultations and meetings (UT, 2002). Like the AAOU QA Framework, comprising 107 statements of best practices, the UT QA framework comprises nine components, i.e. policy and planning, human resource provision and development, management and administration, learners, program design and development, course design and development, learner support, learner assessment, and media for learning. Each statement is further delineated into indicators and methods of achievement such as what sort of policies, systems, procedures, manuals, methods, work instructions, and records are needed to improve quality. This document serves as the foundation for implementing QA system, supplemented with an instrument for self-evaluation and priority setting, and a list of units within the university responsible for assuring the quality of their respective work activities.

At that time the idea of QA system was fairly new to a lot of people at UT, so internalisation through socialisation, training, guidance, supervision, and systematic tryout to the university community were needed to ensure that the main ideas and basic principles of the system were well understood by people within the organisation. Changing attitudes and work habits of people took time to allow for the development of quality culture. The adopted UT credo for QA is "We write what we do, we do what we write, we check, we act, and we improve continuously". QA implementation involved systematic tryout, which was undertaken by writing QA manuals, using the manuals in daily activities, and getting feedback from users directly for continuous improvement. This tryout method involved intensive coordination to enable internalisation process and development of quality culture among staff. Socialisation of

QA framework was conducted for academic and administrative staff as well as managers from all levels of the hierarchy. QA implementation involved self-evaluation and priority setting. Staff awareness of quality had to be established so that everyone realised that UT could no longer wait to start effort on continuous improvement. Integrating QA into annual action plans required careful consideration of resources and cost. Effective integration of QA into annual action plans had to be coordinated by the top level of the management.

QA implementation required the writing of manuals, documenting policies, systems, procedures, work instructions, and records for various work activities. A number of Working Committee were assigned to write these manuals, involving members consisting of managers and staff from different units related to particular activities that they performed in daily work. QA system documents work activities, and ensures that systems and procedures are implemented accordingly. The writing of QA manuals required a great deal of time for discussion and consultation to ensure that clear and precise systems, procedures and work instructions were well understood by staff. A series of activities for writing manuals were conducted, involving tryout and improvement of the manuals. The work on developing 112 job manuals were completed in 18 months during the year 2002-03, involving more than 200 users as developers.

Effective QA implementation began in 2003, initiated with large-scale socialisation involving 200 managers university-wide. These managers had become core agents for change in their respective units. Since then, UT has started to consistently implement a comprehensive QA system to ensure that all management and staff develop quality culture, so that UT becomes a learning organisation with a high spirit for continuous improvement. In the following year, in 2004, the number of QA manuals grew even more, and the UT applied 197 QA manuals for use by staff to perform various activities of distance education provision. In 2005 through to 2006, continuous improvement of QA manuals was further conducted, involving mapping of core activities of UT distance education system. As time goes by, we are learning to be more efficient, precise and effective, and currently the number of QA manuals has been shrinking by half of the previous year down to about 95 manuals.

QA involves the mechanism for internal and external assessments. Internal assessment is conducted through internal audit, monitoring and evaluation. External assessment is conducted by inviting credible external and independent assessors, auditors, and accrediting agencies. External assessment, accreditation and quality certification is an important part of quality assurance in order to ensure public confidence about distance education. Quality is acknowledged by external agencies independent of UT interests. For UT, aiming at continuous improvement and quality enhancement focusing on student satisfaction are the ultimate goals, rather than getting the certification itself. The process of continuous improvement and quality enhancement must be achieved through establishing an effective learning organisation and creating awareness and action-based commitment for quality work culture among staff within the institution.

QA system ensures the quality of distance education provision for students. Stakeholders' interests for quality distance higher education can be met satisfactorily. Quality provision will ensure the sustainability of distance education programs. The competition among distance higher education providers naturally require open universities and distance education institutions to work smarter and have commitment to assure the quality of provision. Quality culture must be internalised to ensure that everyone has the awareness and deep understanding that quality begins with oneself. And last but not least, quality assurance and continuous improvement requires significant resource commitment of the institution.

Step-wise Actions in Implementing Quality Assurance System in UT

The UT implementation of QA system involves a systematic step-by-step process as the following: (1) developing QA framework, (2) conducting self-assessment and setting priorities, (3) integrating QA into action plans, (4) writing QA manuals, (5) implementing QA system, (6) monitoring, evaluation and internal audit, (7) linking quality assurance to staff performance appraisal, and (8) engaging external assessment. Successful and effective implementation of QA system involves changing the people's mindset in terms of quality work values and culture. The challenge for the top leadership is to manage changes of existing organisational culture into quality work culture. Implementing QA system in a very large distance education institution involving networking with participating institutions requires a great deal of effort, strong perseverance, and gradual internalisation. Making new ideas work in practice necessitates constant direction and clear vision of the top leaders. The following is the description of step-wise actions taken by UT in implementing its QA system.

1. *Developing QA framework*. Developing QA framework called "Quality Assurance System for Universitas Terbuka" (*Sistem Jaminan Kualitas Universitas Terbuka* or *SIMINTAS*) was the first step to do for UT to have a systematic and comprehensive approach to quality assurance. To have common perception and platform among the university community was the most difficult phase in QA implementation, in which the existing university community had their established views, values and cultures. The socialisation process of quality management system was conducted encompassing three main stages, beginning from the top level administrators, middle managers, down to all staff. Initially, many of the people were not very much convinced that QA system could improve the quality of UT services. Some staff were afraid of the change, as there was suspicion that would bring about uncertain consequences on their established cultures. Nevertheless, constant effort and sharing of knowledge and experience were attempted, and agreement was eventually reached so that the plan for QA implementation could continue.

2. *Conducting self-assessment and setting priorities*. Once the QA framework was developed, the next step to do was conducting self-assessment and setting priorities. This was done unit by unit and university-wide. Managers from all levels were invited to conduct self-assessment using the QA framework as instrument. After all statements of best practices in the QA framework were self-assessed by managers in terms of the quality, setting of priorities were decided for quality improvement over the next four years. The summary of results indicated that most priorities were set for the years 2002 and 2003. In this way, UT started to integrate QA system into annual plan of activities for the year 2002 and 2003. Management and staff accepted the use of QA as the method for quality improvement. This process was first conducted in 2002, and then it was repeated three years later in 2005, using the same instrument. The results have been encouraging, showing an increase in the average rating score for all 107 statements of best practices from 2.46 in 2002 to 3.83 in 2005 (an increase of 1.37). It seemed that the relatively low increase was attributed more to the fact that there were higher expectations of the staff, and it was not because of the low achievement level the QA

effort. This shows that the whole process seems to have increased the level of quality awareness and culture in the mind of staff.

3. *Integrating QA into action plans*. Integrating QA into annual action plans required careful consideration of resources used and cost needed. An effective instrument has been to link annual funding for activities within units in congruent with the university's strategic plans and operational plans, based on unit performance. This scenario has been developed to achieve effective and successful integration of QA into action plans, and this has to be supported and coordinated by the top level of the management.

4. *Writing QA manuals*. Writing QA job manuals was a long and tedious work involving a lot of staff time. Working Committees were assigned to develop these manuals, consisting of managers and staff from different units relevant to particular tasks. Jobs and activities have been performed every day, some of them have already had proper documentation. These manuals were developed for use by different units within the institution. Manuals are sets of guidelines used as sources of references for performing particular tasks. The manuals elaborate systems and procedures in performing particular jobs and activities, and indicate standards relating to time, output, workflow, resources and competencies needed to perform the task. The system also shows the relationship of tasks among different units. The procedure indicates systematic steps and requirements for task completion and contains objective, scope, definition, reference, requirement and related units involved for task completion. It further describes step-by-step procedural activities to perform the task. Documentation of systems, procedures and work instructions helps improve the quality of distance education product, process, and services continuously.

Writing job manuals was a major step done in QA implementation, involving all operational units. These manuals were developed by users for the users themselves, and therefore the writing process involved a lot of people related to their respective jobs and activities. The functions of the Quality Assurance System Committee, which later become the Quality Assurance Centre, were to facilitate the units and Working Committees in developing and producing the manuals. The process of writing manuals were done in several phases, i.e. (1) determining the manual to be developed, (2) developing the outline of the manual, (3) writing the first draft of the manual, (4) reviewing the first draft, (5) revising the draft, and (6) using the manual.

Developing the QA manuals follow the following steps. The first step in developing the manuals was to develop the outline of the manual. This was done through identifying the work procedures. This phase involved the people responsible in specific tasks. Writing the first draft was done by a Committee comprising a number of people responsible for particular tasks. The writing process was under the coordination and supervision of each of the respective Vice Rectors. The first draft of the manual was reviewed by other Committees whose job was related to the content of the manual. Eventually, the manual was also reviewed by relevant users. The revision of the draft was based on the output of the review process and on careful observation of the actual practice. A final review process was applied to produce the final version of the manual.

5. *Implementing QA system*. Once the QA policy is introduced, implementation becomes the critical step to ensure that the policy can be effectively put into practice. Implementation of

QA requires a step-by-step process and needs to be done carefully. Initially, staff has to have awareness about QA and understand the concept clearly, so that they are sure of what they have to do, where the institutional leaders are taking them to, and where the institution is going into the future. Socialisation of the idea is critical, and needs to be enhanced and repeated from time to time in order to be effective. Effective QA implementation means that the manuals are used consistently by all staff in performing their daily tasks.

6. *Monitoring, evaluation and internal audit.* QA system is a cyclical continuous improvement process which needs to be evaluated from time to time during the process and at the end of the process. The purpose of monitoring and evaluation is to assess to what extent a particular target or task has been achieved and to provide feedback for continuous improvement. The monitoring and evaluation design is intended to observe whether tasks performed are in accordance with the policies, methods, systems, and procedures described in the manuals. Assessment forms have been developed to monitor and evaluate tasks performed by individuals, to record process and outputs of the tasks, to indicate problems encountered during the completion of the tasks, and to offer solutions to the problems.

There are three underlying principles of QA, i.e. customer focus, employee empowerment and involvement, and continuous improvement. QA is an effort to satisfy stakeholders' needs. QA is implemented through empowering and involving all management staff at all levels in the hierarchy. Continuous improvement focuses on each of the step-by-step processes to produce the output. Focusing on process is an important step to ensure standards and improve reliability of the output. UT monitors and evaluates each process to assure that it is "on the right track". Each unit monitors and evaluates its own work process. Every manager is responsible for implementation of QA in the unit, and the roles of the Quality Assurance Centre are to coordinate and facilitate units in assuring the quality mechanism. Reporting of QA implementation is done on a semester basis. Analysis of the report is done by the Quality Assurance Centre, and feedback is given to each unit, relating to particular tasks and accomplishments of the unit.

Internal audit system has been conducted on a semester cycle, following the submission of the semester report. The purpose of audit is to identify consistency in the implementation of systems and procedures, and to ensure that targets and outputs have been achieved in accordance with specified standards. Internal audit results give recommendations for improvement. The internal audit is conducted on a semester cycle in core business process in which UT has acquired ISO 9001:2000 certifications, and in specific areas of significant importance to the UT operations.

7. *Linking quality assurance to staff performance appraisal.* The role of human resources is significant in QA implementation. Resources make things possible, but only people make things happen. For that reason, units and individuals performing high quality processes and outputs should be fairly rewarded. So, UT has designed a fair human resource performance appraisal system. The phases in designing a performance appraisal system comprise the following steps: (1) defining job description, (2) defining standard performance, (3) developing scoring procedure, (4) developing an appeal process, (5) developing an incentive system related to performance, and (6) developing feedback mechanisms about performance. In this way, quality performers will be well rewarded, while under performers will have to be retrained and developed in order to achieve particular levels of quality standards. This means that there is a

fair system of appraisal so that improved individual human performance will eventually lead to improving unit and institutional performance. This is in line with the basic principle of the UT continuous quality improvement effort. A similar exercise performance assessment will also be applied on the performance of individual operating unit. Performing units will be rewarded, while underperforming units will be redesigned and redeveloped.

External Assessment, Quality Certification and Accreditation

External assessment is an important part of a comprehensive quality assurance system. External quality assessment is conducted by inviting external bodies such as the National Accreditation Board of Higher Education (BAN-PT), the International Council for Open and Distance Education Standards Agency (ICDE/ISA), and by a credible certification body for ISO 9001:2000 (the International Organisation for Standardisation/ISO). In fact, the Directorate General of Higher Education (DGHE) of the Ministry of National Education also undertakes periodic assessment of university performance on a semester cycle. Using quality assurance and criteria with international benchmarking will facilitate external assessment of UT distance higher education programs.

UT invited the International Council for Open and Distance Education (ICDE) Standards Agency (ISA) to conduct quality certification and international accreditation in 2005, with successful results after careful preparation and rigid external audit by ISA. The ICDE has awarded UT the Quality Certification and International Accreditation since 2005. It took a while since 2001 for UT to commit serious effort and make all the necessary preparation for the ICDE Quality Certification and International Accreditation.

UT has also been awarded ISO 9001:2000 certificate for course materials distribution from a credible ISO certification agency since 2006. Preparation for the ISO 9001:2000 also began 4 years back in 2001, starting with the implementation of a comprehensive quality assurance system. The development of QA manuals and effective implementation of policies, systems, procedures and work instructions by management and staff have had significant impact on successful quality management certification of ISO 9001:2000. Currently, important work and preparation are also being conducted to improve the quality management systems through ISO 9001:2000 certification in three critical business processes—(1) academic development, covering all aspects of the development, production and reproduction of learning materials as well as the development, production, administration, processing of examination, and returning examination feedback and results to students, (2) operational management and learning services of Regional Offices, and (3) academic administration services.

As it is required by the national stakeholders, UT has also sought accreditation from the National Accreditation Board for Higher Education (BAN-PT). Accreditation by BAN-PT is conducted at Study Program level, and it has to be updated in every three years. National accreditation is important to promote public confidence among national users and stakeholders about the quality of UT distance education programs.

ICDE/ISA Quality Certification and International Accreditation

The ICDE Quality Certification and International Accreditation has a number of assumption upon which it operates. Its purpose is "to promote public confidence that the quality of standards and provision of services to students in Open and Distance Learning are being safeguarded". The ICDE quality audit does not involve an audit of academic standards of courses or qualifications, since there exists no agreed international standards for qualifications, curriculum and academic content, although various elements of these can be regulated by country or region. It assumes that institutions will be operating within the overall national and/or state legislation and guidelines which are applicable to them at any given time. The ICDE audit is concerned with "the quality and standards of services to students at the point of delivery, and an institution's responsibility for what is done in its name". The ICDE audit process involves the following areas: (1) all aspects of recruitment including marketing and general publicity, (2) all aspects of admission, (3) learner support, (4) the integration and maintenance of systems and services, (5) a commitment to educational values, good customer relationship and business practices, and (6) instructional process and student assessment.

In the process of attaining the UT vision to become one of the leading centres of excellence among distance higher institutions in Asia by 2010 and in the world by 2020, UT invited the International Council for Open and Distance Education (ICDE) Standards Agency (ISA) to conduct quality certification and international accreditation in 2005. Preparation for this international accreditation began in 2001, with concrete commitment and actions on quality assurance and continuous improvement. The UT actually wrote a letter to ICDE expressing its interest for the quality assessment in 2004, and then ISA agreed to conduct the external audit leading to quality certification and international accreditation in June 2005. Previously, in late 2004, the ICDE/ISA sent a checklist of distance education activities and operation that it would like to look at critically as part of the quality assessment and audit exercise to be conducted in June 2005.

In the beginning of 2005, UT sent background information and materials relating to various aspects of UT philosophies and operations, i.e. (1) vision, (2) mission, (3) organizational structure, (4) human resources, (5) physical infrastructure, (6) student population and distribution, (7) registration system, (8) course development and delivery, (9) learning support services, (10) examination system, and (11) quality assurance system. In addition to the background information, UT also prepared extended responses to the ICDE Quality Audit Checklist and related documents. There were 18 responses to the checklist relating to: (1) clear institutional quality assurance policies and plans, (2) comprehensive teaching and learning strategy, (3) learning materials, (4) student assessment, (5) validation and approval procedures for courses, (6) existence of capacity, (7) cross-institutional review and co-ordination, (8) evaluation of the outcomes of the use of capacity and co-ordination mechanism, (9) critical review of current teaching and learning practices, (10) effective staff teams, (11) human resources, (12) a supportive learning environment, (13) student induction and support systems which address motivation and learning skills, (14) learning objectives, content, and targets, (15) assessment strategies, (16) range of materials available, both printed and electronic materials, (17) accurate and detailed monitoring and feedback to student on their progresses/performances, and (18) regular evaluation of the effectiveness of the learning process and their practical outcomes.

Meanwhile, all units were making the necessary preparation for the ICDE audit, ensuring that systems and procedures were well implemented. To facilitate the audit process displays and materials were prepared such as documentation of the roles and functions of the units, systems and procedures, work manuals, examples of information for students (such as types assessment and their contribution to the final grades and certification criteria), samples of log process as verification of quality control, relevant statistics (such as number of courses, number of students, number of examinees, numbers of examination papers to be prepared, and number of examinations sites), samples of products (such as samples of curriculum, samples of learning materials, samples of examination papers), and so forth. Relevant documents were translated into English for the audit purpose.

The ICDE/ISA audit processes were conducted by two auditors for five days. The audit process began with an opening presentation, in which the Rector and top management of UT presented the overview of UT, covering vision, missions, organisational structure, human resources, physical infrastructure, student population and distribution, registration system, course development and delivery, learning support services, examination system, and quality assurance system. Afterwards, the auditors visited related units to directly examine the work process, log process, products and the related documents used in the units. Among units to be visited were the faculty, all the operations centres, i.e. Printed Learning Materials Development Centre, Non-Printed Learning Materials Development Centre, Learning Materials Distribution Centre, Examination Centre, Student Support Section, and three Regional Offices in Jakarta, Bogor and Denpasar.

Units also gave short presentations concerning their roles and functions, internal organisational structures, systems and procedures, work manuals, products, and relevant statistics in addition to the physical display of documents, products and log process. During the meeting and visitation, the units responded to the auditors' questions, mostly based on the ICDE Quality Audit Checklist and to other relevant questions that rose during the visit. In the Regional Offices, the auditors met with the Heads of the Office, staff, and with the Regional Offices' partners such as representatives of the education district offices, tutors and students. Extended questions were asked concerning the tutorial processes, student learning, test item production and the security of the examination. After intensive visits to the units, the auditors explained and clarified the results of the audit to the UT top management, with a final conclusion that UT would be recommended to achieve quality and accreditation certificate from the ICDE/ISA. The auditors also perceived that UT staff had outstanding dedication to improve the quality of their work which eventually improves the provision of quality university education to the Indonesian society. The ICDE awarded the Quality Certification and International Accreditation by the ICDE in September 2005.

ISO 9001:2000 Certification for Quality Management System

UT has also been awarded the ISO 9001:2000 certificate for the quality management system of the distribution of learning materials in March 2006. The effort to improve the quality management system through certification of ISO 9001:2000 has been a reflection of a high spirit of UT management to have a standardised management process, leading to standardised high quality output. The management believes that a standardised management system will facilitate in improving the quality of the management processes in most aspects of operational system of distance education, which eventually results in quality products as well as services. The International Organisation for Standardisation (ISO) was introduced publicly in the year of 1987 as an one of the institutions which is dealing with a standardisation of quality management system. At the beginning, this organisation was well recognized in business and industry, but afterwards it was discovered that the system could be implemented in educational system. It was only in 1992 that Indonesia started to adopt ISO certification system for the quality management system of business and industrial companies in the country, and within 10 years, 1300 organisations in Indonesia has been awarded the ISO 9001/2 certification for quality management system.

The effort for the ISO 9001:2000 certification was started in the beginning of 2004, with critical analysis, documentation and evaluation of main business process in the management of learning materials distribution. Hard work and serious commitment from all management and staff was indeed the direct result of such a high accomplishment. The process of acquiring the ISO 9001:2000 award was long and tedious, and it involved many units and personnel, not only from the Learning Materials Distribution Centre being the core unit, but also from other supporting Centres as well as Divisions and Sections from other relevant units which are related to the whole process of distribution management of learning materials. The struggle was not only focused on the improvement of quality management system at Learning Materials Distribution Centre, but also on other supporting Centres that have responsibilities in preparing the learning materials such as the Printed Learning Materials Production Centre, the Non-Printed Learning Materials Production Centre, and the Bureau of General Administration and Finance.

The preparation for standardising the quality management system through ISO 9001:2000 has been conducted as the following. Firstly, the UT as an organisation set up a Working Committee in implementing the quality management system. The Committee had to work with relevant units, and prepared all the necessary documentation, try-out and revision of the quality manuals for the relevant core activities. Secondly, implementation of the ISO 9001:2000 quality management system has been focused on particular core activities which have significant values on UT operations. This is important, as the UT started with something crucially important in particular areas, rather than in all areas which could be unmanageable. Thirdly, UT appointed credible 9001:2000 certification institution. Fourthly, external audit process took place in core activities in which UT sought certification. Fifthly, the ISO 9001:2000 certification has been awarded to UT because of the satisfying result of external audit by the certification agency based on the standard of ISO 9001:2000. The award ISO 9001:2000 certificate lasts for three years since it is awarded, and surveillance audit will be conducted every six months. The surveillance audit aims at evaluating evaluate the effective implementation of ISO 9001:2000 standards.

The extensive preparation in achieving the ISO 9001:2000 certificate for the distribution management of learning materials started in April 2004 up to February 2006. The detailed activities can be summarised as the following. First, the Rector appointed a Working Committee to work on the preparation for the ISO 9001:2000 for the distribution management of learning materials. The Committee with external ISO 9001:2000 consultant to facilitated the process. Second, training and socialisation of ISO 9001:2000 documents to the top level management was conducted with a purpose to develop awareness and commitment to quality assurance and continuous improvement. While the training and socialisation for staff members was meant to build comprehensive understanding of the requirements for the ISO 9001:2000 quality management system.

Third, work then began on revision of quality manuals related to the distribution management activities. These quality manuals include the following: (1) Manuals of Learning

Materials Distribution Management, (2) Manual of Reproduction of Learning Materials, (3) Manual of Receiving and Stacking of Learning Materials, (4) Manual of Compiling Learning Material Packages, (5) Manual of Delivering Learning Materials, (6) Manual of Learning Materials Stock Control, (7) Manual of Reproduction of Learning Materials, (8) Manual of Procurement and Maintenance of Amenities, (8) Manual of Database and Computer Applications, (9) Manual of Staff Recruitment, (10) Manual of Staff Training, (11) Manual of Reporting of Quality Assurance Implementation, (12) Manual of Evaluation of Quality Assurance Implementation, (13) Manual of Internal Audit, and (14) Manual of External Audit. The documentation of these activities as written in each if the Manuals include records, forms, specification table, and work instruction.

Fourth, socialisation and implementation of these manuals are based on the standardisation of quality management system as required by ISO 9001:2000. Revision of quality manuals is based on findings during implementation. A Management Review was conducted, discussing evaluation on the implementation of quality management system, constraints and problems raised during the implementation, surveys on customer satisfaction, and recommended actions for improvement. Then, an internal audit was conducted by the Quality Assurance Centre, and findings of the internal audit recommended some revision of the quality manuals. Then, external audit is conducted by credible certification institution, preceded by pre-audit. Then, revision of manuals was conducted accommodating feedback based on the results of pre-audit as well as external audit. Each of the audit activities, internal as well as external, was followed by verification to ensure that all systems and procedures were effectively in place, implemented and followed by staff in performing their daily activities.

The accomplishment in getting the ISO 9001:2000 award for quality management system of the distribution of learning materials was the result of effective teamwork involving dedicated personnel committed to quality and continuous improvement. The improvement of UT quality management system is a never-ending effort, it has to continue after getting the award. Further effort for continuous improvement has extended to other core business activities of the UT.

In 2007, UT was seeking ISO 9001:2000 certification in the areas of academic development and management of Regional Offices. Intensive preparation process for achieving the quality management systems through ISO 9001:2000 in these areas started in early 2006, involving management and staff from various relevant units relating to the academic development process. The main units involved in the academic development process include the Faculty, and several Centres with significant roles in the process, i.e. the Printed Learning Material Production Centre, the Non-Printed Learning Material Production Centre, and the Examination Centre. Most of the preparation activity process was adapting the existing manuals to the ISO Standard format and adjusting work procedures with the newest processes. However, the adjustment process of the manuals and procedures took a lot of energy and it was time consuming. The preparation process was assisted by an experienced ISO 9001:2000 management and consulting firm. It is expected that the academic development process would be able to get the ISO 9001:2000 certification before the end of 2007, and the hard work will pay-off in terms of improved quality management systems and customer satisfaction. While the preparation process for getting the ISO 9001:2000 certification in the area of operational management and learning services of Regional Offices involved a bigger number of people from 11 Regional Offices of UT. The process continuous quality improvement, including the achievement of ISO 9001:2000 is facilitated by the Quality Assurance Centre.

Currently, UT is still working further to improve its quality management system through ISO 9001:2000 certification for two core activities, i.e. (1) academic development—covering development and production of learning materials as well as development, production, administration and processing of examination, (2) operational management and learning services of 11 Regional Offices, and (3) academic administration services. In 2008, UT plans to wider the scope of certification of its quality management system, which will include the Faculty management, information system management, financial system management, and continuing with the management and learning services of 12 Regional Offices. Through these step by step quality improvement programs, the UT management believe that by 2010 the main business processes of UT services ISO certified and so that UT services can satisfactorily meet customer satisfaction.

Use of ISO 9001:2000 to Improve the Quality of Management System in the Distribution of Learning Materials for Distance Students

To ensure customer satisfaction, UT needs to improve the quality management continuously. One of the strategies taken has been the adoption of the quality management system based on the ISO 9001:2000, which covers eight management principles: customer focus, leadership, involvement of people, process approach, system approach to management, continual improvement, and factual approach to decision making, and mutually beneficial relationship with suppliers (SAI Global, 2002). The main goal of adopting ISO 9001:2000 requirements is significant achievement in improving the UT internal quality management system, which achieving the ISO 9001:2000 certificate has been seen as the instrument to achieve the main goal. However, to ensure that the quality management system complies with ISO 9001:2000, an internal quality audit is needed prior to external audit by an independent and credible certification body. Preparation for the ISO 9001:2000 certification for the distribution of learning materials started in May 2005. For the purpose of UT pilot project, the scope of the certification was limited to the area of learning materials distribution, with the Learning Materials Distribution Centre being the unit with major responsibility of the process.

Since no one has an experience in ISO 9001:2000 certification, UT worked closely with a private ISO 9001:2000 management and consulting firm to help the Learning Materials Distribution Centre and other support units prepare the ISO 9001:2000 requirements. The first step was to define the scope of the certification, which included learning materials reproduction, quality control, warehousing, packaging and dispatching materials to Regional Offices and certain study groups in remote areas. In the business process of learning materials distribution, the Distribution Centre holds the main process, while other support units included (1) the Printed Learning Materials Centre, (2) the Non-Printed Learning Materials Centre, (3) the Institute of Learning Materials Development, Examination, and Information System, and (4) Bureau of General Administration and Finance. The Quality Assurance Centre facilitates the documentation, internal audit, monitoring and control processes, and serves as Management Representatives together with the Head of the Distribution Centre.

The second step of preparation was development of the quality manual, involving revision of the existing work procedures and work instructions. The quality manual contains the vision, missions, structure, quality policy, scope of the quality management system, quality objectives, descriptions of main process, and list of work procedures. Work procedures were improved and supplemented with work instructions to meet the ISO 9001:2000 requirements. It took three months to finalize the quality manual and work procedures and instructions before implementing the process for accomplishing daily tasks. The implementations of the quality manual and work procedures were preceded with staff training to ensure that people at all levels understood their jobs and that their full involvement enabled their abilities to improve the performance of the organisation. Two months after the new procedures were implemented, an internal audit was ready to be conducted in the area of learning materials distribution.

Internal audit is a necessary requirement for ISO 9001:2000 before external audit is conducted by the ISO Certification Body. The objective of the internal audit is to collect information to confirm suitability of system implementation using the specified procedures. For UT distribution of learning materials, internal audit was conducted to examine the whole system of learning materials distribution, to see the implementation of the system in general, and to evaluate the extent to which the level of quality objectives have been achieved. The results of the internal audit are considered to be significant inputs to improve implementation of the system. In order to conduct a valid and reliable internal audit in accordance with the ISO 9001:2000 requirements, an internal audit team was prepared through intensive training. Some of the staff undertook external training programs to prepare themselves to become internationally certified Lead Auditors.

Coordinated by the Quality Assurance Centre, an internal audit team consisting of staff from various units within UT with audit certification, conducted internal audit of activities related to the distribution management system of the learning materials in August 2005. All aspects in the learning materials distribution process were audited. The audit started with evaluating quality manuals, followed by the audit of the management involvement and support functions, procedures of learning materials printing estimation, reproduction of learning materials, quality control, warehousing (receiving and storing), assembling and packaging, producing the delivery order (DO), dispatching, stock control, administration support, training, maintenance, monitoring of quality objectives, customer satisfaction measurement, and customer complaint handling. Internal audit has contributed significant inputs to improve the system. Detail findings noted in the internal audit were consistently followed up by the management and the organization. Findings should be closed before an audit for certification was conducted. To maintain the consistency of the process and to ensure continuous improvement, an internal audit mechanism has been regularly conducted in every six month.

For the ISO 9001:2000 certification audit, the UT appointed an internationally accredited certification body, which is a member of IQ-Net (International Quality Network), to ensure worldwide recognition of the certification. Before the certification audit was conducted in December 2005, preliminary audit was performed in October 2005. Preliminary audit was conducted to confirm that key ISO 9001:2000 requirements were in place and supported by suitable documentation. The preliminary audit provided feedback and information on the status of compliance to the ISO 9001:2000 requirements which would help prepare for future external assessment. The preliminary audit involved the following activities:

- Reviewing issues arising from the auditor assessment of self evaluation check list.
- A review of management system documentation to assess whether key requirements of ISO 9001:2000 have been adequately addressed.
- Assessment of the organization progress in implementing the system through discussion and sampling of procedure, record, etc.
- Checking adequacy and reliability of ISO 9001:2000 auditing, procedure and programs.
- Reviewing ISO 9001:2000 audits and follow up activities.
- Planning resources and determining the scope of the Certification Audit.

The audit for ISO 9001:2000 certification was conducted in December 2005. The purpose of the audit was to focus on issues pertaining to the following areas:

- Management involvement.
- Management support function.
- Training.
- Maintenance.
- Learning materials printing order estimation.
- Reproduction of learning materials.
- Incoming inspection of learning materials.
- Warehousing, i.e. receiving and storing of learning materials.
- Stock control.
- Assembling, packaging and dispatching of learning materials.
- Administration support.

The findings of the audit for the ISO 9001:2000 certification are classified into three categories: non-conformance, areas of concern for improvement, and opportunities for improvement (SAI Global, 2005). Non-conformance findings is a breakdown, total or to a significant level, in the implementation and/or maintenance of a management system. Such failure requires urgent correction. If a system failure is not addressed within the term of the corrective action agreement then the actions are taken not to issue the ISO 9001:2000 certificate. While, areas of concern for improvement are areas of the system for which it is required to investigate the potential or actual non-conformity of minor significance and apply corrective action within the management system. Opportunity for improvement contains documented statement that may identify areas for potential improvement, but do not make specific recommendations. When solutions are developed and implemented they may add value through enhancing the organization's operations and/or management system.

Even though the system has demonstrated compliance with the requirements of ISO 9001:2000 standards and the issues raised during the preliminary audit have been generally well addressed, some cases still need attention for improvement. The recommendation for certification could not be given since two non-conformance findings were raised during the audit, a follow-up audit should be performed. Follow-up audit was conducted in February 2006. The aim of the follow-up audit was to verify compliance of the implemented quality management system to the requirements of ISO 9001:2000 standards. After closing of two non-conformance findings raised during former audit, it is concluded that the organization has implemented a quality management system, which meets the requirements of ISO 9001:2000 standards. A recommendation for issuing ISO 9001:2000 certificates has been made. ISO 9001:2000 certificate was awarded in March 2006 during the occasion of the UT National Coordination Meeting attended by UT Management and Heads of Regional Offices throughout the country. After the ISO 9001:2000 certification has been achieved, surveillance audits are required twice a year to ensure the system is being maintained. Many recommendations have been made by the auditors for continuous improvement. The auditors also identified some issues that would be reviewed during the following audit to ensure that they have been adequately addressed. Since there has been no non-conformance finding raised in the surveillance audits, the certification may continue.

Significant improvements have been made by implementing the ISO 9001:2000 quality management system. This has to support by strong commitment of the management for the improvement of quality management system. This commitment is reflected in the quick response and follow up of the results of internal external audit findings. External auditors have reported that the top management has stated the vision and missions for the organization as well as the quality policy to be one of the centres of excellence in distance higher education. The strong commitment has been demonstrated by the top management through communicating this policy and determining several functional objectives in relevant areas (SAI Global, 2005). Long-term and short-term strategic plans have also been established and reviewed as necessary. Actions have been taken to improve organizational performance including monitoring activities. Necessary resources needed for continuous improvement have been identified and later fulfilled by the organization to support operational activities and ensure effective implementation of quality management system. The management has also attempted to improve staff performance and motivate staff to work more effectively and efficiently, with clear and measurable objectives and targets. Customer survey results have indicated increasing satisfaction of Regional Offices in the distribution management services of the learning materials distribution.

Conclusion

Quality is a significant investment and it necessitates resource and funding commitment. Establishing and sustaining quality work culture within an organisation are significant challenges for any distance education institution. QA should bring about positive changes in organisational structure and culture that lead to improved results in terms of how distance education institutions operate effectively and to enhance the development of a learning organisation. QA provides management with an effective instrument to help distance education institutions achieve quality brand from stakeholders. Institutions will be better prepared to be engaged in collaboration and competition with other providers when they have high quality programs. Implementation of quality management in UT works hand in hand with the establishment of good corporate governance within the institution.

The UT QA approach has had constructive significant effects on the establishment quality culture as "lifestyle" of its people, quality products and services. Implementation of quality management system is linked with human performance appraisal system, in which the quality performance of staff and unit is well rewarded. For staff members, job manuals have become an important tool to guide them in performing daily tasks. Writing job manuals is more than just documenting daily activities of staff. It has involved team building and establishing *esprit de corps* among staff members, improving the work systems and procedures, and changing the work culture of the staff.

Assessment plays crucial roles in quality assurance, and it is done continuously through self-assessment, internal assessment and eventually external assessment. Self-assessment is conducted by individual units, so that units have ideas about what they have and have not yet achieved, and which systems and procedures can and cannot work, and which areas need improvement based on the assessment results. For the institution as a whole, self-assessment provides information about which units do and do not perform well. And if particular units perform less, the university can take the necessary actions to help improve their performance. QA can serve as an effective instrument to improve staff performance, target achievement of units, and institutional achievement of the stated vision, missions and goals of meeting customer satisfaction.

Quality in Flexible, Online and Distance Education at Deakin University, Australia

14

—*Dale Holt* and *Stuart Palmer*

Introduction

This chapter presents an overview of the management of quality for flexible, online and distance education (off-campus education) at Deakin University in Australia. In 1974, Deakin University was established as a dual-mode institution educating large numbers of both on- and off-campus students. From its foundation it has increasingly sought to provide the same learning resources, equivalent learning experiences and parity of outcomes to students studying in all modes (Hay et al., 2002). While this was the ideal on which Deakin was founded, in practice approaches differed across various schools and courses where in some areas integration was achieved through an open-campus model, while in others the tendency was towards separation of the modes of delivery by course. Deakin's history can be characterised as moving from dual-mode approaches to educating its student cohorts, to now a well-articulated, integrated and institution-wide approach to assuring and improving the quality of all modes of educational delivery for an extremely diverse and complex set of student cohorts. In this regard, it makes no particular distinction between these student groups in its policies, procedures and processes relating to educational matters. The move to such an all-encompassing approach to it quality practices can be seen in the context of four fundamental forces in the university's historical development:

- First, the growth of the university from a one-campus regional operation to a multi-campus/multi-city organisation underpinned by a unitary merger model and shaped by national government policy interventions which demanded larger scale operations.
- Second, the explosive growth of information and communications technologies (ICT) throughout the 1990s and the new millennium of relevance and value to all student cohorts both on- and off-campus.
- Third, the increasing diversity and spread of student cohorts studying on-campus, cross-campus, nationally and through partners internationally, much of which is driven by the university's need to generate student fee income directly and all of which needs to be carefully managed to ensure quality learning opportunities and outcomes.

Over time there has been a proportionately larger number of school-leaver, on-campus students studying across Deakin's major teaching campuses compared with off-campus undergraduate and postgraduate student enrolments.

- A growing recognition that a common set of attributes of excellent teaching and student-centred learning approaches could be enacted which would benefit the education of all students, and that the newer technologies could allow students enrolled in different modes of delivery to interact as one community of learners in mutually beneficial ways.

These four forces have reshaped the university's strategic commitments to on-campus, online, flexible and distance education, along with associated approaches to quality practices. Before presenting the details of Deakin's strategic and operational responses to quality we provide some background information on quality in higher education, Deakin's historical development and some aspects of the Australian national higher education environment which form the context that influences Deakin's operations.

Contemporary Views of Quality in Higher Education

Defining who the user is and what we are offering to them provides a framework for identifying what aspects of quality we would seek to control and/or improve and which areas of the organisation contribute to impact on that quality as perceived by the user. In any conception of quality in higher education, students must be viewed as a principal user group. Some may argue that many undergraduate students are comparatively naive 'customers' with a limited conception of the knowledge and skills necessary in their field of study. However, ignoring the needs and expectations of any important customer group is a recipe for organisational failure, and the modern university undergraduate student (particularly those studying part-time, on-campus or by distance education) is just as likely to turn out to be a mature age student (with significant experience of their field of study and/or prior experience in higher education) rather than an 18 year old directly from secondary school. This is inevitably the case for those mature aged students undertaking postgraduate coursework or continuing education studies by distance education. Over the course of their studies, students will experience a wide range of teaching and learning, and be well placed to make comparative judgements of quality, and, as novices in their discipline, will also be qualified to judge whether their involvement in education is assisting them to learn (Ramsden, 1991).

In Australia, each year, all university graduates are surveyed about their course experience. A large analysis of open-ended comments made by university graduates on their studies as part of the course experience questionnaire has recently been completed (Scott, 2006). Apart from highlighting the complex and multi-faceted nature of quality that arise from such a diverse group of users, graduates indicated that it is the total university experience that counts. This finding confirms the idea from total quality management that all areas of an organisation contribute to the final quality of the services and products (Juran, 1988). There is a system-wide 'quality function' that exists and impacts on quality. In a distance education context, this implies that the student perception of quality is likely to be influenced just as much by the late delivery of materials, the amount of network downtime, the promptness of replies from student services and the availability of titles for borrowing from the library, as it is to be influenced by currency of course material. Increasingly, with the services traditionally offered to distance education students now being made available to their on-campus counterparts through electronic means (and vice versa in the case of recorded lectures delivered over the WWW) quality failures can adversely affect all types of students' learning experiences in the system. Equally, quality improvements can benefit the full spectrum of students in the organisation as well. The unifying philosophy is well summed up in a motto accompanying Deakin's national institutional teaching award for the provision of support services that assist student learning through Library off-campus services, "If this works for off-campus students, then it will work for all students".

Institutional Context

Deakin University was established in Geelong, in the state of Victoria, in Australia in 1974, and began teaching in 1977. Deakin was created from the merger of the Geelong State College and the Gordon Institute of Technology. Later, Deakin merged with the Warrnambool Institute of Advanced Education and Victoria College, to create a multi-campus university with on-campus teaching operations in metropolitan, regional and rural areas of Victoria, spanning more than 220 km as the crow flies. From its inception as a single campus university, Deakin was conceived as a 'dual-mode' institution, servicing both traditional on-campus students as well as students studying by distance education (Jevons, 1982). However, the 'dual-mode' philosophy was somewhat inconsistently in operation in the early years of Deakin's development given the various teaching approaches inherited from the antecedent institutions. The original philosophy of an 'open campus' was heavily influenced by the Open University in the UK, with unit teams developing print, audio, video and other resources for use by all students (Hay et al., 2002). In the 1980s, Australian government policy supported distance education as a vehicle for providing opportunities for groups not traditionally well represented in higher education. In 1988, Deakin was one of seven Australian universities designated as Distance Education Centres (DEC), and who received funding to specialise in the delivery of open and distance education (Reid, 2005). The late 1970s and 1980s, therefore, saw Deakin being positioned as a new generation distance education provider in the country and where new course developments all had to be offered in off-campus mode.

Despite being formed from a number of antecedent institutions, Deakin is not a federated university—all principal academic and administrative functions are centralised and standardised, with the same programs of study and services being available to all students and staff, regardless of location (Calvert, 2001). As is common in distance-only institutions, Deakin has central resources (currently two separate units) responsible for the educational design and development of learning resources. The multi-campus-but-identical-program nature of Deakin's academic programs means that it has a tradition of unit development by teams and a common presentation of the unit to all students that is also similar to distance-only institutions. Generally, off-campus students study the same syllabus, complete the same assessment and sit the same examinations as on-campus students. In 2006, the total student enrolment at Deakin was 32,374 students, of which 35% (11,264) were off-campus students.

Over time, the nature of off-campus study has changed. Initially, Deakin's off-campus students were predominantly distance students, who received study materials and studied primarily by themselves remotely. The introduction of computer/multi-media technology meant that greater levels of student interaction were possible with learning materials. The wide-scale availability of computer communication technology meant that off-campus students could take part in computer-mediated communication forums open to all students. In fact, making educational technologies equally available to off-campus and on-campus students to use has helped to justify ever-expanding investments in online systems to this very day. By 1994, Australian government policy no longer gave special status to open and distance learning, and the DECs were disbanded. The growth in part-time study, by both on- and off-campus students, and Deakin's partnering with other institutions internationally to deliver its programs 'off-shore' led to the conception of 'flexible learning' based on equivalency of syllabus and learning outcomes emerged strongly in the mid-1990s as organisational vision, but delivered in the combination of modes best suited to the circumstances of the student. The pervasive growth on online systems has meant that in many areas 'distance education' has become synonymous with 'online learning' (Calvert, 2005). In 2003, Deakin sought to formalise and gave even greater strategic direction to its growing use of online teaching and learning under a project entitled 'Deakin Online' (Corbitt, Holt and Segrave, 2006), which aimed to establish a university-level system with a consistent, single interface to provide:

- Access to information about the university to the general and academic communities;
- A basis for university-wide knowledge management via an online portal; and
- A basis for online student access to general services and the Deakin e-learning environment (Deakin University, 2004a).

While elements of online delivery and interaction are now central to most Deakin off-campus programs, and all Deakin undergraduate students must complete at least one unit in their programs that is delivered wholly online, the postal delivery of print and other study materials still remains an essential element of most off-campus study at Deakin. The intermingling of online, on-campus and off-campus education should not be seen as unique to Deakin in the Australian higher education system. A meta-analysis of 2002 institutional audit reports undertaken by the Australian Universities Quality Agency (AUQA) that:

Forms of off-campus teaching, whether called distance education, flexible learning or online learning, are now widespread among the institutions, including those which do not have a distinctive distance education mission. Much institutional effort is currently on developing flexible delivery modes and, in particular, online capabilities. A number of the Audit Reports make specific recommendations on improvements in this area, without any particular focus emerging, apart from a need to ensure overall co-ordination of developments and parity of standards across different modes of delivery (Martin, 2003).

However, the shift, nonetheless, has been pronounced in the case of the development of our own university.

External Drivers

There are a number of external drivers of quality assurance and quality improvement in Australian higher education which impact online, distance and flexible education, namely national quality audits, a national graduate course experience survey and related learning and teaching performance fund, a national body to recognise, reward, promote and develop quality learning and teaching, national patterns of change in student work/study mix across all cohorts, professional accreditation requirements, and the steady move to student user pays systems. Each will be discussed in turn.

In Australia, the Australian Universities Quality Agency (AUQA) referred to above plays an important role in quality in higher education. AUQA is a national body that is independent of the government and the higher education sector. It was established in 2000 and conducts audits and reports on QA in Australian higher education. Audits are conducted on a five-yearly cycle, and require institutions to prepare a self-report around a series of structured criteria, which is then followed up by an on-site audit of the institution. Audits are primarily norm-referenced, taking into consideration the individual goals of the institution as well as commonly accepted practice in the sector. AUQA principal function is in the assurance of quality, though it does incorporate elements of quality improvement/enhancement through:

- The inclusion of commendations, affirmations and recommendations for improvement in its audit reports;
- The hosting of a 'good practice database' to disseminate good practice; and
- Hosting the Australian Universities Quality Forum to facilitate sharing of good practice in higher education in Australia.

Since 1993, Australia has surveyed all completing undergraduate students (on- and off-campus) using an instrument known as the Course Experience Questionnaire (CEQ) mentioned earlier (Graduate Careers Australia, 2006). The CEQ has a long history of development and research that confirms that it is a reliable and valid measure of students' perception of their learning environment, and is based on earlier work which shows there is a strong link between this and quality of student learning (Wilson, Lissio and Ramsden, 1997). Consolidated institutional results from the CEQ are publicly available, hence a good ranking on CEQ performance is considered desirable. Another reason the CEQ is important in Australian higher education is its relationship with the Learning and Teaching Performance Fund (LTPF). The LTPF aims to reward those Australian universities that best demonstrate excellence in undergraduate learning and teaching in four major discipline clusters. Eligibility to participate in LTPF funding is currently determined by a combination of performance indicators, including the core 'student satisfaction' indicators from the CEQ, 'outcome indicators' from the Graduate Destination Survey (GDS) (an Australian national survey of employment or further education status of graduates), and 'success indicators' (student progression and retention rates) from the Federal Department of Education, Science and Training student statistical information. The quantum of funding that is contingent upon the results of the LTPF (over $AU82 million was available for allocation in 2007) means that it (and by implication the CEQ) will remain an important concern for Australian universities.

Launched in 2004 and succeeding a sequence of predecessor institutions, the Carrick Institute for Learning and Teaching in Higher Education provides a national focus for the enhancement of teaching and learning in Australian higher education providers. Included in its published objectives are that it will:

1. Promote and support strategic change in higher education institutions for the enhancement of learning and teaching, including curriculum development and assessment (through a scheme of competitive national teaching grants up to $AU220,000 each).
2. Foster and acknowledge excellent teaching in higher education (through a scheme of national teaching awards of up to $AU75,000 each and Fellowships valued up to $AU330,000 each).

3. identify learning and teaching issues that impact on the Australian higher education system and facilitate national approaches to address these and other emerging issues (by funding a range of 'discipline-based initiatives' investigations in the range $AU100,000-$AU200,000 each).

This funding is highly prized, and Australian universities compete and collaborate to win it by demonstrating the quality of their teaching, teachers and teaching enhancement project ideas. Deakin in recent times has been a joint winner of an institutional national teaching award for the provision of quality off-campus services through the Library, and was a short-listed nomination for assisting quality student learning in the university's community of learners through Deakin Online.

When Deakin first opened its doors there was a clear distinction between on-campus and distance students. The former primarily came direct from secondary school and studied full-time, and the latter were primarily 'second chance' female or mature age students, who had not previously had the opportunity to access higher education, and normally studied part-time (Hay et al., 2002). In reality, the nature of 'full-time' undergraduate on-campus study has changed radically in the last three decades. Internationally, the increase in student term-time employment has paralleled the decline in state support of higher education and the shifting of more of the cost of higher education to students. Long and Hayden, in a survey of more than 30,000 Australian undergraduate students in 2000, found that 70% of students had employment during the semester (a 50% increase since 1984) and the average hours worked per week was 14.5 hours (a threefold increase since 1984) (Long and Hayden, 2001). McInnis and Hartley, based on a 2001 survey of 1563 working Australian undergraduate students, found that the average hours per week of work was 14.7 hours (McInnis and Hartley, 2002). The modern study-plus-work arrangement of the typical on-campus student is moving closer to the work-plus-study pattern of the typical off-campus student. The boundary between on- and off-campus studies is now significantly blurred, with many on-campus students making use of any available off-campus learning resources to enhance their learning and/or reduce their reliance on attendance at formal classes, and developments in distance education leading to transformations in on-campus teaching. The historical dichotomy between on-campus and off-campus students is disappearing, as the two groups become more like each other—sharing work patterns and study resources.

A group with important influence on the content and delivery of a range of undergraduate programs in Australia, and off-campus programs in particular, are the national professional bodies that accredit professional degree programs such as architecture, engineering, education, nursing, psychology, law, etc. In some circumstances they permit off-campus studies, but may mandate special additional conditions such as minimum compulsory residential attendance periods, which can act as a significant practical barrier for some students to consider distance education in these disciplines.

In the 1980s, access to higher education was dramatically expanded in Australia. Since 1989, all undergraduate students have been required to pay at least part of the cost of their university education through the Higher Education Contribution Scheme (HECS). Making students pay part of the cost of higher education has turned them into customers, and the expansion of higher education has presented students with more options as to where they might undertake their studies. The Australian higher education environment has become highly competitive, forcing universities to place an emphasis on quality assurance and quality improvement (Reid, 2005).

Internal Responses

Acknowledging that 'quality' is a system-wide function that arises from all aspects of the organisation's operations, Deakin employs a wide-ranging conception of quality. Deakin's historical foundation as a dual-mode institution with a focus on distance education is still reflected today in the three 'core commitments' articulated in its strategic plan, they are:

- rural and regional engagement;
- continuing education and life-long learning; and
- equity and access for individuals and groups who might not otherwise enjoy the benefits that flow from participating in higher education (Deakin University, 2004b).

An on-going involvement in distance education is specifically re-affirmed in the explanation accompanying the second core commitment, "Deakin is committed to continuing education and lifelong learning, especially, but not only, as a provider of high-quality distance education..." (Deakin University, 2004b).

Cognisant of the AUQA audit framework, Deakin has embedded its strategic and operational planning processes within a cycle of continuous quality improvement (CQI) that can be shown in Fig. 14.1.

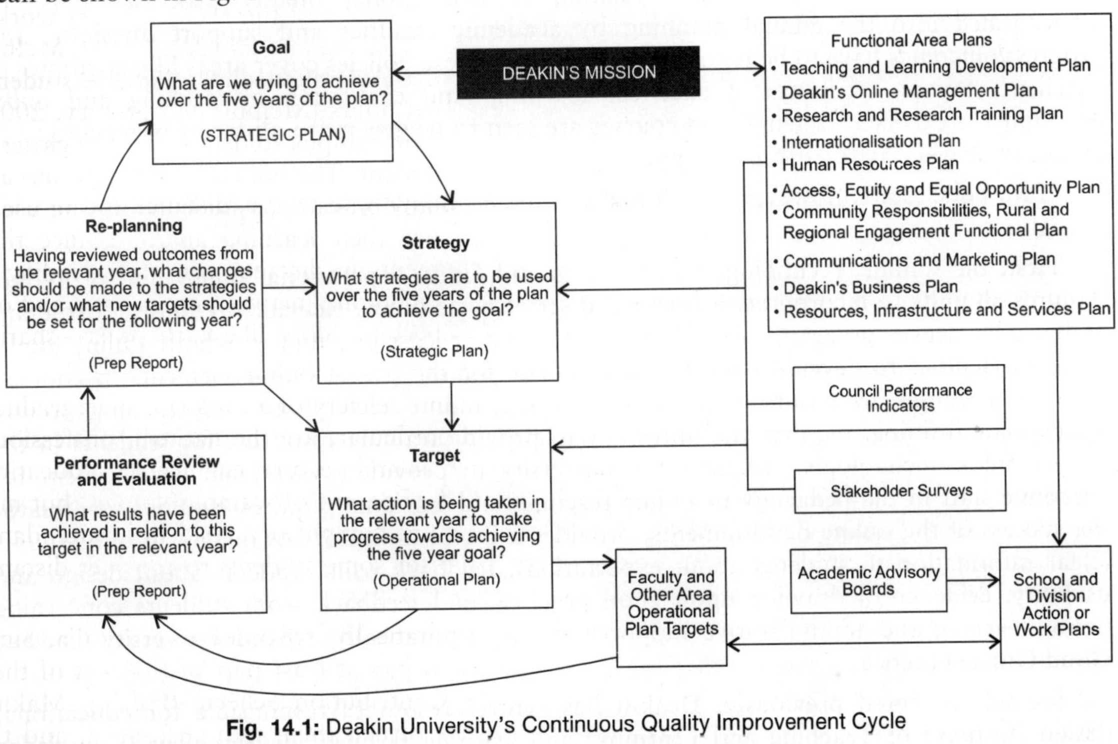

Fig. 14.1: Deakin University's Continuous Quality Improvement Cycle

The AUQA audit process requires that auditee institutions develop an action plan to address audit recommendations, and that the auditee make a progress report against the action plan publicly available no later than 12 months after the completion of the audit. Deakin has done this, and has embedded updating the audit action plan progress report into its annual planning cycle. The university strategic plan, and university and faculty annual operational plans have sections devoted to teaching and learning goals, objectives, strategies and targets. Since the new continuous quality improvement cycle was established in 2003 a number of key objectives, strategies and targets have related to Deakin's commitments to flexible, online and distance education. As can be seen in Fig. 14.1, there are also a series of specialist functional plans outlining more detail on matters to do with teaching, learning and online directions for the university (note from above the teaching and learning development and online Management plans). All of the university plans have emphasised the integrated approach required to design and operate quality teaching and learning environments to meet the needs of all of the university student cohorts.

However, in the context of online (Oliver, 2003) and open and distance learning (Inglis, 2005) at dual-mode universities in Australia, it has been identified that quality issues and measures, while being substantially identical for on- and off-campus teaching and learning, also need to take into account the practical differences between the different modes. Deakin's quality processes and measures are generally universally applied to all modes of delivery, though there are some exceptions in the area of online teaching and learning, where additional policy and procedures have been developed. Key university policies (generally with accompanying detailed procedures) relating to institutional quality processes must be incorporated into the annual planning by academic faculties and support divisions, and progress/outcomes have to be reported on annually. These policies cover areas like attributes of excellent courses, attributes of excellent teaching, and evaluation of teaching and units. Attributes of excellent teaching and courses are seen to be generic to all forms of teaching and modes of delivery across the university.

Two policies are, however, worth highlighting as applying to online, distance and flexible education.

First, the Online Technologies in Courses and Units—operational policy and procedure requires all units to incorporate a prescribed set of basic online elements; requires all students of Bachelor degree programs to undertake and pass at least one unit in wholly online mode; requires faculties to develop educational rationale for the use of online elements in courses; requires Faculties to ensure that all staff using online technologies in teaching receive appropriate training; requires the university to provide training resources for students in the use of online technologies; requires the university to provide professional development for academic staff in the pedagogy of online teaching and learning; requires faculties to monitor the success of the online developments; provides a list of indicators of quality in online units (clear information to students about expectations, feedback from students about design and usability, evidence of drawing upon good practice, and feedback from students concerning online teaching and administrative support); and incorporates the Deakin University Code of Good Online Practice.

Second, as noted previously, Deakin has central resources responsible for educational design (Institute of Teaching and Learning) and learning resource development (Knowledge Media Division). While providing assistance to all areas of the university, these resources have a particular role in the development of off-campus learning materials. As a common point in the materials production process, the Knowledge Media Division (KMD) provides a consistency of style that is an important element of quality assurance. In addition, KMD have developed ten core quality principles for quality course materials:

1. **reliable**—Content is accurate, current, appropriate and relevant
2. **informative**—Relevant administrative and technical information is provided
3. **well communicated**—Content uses appropriate tone/level for audience, is logically structured and well communicated
4. **acknowledged**—Content is clearly identified, acknowledged and accurately branded
5. **navigable**—Navigation through content is clear, accurate and consistent
6. **presentable**—Content is formatted and presented appropriately and meets technical standards
7. **compliant**—Content meets legislative requirements (copyright, accessibility, privacy, plagiarism)
8. **appropriate in media mix and quantity**—Content is delivered in appropriate media and quantities (media mix and volume)
9. **learner-centred**—Learning content employs appropriate learning approaches
10. **explained**—Learning approaches are explained (Knowledge Media Division Deakin University, 2006).

Accompanying the core quality principles are detailed best practice guidelines that provide exemplars of the application of the quality principles in a range of media formats. During 2006, KMD conducted a large-scale quality audit of all unit learning resources against these principles and provided detailed feedback to unit chairs outlining any areas where learning materials required improvement to meet the quality principles and guidelines.

One of the responsibilities of the Institute of Teaching and Learning (ITL) is the provision of system management and staff training for the university online course management system (CMS), currently Blackboard. The move from a wide range of local online delivery systems used in different schools and faculties to a corporate centrally supported CMS in 2004 has helped to bring about and assure a consistent level of quality in the student experience of using the CMS. The need to become familiar with the navigation of only a single online system, and ability to be able to find a core set of learning resources online in every unit studies is of particular benefit to off-campus students.

Looking Forward

To maintain currency, a quality management system (QMS) must undergo periodic evaluation and revision. At the time of writing, Deakin's strategic plan is undergoing a process of revision, along with the development of a new Teaching and Learning Functional Plan and the consideration of outcomes of an external review of teaching and learning at the university initiated by the Vice-Chancellor. The new round of strategic planning involves a re-assessment of the university's mission and objectives, and of developments in the external environment that offer opportunities for and threats to the achievement of that mission. Four major external forces identified for planning purposes cover:

- The massification of higher education which, in Australia, has taken place at the same time as cuts in the Commonwealth Government's public funding for universities.

- The globalisation and internationalisation of higher education (in terms of both student mobility to and from Australia, curriculum development and the desire for internationally-recognised credentials).
- The communications' revolution.
- The changes in working patterns which demand that workers are lifelong learners.

While the strategic plan for the period 2008-12 is still a work-in-process, the university has re-affirmed the three core commitments of the current strategic plan, ensuring a long-term commitment to the delivery of off-campus education via a range of means and media. In addition, Deakin is currently in the process of developing a teaching and learning quality framework that has as its aim the improvement of teaching and learning at Deakin through:

- A coherent framework to provide the basis for an extensive review of all existing policies that relate to quality in teaching and learning, and their interrelationship to each other.
- An integrated quality enhancement strategy for all faculties based on using the quantitative and qualitative data from the CEQ, GDS and Student Evaluation of Teaching and Units (SETU) surveys in a proactive way.
- Incorporating clear systems of accountability for the quality of teaching and learning into faculty management structures and academic leadership roles.

The primary role of a QMS is the assurance of quality. But, for both its own sake and in response to a competitive environment, we should also be concerned with the improvement of quality (QI). The higher education literature notes that QA and QI (or quality enhancement) are not the same thing (Avdjieva and Wilson, 2002; Knight, 2006). A short-term 'tactical' response to quality in higher education may be adequate to satisfy external QA auditing bodies, but a 'strategic' approach to quality is needed for the development of an organisation-wide culture of QA and QI (Gordon, 2002).

Chalmers and O'Brien (2005) identify four concerns of central education development units:

- Building up a corporate memory and sustaining engagement in teaching and learning developments.
- Supporting and guiding the comprehensive implementation of educational initiatives.
- establishing and maintaining communities of practice to enable to organisation to generate, share and promote knowledge of developing teaching and learning approaches and practices.
- Supporting, undertaking and disseminating research and evaluation on teaching and learning issues, innovations and developments.

Deakin's newly established Institute of Teaching and Learning (ITL) has been proactive in providing direction and resources for the wider university academic community for the improvement of quality. As overseen by ITL, Deakin provides a range of annual awards for the recognition of excellence in teaching by individuals and teams. Apart from providing a significant incentive for staff to excel in their teaching activities, these internal awards have been strategically aligned with the Carrick Institute National Teaching Awards by adopting the same criteria for teaching excellence as employed by Carrick, and requiring recipients, with the assistance of ITL, to apply for a Carrick national teaching excellence award. The ITL site has a complete listing of all previous Deakin and Carrick teaching award winners thus contributing to the 'corporate memory' and enabling interested parties to easily contact successful applicants with similar teaching interests.

ITL administers the university's strategic teaching and learning grant scheme (STALGS: faculty and reserved components), and supports staff applying for funding and in implementing successfully funded projects. STALGS is aimed at enabling major development and research projects to be undertaken in strategically important areas of teaching and learning for the university. Under the STALGS Faculty component, each year, staff are invited to bid for funding of up to $AU50,000 of strategic relevance. Bids for the total available STALGS funding of approximately $AU250,000 has become very competitive, with about 25% of applications receiving some funding in 2007. Projects must include a strategic rationale for the project, a research/evaluation component and a dissemination strategy. Again, all successfully funded STALGS projects appear on the ITL website, along with links to various project outcomes as contributions to corporate memory formation of achievements and as stimulus for new STALGS funding applications. Many of the successful projects relate to progressing developments in online, distance and flexible education. The STALGS scheme is a springboard to developing applications for a national Carrick grants and STALGS project leaders are designated as Teaching Fellows of the Institute. A component of STALGS funding of around $AU300,000 is held back by ITL to fund projects of clear institution-wide application, with areas supported to date including e-simulations, e-portfolio adoption, social software environments and online self- and peer-assessment systems. All of these developments are of equal value and use by on- and off-campus students, and all need to be quality assured as they move from pilot to mainstream use by the general student body.

In addition, ITL has developed a robust suite of online professional development and training materials, and case study resources of good teaching-in-action to support just enough/just-in-time staff learning as related to various e-learning technologies and general teaching and learning issues. Online resources are created by faculty teaching staff seconded to ITL, as Professional Development Fellows, and represent another avenue for teaching expertise to be captured and distributed throughout the organisation. ITL's online professional development environment has been conceived within a framework articulating connections amongst areas of educational value adding, staff capacity building and strategic academic professional initiatives (Segrave et al., 2005). Online professional development resources are being complemented with various initiatives to establish staff online-supported communities of practice, an imperative for an organisation so geographically dispersed dealing with so many different student cohorts. A notable development in this area is the formation of a Fellowship of Distinguished Educators representing the best of the university's teachers and teaching expertise. These communities of practice are being designed to make a substantial contribution to improving the quality of teaching and learning across the institution.

Conclusion

As Deakin has grown in operation and expanded its course and student population base, so has its mission, vision and quality practices changed. The present Deakin is in some ways unrecognisable from its original predecessor. An original commitment to dual-mode teaching has evolved into an integrated, institution-wide set of educational approaches and practices encompassing all staff, all students and the use of a growing range of media and technologies for the benefit of all parties. When quality was first raised, it was seen in the context of distance education and progressive forms of on-campus, face-to-face teaching. Then it was seen in the context of flexible delivery for different student cohorts and finally online provision for all students using the same environments. Descriptions now of commitments in progressive on-campus, flexible, distance, online, and even, blended learning seem less than convincing in providing future frameworks for enacting quality. Increasingly, focus is turning to learner/learning experience design, selectively enabled through different combinations of e-learning technologies, and customised to meet the needs of different student needs and circumstances, as an emerging frame of reference for quality practices in higher education.

Quality Management System at the Open Polytechnic of New Zealand

15

—*Rowan Anderson, Axel Laurs, Caryl-Louise Robinson* and *Sally Rawnsley*

Introduction

With its specialized Open and Distance Learning (ODL) capability, the Open Polytechnic (OP) plays a distinctive role in New Zealand's tertiary education sector, making a substantial contribution to the NZ economy, delivering a net annual economic benefit of around $320 million to the country. Currently with over 30,000 learners it is the largest institution in the Institute of Technology and Polytechnics (ITP) sector for domestic students accounting for 20% of individual students and 10% of equivalent full-time students (7950 EFTS in 2006). It enrols 91% of ITP distance learners at diploma level and 85% of ITP distance degree students. Two-thirds of the polytechnic's students are in the workforce studying to up skill or re skill. Student responses to annual surveys cite convenience and flexibility of study as key reasons for enrolling with the OP.

Since its inception sixty years ago, the OP has developed its vision and currently strives to be "New Zealand's first choice for vocational and lifelong learning from foundation to degree level". Its mission is "To support national development goals, build workforce skills and empower New Zealanders as individuals and citizens by providing flexible, nation-wide access to education that meets the changing vocational needs of lifelong learners". To achieve this vision and mission, the OP has taken a structured approach to ensuring quality for its students and other customers.

This chapter sets out to sketch the OP's progress in developing and maintaining a best practice Quality Management System (QMS) by providing the context and evolution of the institution's QMS leading up to the major ITPQ Academic Audit in late 2006. Significant stages identified include a pilot programme, involving the institution's Printshop, engagement with ISO 9001, external academic audits, internal quality audits culminating in the current integrated process. This is followed by consideration of Quality Management of Materials Development, critical in the ODL context. The Appendix, Lessons from LifeWorks, provides discussion of modified QMS practices applied to the distinctive LifeWorks programme.

QMS at the OP

Since the early nineties, a QMS has evolved at the Open Polytechnic to improve capability and ensure quality provision for its students, customers and stakeholders. To underpin the achievement of its business objectives and to drive business improvement, the OP has incrementally adopted a systematic approach to quality management to foster quality strategies and to give effect to quality management principles. These principles were identified as focusing on:

- customer orientation,
- management excellence,
- academic excellence,
- process excellence through a systems approach,
- people commitment,
- quality information and continual improvement.

Four broad stages for implementation of the QMS were identified with the following imperatives: plan, do, check and improve. All polytechnic managers have responsibility to improve the OP's business through implementing and maintaining the QMS within their areas of responsibility.

External Audits

As of the early nineties, to qualify for government funding, polytechnics and technical institutes within New Zealand were required to have their quality management systems validated by a central body responsible for qualifications and accreditations, the New Zealand Qualifications Authority (NZQA). In turn, NZQA delegated validation for the sector to another body, initially called the New Zealand Polytechnic Programmes Committee (NZPPC), and now known as ITPQ. In essence, an ITPQ audit encompasses a pre-planned systematic and independent examination to determine whether an institution's activities comply with planned arrangements. Part of the process of continuous quality enhancement, the ITP Quality audit process is based on 12 ITP New Zealand Academic standards (Appendix 1). This involves a 3-5 day on-site visit by an audit team of 3-4 members, scrutinising a cross section of up to 12 selected programmes. It seeks to evaluate effectiveness and continuous improvement of the institution relative to its own objectives and indicators and identify best practice, with a summary report of findings and recommendations published on ITPQ's website.

The approach taken by the Polytechnic in relation to quality management has always been that the organisation's business needs must drive the system. The quality system was set up to meet the needs of the business, and to ensure that service to our primary customers (i.e. students) met their needs as well as those of other stakeholders such as industry including employers. Hence, though the need to meet external quality standards was seen as important to be able to continue in business, it was not considered the prime driver for our vision and mission.

In addition, the Polytechnic considers interaction and co-ordination of work activities through staff performance to be critical. The formal documentation of the QMS on an intranet site was only part of the strategy adopted. Without co-operation and understanding of the quality approach, any quality system is doomed to languish as theoretical rather than operational. Considerable effort was invested in involving staff within the system, training them in their responsibilities, and ensuring they were able to change processes effectively when necessary.

The Polytechnic is the one specialised distance provider in New Zealand that is required to meet the ITPQ academic quality standards. As a distance provider, the Polytechnic's systems for key processes such as enrolling students and providing learning support and assessment are different to those of providers who teach mainly in classrooms. From the inception of external validation, the Polytechnic has provided a written description of its quality management system, known internally as "the mapping document". This was, inter alia, designed to educate external auditors about standards met through systems that differ from those of contact institutions, where the auditors tended to derive most of their experience.

Over the years, this mapping document has proved an invaluable tool for external auditors. It is also useful for the staff, to understand their particular role within a large and complex organisation, with regulatory requirements set by the Polytechnic's Academic Board and Governance Council, and by the New Zealand government through the Ministry of Education and latterly, the Tertiary Education Commission. In addition, this approach of separately mapping activities against the external standards ensures that those standards did not "drive" business operations.

ISO Certification

In 1992, the Management and Council of the Polytechnic undertook a pilot programme seeking to achieve ISO 9002 certification for the Polytechnic's Printshop. A large proportion of the staff in the Printshop were non-native speakers, and the Polytechnic believed that a strongly structured approach to quality improvement would advance effectiveness and efficiency gains. This project took some time to implement, but ISO 9002 certification was finally achieved in 1995.

Strong emphasis was placed on the basic quality improvement idea of "fix the problem, fix the system". Printshop staff were trained to handle complaints by considering what needed to be done to fix the immediate problem, and then to look at the way the work was being processed to see if change was necessary so that the problem did not arise again. Process improvements frequently came from this attention to process, as staff had more ownership of their processes.

During the pilot, many problems between the Printshop and its main internal customer, the Production Unit (the area of the Polytechnic responsible for developing course materials to final print stage), were identified and remedied. Over the term of the pilot, the number of complaints reduced considerably as work practices were standardised and improved to better meet the customers' needs.

During 1995, the Polytechnic gained interim acceptance of its quality management system from NZPPC. At that time technical institutes and polytechnics in New Zealand were required to seek external approval for course and programme accreditation. Over the next years until the Polytechnic was granted quality-assured status by ITPQ in 2002, it maintained a 100% success rate for its approval applications.

In 1995 at the Chief Executive's request, a small working team within the Polytechnic investigated the appropriateness of ISO as a quality standard for the whole organisation. Although ISO was seen as appropriate, and desirable to drive continuous quality improvement, the working team concluded similar gains could be achieved without ISO certification.

However, the expected independent drive for continuous quality improvement did not eventuate throughout the Polytechnic, and in June 1996 management decided to set up a project team tasked with achieving ISO 9001 certification for the whole Polytechnic, by 31 December 1997. This project team (Project Leader, four full-time staff and other support as required) documented and published standard work procedures, and established new systems across the Polytechnic, including:

- Internal audit.
- Central complaints recording.
- Central document management including publication of process and policy information to all staff.
- Annual reviews by management of the quality management system.

A software package called "Qpulse" from Gael Quality in Scotland was selected as the electronic system for managing aspects of the quality system, including complaints, non-conformances, document control and internal audit. This package has supported the quality management system since 1996.

The Polytechnic achieved full ISO 9001 certification in January 1998. The organisation viewed this as an outstanding result, given the size of the organisation (719 staff in a range of roles and under varying employment arrangements; teaching an average of 30,000 students each year). The auditors commended the Polytechnic on its innovative use of the campus intranet for enabling staff to access management system procedures, and noted that the Polytechnic had achieved certification in one of the fastest timeframes seen at the time in New Zealand.

Work processes were published on an internal intranet site called Manage, and updated and managed through a central system. All staff now had access to clear descriptions of how each process worked, and the business rules or academic policies relating to that process. A team of internal auditors was established and trained, and regular ISO audits began in accordance with an audit plan agreed by management. In February 2001, the Polytechnic gained full certification against the new ISO 9001:2000 standard. Only one non-conformance was identified (relating to record-keeping), which was seen as an outstanding achievement for the Polytechnic, particularly as the new full standard was only issued in December 2000.

The Polytechnic was the subject of twice-yearly ISO surveillance audits carried out by an external auditor from 1998 until the end of 2005. At this time management decided to let the ISO certification lapse, as the Polytechnic was no longer identifying improvement opportunities through the surveillance process. Practices put in place to achieve ISO certification were now embedded in organisational practice, and the same pattern seen with the Printshop pilot (a dramatic reduction in the number of complaints from customers) had occurred for the Polytechnic as a whole. The Polytechnic withdrew from ISO certification in 2006.

NZPPC carried out a full academic quality audit in October 2002, and the Polytechnic received quality assured status from November 2002. This gave the Polytechnic delegated authority to approve its sub-degree programmes for the next four years. One low risk corrective action was identified, and a number of commendations were made around good practice. A mid-term review followed in February 2005, which provided assurance that the

Polytechnic's internal audit and review processes were effectively maintaining academic quality consistent with its quality assured status.

ITP Quality Auditors carried out a second full audit in December 2006, to examine compliance with and effectiveness against the ITP NZ academic quality standards. This audit confirmed that the Polytechnic continued to meet all 12 standards, and found no areas where it was necessary to seek corrective action. Eight recommendations were made suggesting further improvements to policies and procedures already operating successfully. The most significant recommendation was that the approach to the re-configuring of the intranet system Manage be from the policy level down, to ensure a logical match was achieved with work procedures.

Eleven good practices were also identified, in particular the annual review of the quality management system and its continuing development, and the quality and effectiveness of the internal audit process led by an independent internal auditor (an employee of the Governance Council rather than the Chief Executive of the Polytechnic). The external auditors saw this as maintaining a robust and meaningful audit process. The external auditors also commented on the positive contribution of the internal audit programme where the efforts of staff ensured that the process was not regarded merely as a formalised compliance exercise.

Consequently, the ITP Quality Board approved the continuation of the Polytechnic's quality assured status for another four years.

Internal Audit

Since 1998, the Polytechnic has carried out a full programme of internal quality audits. Two parallel internal audit processes were implemented, one focussing on the audit of compliance with the ISO standards, and one focussing on internal controls in place for specific risks identified by management. The compliance audits were managed and carried out by Polytechnic staff members.

The audits on risk were directed by Council and led by an external Lead Auditor employed by the Council. These replaced an earlier audit regime based largely on financial processes (e.g. Accounts Receivable, Accounts Payable). At the time of the first external academic audit in 2002, the Polytechnic was completing a project designed to align all internal audit processes, to mitigate overlap and ensure they covered ITP Quality academic standards, ISO 9001 and the risks identified for the business, by management. The external academic audit identified this alignment as a good practice, unique in the tertiary education sector in New Zealand.

Later in 2002, Council took ownership of all internal auditing activities, and approved a three yearly rolling audit plan covering all activities within the Polytechnic. The audit plan continues to be structured around the main business processes of the Polytechnic, and the Fig. 15.1 shows the Polytechnic's business process model, adapted from Porter's Value Chain by Colin P. Bond.

The documentation intranet site "Manage" was subsequently rewritten reflecting the aligned approach in the new business process model. Transparent at all stages, the audit process is formally documented within the quality management system.

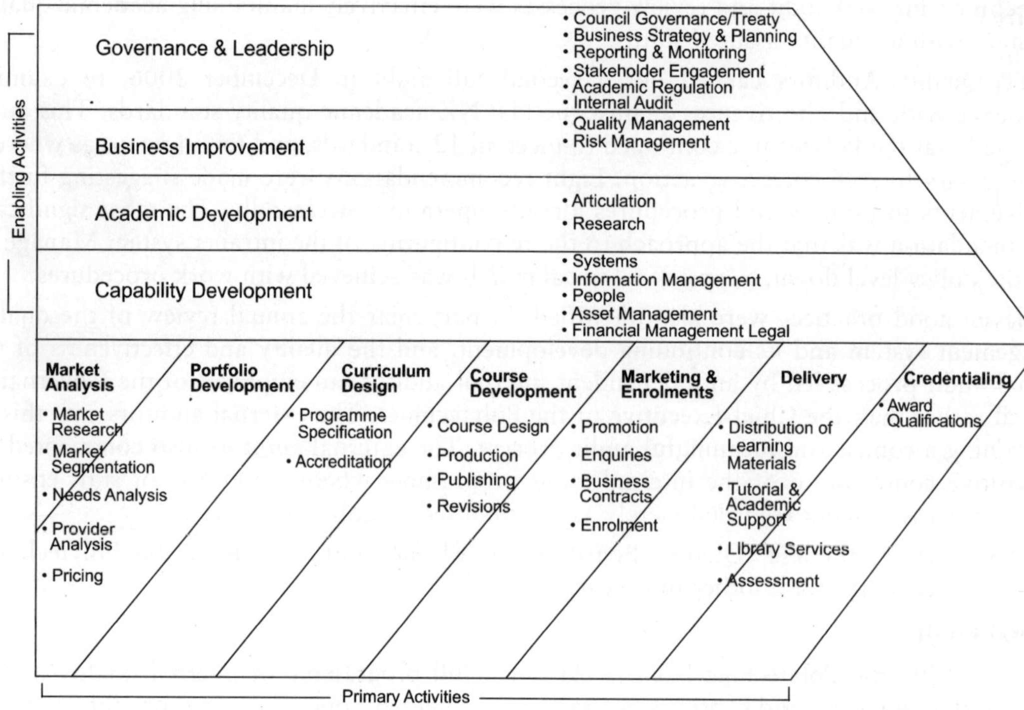

Fig. 15.1: The Open Polytechnic of New Zealand: Business Process Model

The Lead Auditor develops a formal audit plan before each audit, covering the scope of the audit, its objectives and recording any prior relevant audit findings. The Academic Manager reviews and approves the final plan to ensure it will provide adequate coverage of the matters being audited, which is then published to the managers of the areas to be audited. The Internal Auditor(s) carry out the audit and prepare a draft report, which contains any findings of significance, and identifies good practices. The draft is reviewed for quality by the Academic Manager and circulated to managers so they and the auditors can resolve any inaccuracies.

The final report is viewed by senior staff (members of the Executive) and managers, who provide a response to each finding. The Auditor must find the management responses acceptable in terms of appropriateness, commitment to action and timeline.

The final report and management responses are then forwarded through the Polytechnic's Executive and Academic Board, with a copy going to Council so they can be alerted of any areas of major concern. The Lead Auditor has full access to the Council to ensure further transparency around audit activities.

The Polytechnic records and tracks audit findings, responses, and actions taken through the Qpulse recording system, to ensure that audit findings are given due weight and actioned. This system is still in use in 2007.

Quality Principles

During the audit alignment project between 2001 and 2003, the Polytechnic explicitly defined the quality principles underpinning the quality management system. Though agreed and understood, these had not been explicitly articulated to that point.

Each principle has a specific strategy for achievement, and the principles are given in the Table 15.1.

Table 15.1: Quality Principles

Principle	Detail
Customer orientation	Customers define their requirements for products and services. We aim to work closely with our external customers to ensure that products and services are provided that fit customers' purposes.
Management excellence	A systems approach to "management".
Academic excellence	Developing a reputation for excellence to give value to The Open Polytechnic's qualifications.
People commitment	We acknowledge the importance of effective teamwork in supplying quality products and services in a way that ensures the customer has a straightforward relationship with the Polytechnic. We strive to ensure that all staff have a clear sense of purpose and understanding of the Vision and Mission of the Polytechnic. We invest in our staff by providing training, personal and professional development time and opportunities to undertake and participate in research activities.
Quality information	We seek high quality information to be able to provide quality products and services.
Continual improvement	We have a systematic and managed approach to continual improvement through: • Specific tools • Agility.

Quality Management of Materials Development

The success of an institution dedicated to open and distance learning is very dependent on the design and delivery of learning materials and the support given to the student studying in their own location. The Open Polytechnic of New Zealand has a long history of learning materials development and has invested significant resources in establishing a Design and Development Centre (DDC) that is considered one of the strongest of its type in New Zealand.

The DDC is a specialist unit within the Open Polytechnic dedicated to planning, designing, developing and publishing learning materials in a range of media. It provides services in project management, instructional design, editing, educational technology, multi-media, typesetting and graphic design. These services are supported by centralised processes, which aim to ensure that Open Polytechnic learning materials are developed efficiently and to a consistently high standard.

DDC works in partnership with internal and external stakeholders to develop well-targeted, inclusive learning materials that:

- Enhance students' learning experience by structuring and supporting their learning.
- Optimise teaching and learning by incorporating appropriate media and technologies.
- Are developed through processes that achieve the appropriate balance between quality, timeliness and cost.

The team developing or revising the teaching materials chooses appropriate teaching methods, case studies, practical activities and other strategies. Teaching and learning strategies are selected that are appropriate to:

- The OP's academic philosophy (in its Charter).
- The learning outcomes of the programme/course under development.
- The profile of students who are expected to undertake the programme including their access to particular learning options.

The appropriateness of the level is determined during the course approval and development processes.

Team Approach

The Open Polytechnic uses a team approach to course development. After a preliminary discussion with faculty to identify a suitable writer or content expert, the Project Coordinator sets up a team for the particular project, drawing on the following roles:

- Project Coordinator—Manages the project to meet time, quality and budget requirements.
- Content Specialist(s)—Writes course content.
- External Industry Advisor—Usually a recognized expert from the discipline area. Ensures that the course reflects the current practice and that the assessment processes are acceptable, relevant and appropriate to the level.
- External Moderator—Ensures that assessments produced alongside learning materials address the learning outcomes, and are accurate and appropriate for the level of learning.
- Technical Editor—Ensures that the content is technically correct and meets the requirements of the unit standards or teaching prescription. This role may be filled by the external industry advisor
- Instructional Designer—Ensures that the learning materials and assessments are at an appropriate level for the learner, match the learning outcomes and are educationally sound. Assists with the selection of appropriate media and technologies for delivery of course material.
- Cultural Adviser—If the target market for the development is made up of a group with different cultural needs or perspectives, appropriate Cultural Advisers will be used; for example, Maori, Pacific Islands, international.
- Editor—Provides final quality check on language, punctuation, formatting, copyrights acknowledgements and referencing.
- Mac Operator/Typesetter—Puts raw material into style, inserts graphics and prepares files for print or online delivery.

A team approach using specialists for each part of the process has the advantage of ensuring that a high quality product is developed. The possible disadvantages of such an approach are: higher costs of materials development, longer timeframe for materials development, increased need for project coordination.

The Course Development Process

From the design brief included in the course or programme proposal, the Design and Development team develops working plans, a prototype of a small section of the course for approval by the 'client' (a school or external client, and then proceeds to complete the course with a final sign-off by the clients).

The process ensures:

- Professional industry and academic advice is sought where necessary.
- Representation of specific groups (for example, consumers) both at the point of development and the point of evaluation.
- Compliance with legislative requirements.

Approvals

Quality management of the learning materials process starts with the approvals process. This phase is 'owned' by Faculty and Academic Office. It involves getting academic case and business case approval for new materials or for a major redevelopment of existing material.

Planning and Writing

Once approval has been obtained, the DDC Project Coordinator organises a planning meeting attended by the writer (who is chosen because he or she is a subject matter expert), Instructional Designer, faculty representative and other team members as appropriate (see team approach above). The output from this meeting is a detailed course plan, which faculty signs off. the writer then starts drafting the course and, at a pre-arranged point, sends draft material in to the ID for review. During this phase a Technical Editor reviews the material for content accuracy. The average cost of the planning and writing phase is around 40%-45% of the total project budget. This is a significant figure given that one of the chief determinants of the speed and cost of a project is the quality of the initial writing.

Instructional Review

The Instructional Designer is pivotal in ensuring a quality learning experience for the student. The ID acts as an independent 'champion' of the distance education student and reviews the writer's first (and sometimes second and third!) draft to ensure that it will provide an effective and relevant learning experience for the student. The role of the ID is to ensure solutions devised are appropriate to student learning needs, meet the Open Polytechnic's delivery requirements and are acceptable to the tutorial staff involved. Time and budgetary constraints and workload balance issues must also be taken into account. The ID negotiates suggested improvements with the writer and, in some cases, assists with rewriting of the material. When the ID and faculty have approved the draft, it may be sent out for external peer review or bi-cultural review where appropriate. The average cost of ID work is approximately 18%-20% of the project budget. Peer review and bi-cultural review add around another 5%.

Production, Publishing

Once all stakeholders have approved the draft, it is sent to Mac Ops for typesetting, layout and composition, formatting, image processing, insertion of graphics, print preparation and pre-press. The average cost of Mac operating is around 10%-12% of the project budget. The material is then sent to the Editor who checks for grammatical errors, typos, unclear use of language, continuity errors, copyright clearance and acknowledgements, accuracy of referencing, etc. Once the Editor has finished, the file is signed off by faculty and prepared for print. The average cost of editing work is around 10%-12% of the project budget.

e-Learning

While the bulk of the Polytechnic's learning materials are print-based, the sector-wide adoption of digital communication technologies for e-learning has led to the creation at the Polytechnic of an e-Learning Unit. e-Learning staff work in close partnership with the DDC to design and develop mixed media learning materials using the most appropriate medium in order to achieve the desired learning objectives. These projects offer a strong future direction for the design of courses at the Polytechnic through the creation of resources that can be reused, and processes and training to develop instructional design capability and enable their effective use by staff and teaching faculty.

Summary of Good Practice of Material Development

The recent 2006 ITPQ audit made the following comments relating to materials development at the Open Polytechnic:

- Instructionally designed learning materials pass through a rigorous approval and planning process.
- As the levels of programmes advance, more use is made of techniques, including online methods, to encourage students to explore, critique and generally direct their own learning. Some of the developments in e-learning that shift the learning approach from a content-based to a collaborative approach are particularly noteworthy.
- While increasing use is being made of online delivery, print materials remain the dominant mode. Quality of content and presentation for all modes of delivery is maintained by 'enforcing' the use of centralised processes designed to make best use of the specialist expertise available within the institution.
- Learning materials are developed in parallel with other learning resources (such as supplementary online materials) and are delivered to students as a high quality integrated learning package.
- Assessment tools are developed in parallel with the main package of learning materials and students are encouraged to use these together in ways that will help them identify and achieve the key learning objectives.

For smaller institutions, the cost of using large project teams of specialists as described above could be a major constraint. Even finding the specialists might be a difficulty. However, experience has shown that where one or two people only are solely responsible for the planning, design and development of learning materials, the results can be highly variable. The effect of a proscribed, centralised course development system is to produce learning materials that are of a consistently high standard. The highs and lows are ironed out, but a consistent level of quality is assured.

Conclusion

In November 2006, the Polytechnic introduced a new electronic student management system to replace an aging system. The new system meant that work processes changed and it was necessary to redocument these to show overall work processes, any applicable business rules and step by step instructions for data entry for the new system. Consequently a new website was introduced to support the new system, and the earlier site known as Manage is being reviewed to ensure that all information relating to operational processes is held on one site, and that governance and management policy statements, and governance/management processes (such as audit) are linked to the new site.

Concurrently within the context of significant reform underway for the tertiary sector in New Zealand, the Open Polytechnic continues to modify its business model to best meet 21st century learner needs and national imperatives. The overall approach to QMS continues to move from "compliance-driven" practice to "reflective" practice, as illustrated by the case studies from LifeWorks and the Design and Development Centre, developing and refining innovative and effective ways of meeting (and often leading) changing student and societal expectations.

***Appendix* 1**

ITP New Zealand Academic Quality Standards (2006 Revision)[1]

1. Institutional Academic Quality Management
   - 1.1 The institution has documented academic quality systems, policies and evidence of their effective application.
   - 1.2 Authorities and responsibilities for academic quality are clearly assigned in accordance with institutional policies.
   - 1.3 The institution's commitment to principles of the Treaty of Waitangi is clearly evident throughout its operations.
   - 1.4 The institution's commitment to attaining the highest standards of excellence in education, training and research, with due concern for the public interest and the well being of students attending the institution, is evident in the way it conducts its academic functions.
2. Development and Review of Qualifications and Educational Programmes
   - 2.1 An educationally sound, effective process is used for the development, approval, and review of all qualifications, programmes and courses associated with the institution.
   - 2.2 Stakeholders have appropriate opportunities to give feedback on programmes and to be involved in the development and review of programme outcomes.
3. Financial, Administrative, Human and Physical Resources
   - 3.1 An effective process is used to identify and allocate adequate resources (including physical resources) to achieve the outcomes of qualifications, programmes and courses and to implement, maintain and improve the institute's QMS.
   - 3.2 Effective policies and procedures are in place to meet the institute's health and safety requirements.
4. Staff Selection, Appraisal and Development
   - 4.1 Staff qualifications and experience enable quality delivery of programmes.
   - 4.2 Appropriate staff development plans, based on identified needs, are implemented and outcomes monitored to ensure effectiveness.
5. Student Information and Admission to Programmes
   - 5.1 Prospective and continuing students receive effective information and guidance to assist with making informed decisions on their programme of study.
   - 5.2 Appropriate entry and selection criteria for each programme of study are well-publicised and applied consistently.
   - 5.3 The institute has effective credit transfer and recognition of prior learning policies and procedures, consistent with NZQA Credit Recognition and Transfer Policy.
6. Student Guidance and Support
   - 6.1 Students are provided with learning and pastoral support, which is timely, effective and appropriate.

6.2 Safeguards are in place to protect students' physical and emotional well-being.

6.3 The institution has effective policies and procedures, which are accessible, appropriate and fair, for resolving student complaints.

7. Programme Delivery

7.1 The institution defines and implements effective teaching and learning practices that are educationally sound, and appropriate to the programme of study and mode of delivery.

7.2 Programme delivery undertaken in partnership with, on behalf of or by another organisation, meets the standards set in the quality management system.

8. Off-Site Practical/Workplace Components

8.1 Off-site practical/workplace components are effective and integrated into curricula.

8.2 Clear criteria are used to select off-site placements, and clearly identified roles and responsibilities for all parties are stated and agreed.

9. Assessment and Moderation

9.1 Systems are in place for ensuring the assessment of learning outcomes is fair, valid and consistently applied.

9.2 Student learning outcomes are accurately, effectively and fairly assessed.

9.3 Students receive accurate and timely advice on their learning progress.

9.4 Effective and appropriate policies and procedures enable students to appeal assessment outcomes.

10. Reporting and Certification

10.1 Students and appropriate external stakeholders receive accurate and timely advice on students' achievement.

10.2 The appropriate awards are accurately documented and issued, in a timely manner to all students who meet the stated requirements.

10.3 Student results are safely stored, with final records accessible for future reference.

10.4 Awards issued by the institution are consistent with internal and external requirements and definitions.

11. Research

11.1 The institution has defined research objectives, appropriate to the level and type of qualifications delivered.

11.2 The institution ensures adequate resources and support are available to meet the defined research objectives.

11.3 The institution systematically evaluates and reports its achievement of research outcomes.

12. Internal Audit and Review

12.1 Internal academic audit, and improvements arising from audits, are effectively managed.

12.2 The quality management system is reviewed, by senior management, and updated on a regular basis.

Appendix 2

Lessons from LifeWorks

This section deals with insights into the quality management system of the LifeWorks Programme of the Open Polytechnic of New Zealand. It describes how the programme operates, how changes were made and the results of changes, and further action arising from analysis of the results. The LifeWorks experience affirms that good quality management systems are a benefit when used as an ongoing way of operating rather than one-off interventions.

Graduates of the LifeWorks Programme are prepared for entry level employment, further study or training and lifelong learning. They become more confident to pursue work and personal goals and they increase their contribution to their communities and society. Of those who graduate, 96% would recommend LifeWorks Programme to others, and 53% of them have gone on to either full or part study or training.

The delivery method used is a combination of distance learning and face to face, one on one support from coaches and support from the Contact Centre. There are several critical factors in the success of the LifeWorks Programme. The fundamental factor is that the programme has been designed and is operated with a very strong learner-focus, which is reflected in the materials, the contact centre, the staff support, and the coaches who deliver services to the learners. Success is due to the coaches who are community-based and locally employed and able to interact effectively with typical LifeWorks Programme learners. Success is also due to the quality of interaction from the central Call Centre, which acts as a first point of contact messaging service and support system for learners and coaches. The materials are an important part of the programme but the essence of success is the human interaction where learners are engaged and want to learn to learn.[2]

Community-based organisations are contracted by the Open Polytechnic of New Zealand to be providers of the LifeWorks Programme and in so doing are required to employ community-based coaches. The mechanism for this arrangement is a contract document, which specifies the obligations of each party.

Issue

For the initial period of delivery of this programme, the Open Polytechnic's formal contract with LifeWorks was used as the key documentation for accountability. For most of the time, the results were sufficiently satisfactory. However, at contract review time and once data was analysed to determine to see if there were ways that the LifeWorks Programme could be operated to give the learner better service, it became apparent that greater clarity was needed around the OP's expectations for the role of the provider and the coach.

Some of the data showed that the administration processes were not providing the necessary quality management of learner records and achievements and that in some cases learners were missing out on what was their rightful achievement. While the contract implied expected actions on the behalf of providers and coaches the actual 'how' was missing. Staff supporting the LifeWorks Programme believed that greater clarity of expectations and some simple changes would have a positive impact on the quality of management of delivery.

Action

Staff agreed internally to draw up a document alongside the contract to incorporate the elements of the contractual obligations. They agreed that it should specify exactly what was required, and that the process needed to reflect the aims of the LifeWorks Programme. It was important to engage and capture the imagination of the providers and their administrators and coaches.

A draft concept was floated at a national meeting of providers and, after discussion and useful input from them, a working document for consultation with providers was drawn up. This support document was called 'Achieving Excellence'[3]—carefully crafted to focus on the here and now, and ongoing using the present participle of 'achieving' and 'excellence' to emphasise the stretch from just meeting contractual obligations.

The 'Achieving Excellence' document outlines procedures—for example, in monitoring retentions and completions, it specifies step by step for supporting coaches, how to interpret online reports, student withdrawal processes and provider action timelines. It was important to embed the principles agreed to carefully in writing. The new document was introduced face to face with each provider by one of the programme staff—walking through every element so that it was a joint commitment to use as the basis for quality delivery. Once the providers had been introduced to it then the programme staff ran a national meeting for all coaches with Achieving Excellence as the theme and underpinning action for all events at the meeting.

After this introduction, the Achieving Excellence document has now become the basis for regular interaction between programme staff and providers and a means to keep action and performance on-track. Programme staff use a check sheet derived from the Achieving Excellence document in the process of formally reviewing each provider's contract, acknowledging achievement and noting areas for action.

Results

In March 2007, having used the Achieving Excellence document for some months in 2006 and with an eye to future developments, the programme staff assessed what had been achieved and what could be done differently.

The fortnightly telephone meetings have ensured that providers know their targets and can be advised by programme staff on a regular basis. The Achieving Excellence document, which outlines expectations for providers about student records and files, has contributed to a noticeable increase in file return compliance and in the timeframe for visits to students.

Feedback from participants in the national coach conference was very positive. Coaches reported that they were more motivated, better-informed and felt part of a wider team. (This is an important aspect as most coaches work in the community with little interaction with colleagues on a daily basis.) However, the coach provider network website is only being used by a small number of coaches and cannot therefore be a guaranteed way of reaching coaches with information. Training (for new coaches) has been carried out at the programme offices and this has strengthened the commitment from new coaches and introduced them to programme staff and resources.

The withdrawal rate for students is within acceptable limits at less than 30% of enrolments, and the number of visits within the expected timeframe is being achieved by more than half the providers.

The award achievement rate has increased marginally but it is still below the government target (although it is within the achieved results for similar courses at a similar level).[4]

Considerable variance remains between coaches in terms of student achievement. However, as with many results, all is not well as it could be. To that end the programme staff have set in place further achievement targets to ensure ongoing improvement.

They have conducted a qualitative research project with coaches to determine how those who get the highest results for their students are achieving that. Fifteen coaches have been interviewed with a selection of high, average and low performers and results are due after April 2007. Focused training support for coaches of up to two to three times per year—written into the provider contract but seldom invoked—is to be brought to providers' attention so that they can seek advice and support for individuals or groups of coaches.

Streamlining the administrative systems used, so that discrepancies between user systems are diminished or removed, is to be considered for future development. Training for provider administrators once or twice per year to ensure that system changes and administrative procedures are appropriately understood and used, is to be considered for introduction in 2007 and subsequent years.

One of the most inspiring and motivating ways for programme staff and provider staff to stay engaged in their work is the direct feedback from LifeWorks Programme graduates.

The results achieved with the LifeWorks Programme reflect the effort put into it by programme staff:

- Overall, 51% of graduates go on to further study.
- 43% of those who go on to further study credit the LifeWorks Programme as the reason for them taking up studying.
- 71% of students who have not yet begun study since completing the LifeWorks Programme intend to do so in the future.
- 65% are in full or part time paid employment post LifeWorks Programme (an increase of 14% from pre LifeWorks.
- 28% of graduates are receiving a government benefit post LifeWorks Programme (a decrease of 4% from pre LifeWorks).[5]

The quality management systems used in the LifeWorks Programme have been beneficial to all stakeholders as a means to ensure that better and different ways of reaching, engaging and retaining students are part of the business as usual operations of the programme.

Notes

1. http://www.itpq.ac.nz/auditOverview.html
2. Data sourced from commissioned surveys conducted by TNS Ltd., 2005-06
3. 'Achieving Excellence 2006'—provider procedures for monitoring student retention and completions, the Open Polytechnic of New Zealand, internal publication, 2006.
4. Provider Best Practice Review, TOPNZ LifeWorks Programme, unpublished internal report, March 2007—see Appendix III.
5. Data sourced from commissioned surveys conducted by TNS Ltd., 2004-06.

Role of Distance Education Council in Promoting Quality in the Distance Education System in India*

16

—*Manjulika Srivastava, Nalini Lele* and *Bharat Bhushan*

Introduction

Distance education (DE) has become a major form of teaching and learning around the world. It is regarded as a truly innovative educational phenomenon, vital to the transformation of education. It is no longer looked upon as the second best mode of delivery. It is considered as the most invaluable strategy for providing opportunities of education to all people at the levels. In India too four and a half decades of DE has seen a phenomenal expansion and growth of the system, not only in terms of number of institutions but also in terms of number of programmes and courses on offer and student enrolment. Today, India has one the largest DE systems in the world. Presently, there are 355 universities of these 127 are dual-mode universities offering both classroom-based education and distance education. Besides, there are 14 open universities exclusively offering programmes through distance mode. Thus, nearly 40% of the universities in India are offering DE programmes.

With such huge network, spanning across the country, and the growth being exponential in a comparatively short period of time, there is a growing concern for the quality in education being imparted through such institutions.

Distance Education Council

The Distance Education Council (DEC) was established in 1991 under Section 5(2) of Indira Gandhi National Open University (IGNOU) Act (1985) passed by the Indian Parliament. It is responsible for promotion, coordination and maintenance of standards of DE system in the country. Section 5(2) of the IGNOU Act (1985) stipulates that:

> Notwithstanding anything contained in any other law at the time being in force, but without prejudice to the provision of sub-section, it shall be the duty of the University to take all such steps as it may deem fit for the promotion of the Open University and distance education systems and for the determination of standards of teaching,

* The data presented in this chapter has been taken from the unpublished records and documents of the Distance Education Council where the authors are working.

evaluation and research in such systems, and for the purpose of performing these functions, the University shall have such powers including the power to allocate and disburse grants to colleges, whether admitted to its privileges or not, or to any other university or institutions of higher learning, as may be specified by the Statutes.

The following powers and functions of DEC are defined under Clause 4(a) of Statute 28 of the Indira Gandhi National Open University Act (1985):

"It shall be the general duty of the DEC to take all such steps as are consistent with the provisions of this Act, the Statutes and the Ordinances for the promotion of the open university/distance education systems, its coordinated development, and the determination of its standards, and in particular.

- To develop a network of open universities/distance education institutions in the country in consultation with the State Governments, Universities, and other concerned agencies.
- To take such steps as are necessary to ensure the coordinated development of the open university/distance education system in the country.
- To advise State Governments, Universities and other concerned agencies on their proposals to set up open universities or to introduce programmes of distance education.
- To appoint Review Committees from time to time to study and assess the performance of the open universities/distance education institutions participating in the network of any respect relevant to the functioning of the network.
- To prescribe a broad framework for courses and programmes including their pattern and structure.
- To evolve norms, procedures and practices in respect of admission, evaluation, completion of course requirements, transfer of credits, etc. of students admitted to the programmes of the open university/distance education network and for the award of certificates, diplomas and degrees to them.
- To evolve guidelines for the organization of student support services for the open university/distance education programmes.
- To appoint Committees for advising and assisting the DEC in the performance of any of its functions or exercise of any of its powers."

Initiatives Taken by the DEC

A beginning was made to bring in quality in distance education system by interacting with international bodies like the Commonwealth of Learning (COL) to develop a blueprint for DEC and its operations. Experts deputed by the COL visited DEC and participated in discussion on issues like transfer of credits, grading system, etc. with a view to improve the quality of programmes offered through distance mode in the country. The COL later funded a project for an Indian team to visit Australia, Canada and the UK to study the mechanisms instituted by distance education institutions in those countries to assure the quality of their products and processes. A three member team comprising the Director, Distance Education Council; a senior Professor from a State Open University (BRAOU, Hyderabad) and the Head of the Correspondence Institute of Madras University visited these countries in November-

December 1993. On their recommendations, a major round table-cum-workshop on quality assurance was organized in 1994. The UGC, IGNOU and the COL supported this project and all the Vice Chancellors of State Open Universities (SOUs) and the Directors of Correspondence Course Institutions (CCIs) of conventional universities participated in this workshop.

COL assured full support to DEC for staff development, capacity building and technical support on quality assurance.

The DEC was of the view that being a facilitating body, all major decisions should be taken on a participatory basis. Therefore, all its initiatives have been undertaken through the medium of committees with representation from different DE institutions.

In its early years, the DEC had constituted a committee in 1993 for 'Database and Networking of Open Universities'. The committee devised formats that would be shared by all universities. The formats included those for storing institutional information, information on teachers and academics, student admission, etc. The DEC was of the opinion that uniformity in collection of data would make coordination and networking with different open universities an easier task for it.

The DEC has been appointing various committees in advising and assisting DEC in its functions and developing policies thereof. A Quality Assurance Panel was constituted in the year 1994 with an intention that it can advise DEC on various activities that the DEC can take up to induce quality in the system. A number of times committees have been formed to develop guidelines on how to go about institutional assessment; develop strategy for assessment by peer teams; develop strategies for institutional recognition and programme approvals, develop guidelines for establishing DE institutions, etc. as per the needs and requirements of the time. The DEC has also been appointing review committees from time to time to assess performance of institutions, evaluate their utilization of grants, etc. The different expert committees constituted for major activities over the years can be listed as under:

- Committee for Database and Networking of Open Universities 1993-1994.
- Committee for Standardizing Grading for Credit Hour/System 1993-1994.
- Expert Committee for Promotion of D.E. System, 1994.
- Quality Assurance Panel –1994-95
- Committee to Develop Norms and Standards for Management Education Programmes through Distance Mode, 1996.
- Committee to Develop Norms and Standards for Computer Education Programmes through Distance Mode, 1996.
- Committee to Develop Norms and Standards for Library Science Education Programmes through Distance Mode, 1996.
- Committee on Sharing of Materials from Common Pool of Programmes, 1996.
- Committee on Development of Performance Indicators, 1996.
- Working Group for Development of Self Assessment Manual for Open Universities, 1997.

- Working Group for the Development of Manual for Research in Distance Education, 1997.
- Committee to Develop Norms and Standards for B.Sc. (Nursing) programmes through Distance Mode, 1998-99.
- Committee on modalities for Financial Assistance to State Open Universities (SOUs) and Correspondence Course Institutions (CCIs), 1998.
- Task Force for Assessment and Accreditation of Distance Education Institutions (DEIs), 2000.
- Task Force on Honorarium for Resource Persons for Different Activities in Distance Education, 2000.
- Expert Committees on Research Projects have been constituted with tenure of 2-3 years. The committees have helped in formulating guidelines, modifying them, screening of the research project proposals and recommending proposals for financial assistance. Such Committees were formed in 1996, 1999, 2000 and recently in 2007.
- Task Force for Personnel Policy for Academic Staff in D.E., 2000.
- Committees for Peer Team Visits to Institutions for Institutional Assessment, Impact Assessment of Grants etc., 2005.
- Committee for Development of Proformas for Assessment of Institutions, 2006.
- Committee for Area of Jurisdiction for Operation/Offering of Distance Education by DE Institutions, 2007.
- Committee for Development of Strategy for Assessment and Accreditation, 2007.
- Committee for Development of Proformas, Guidelines, Handbooks for Recognition Purpose, 2007.
- Committee for Development of Minimum Norms for Ensuring Quality in DE Institutions, 2007.

Organization of Round Tables/Workshops/Seminars

The DEC has been organizing seminars/round tables and workshops at a national level on very pertinent issues in order to usher in quality in the system and also for developing mechanisms for quality assurance. The DEC has also been promoting seminars/conferences by giving financial assistance to DE institutions to support organization of such events. The details are as follows:

- Workshop/Round table on Quality Assurance in Distance and Higher Education was jointly organized by DEC-UGC, at New Delhi, 30 June-2 July 1994. It was the beginning of the dialogue with DE institutions.
- 'Open Learning—A Rededication to Innovation' was organized in 1995 as a part of the decennial celebrations of IGNOU.
- UGC-IGNOU Conference of the Vice Chancellors of universities offering correspondence courses, was organized at IIPA, New Delhi, 11 December 1995. This was organized to educate the so-called Correspondence Course Institutions (CCIs) of conventional universities on transforming them to DEIs. Till then, the study material

provided to the students was only in the form of print like the textbooks were prescribed and were same as that used by regular students with or without a few handwritten notes or cyclostyled ones, and no face-to-face teacher-student interaction. The concept of Self Learning Materials and supporting materials in audio/video forms, etc. was introduced for the first time.

- Workshop was organized on Performance Indicators and Accreditation in Higher Education Association of Indian Universities, at New Delhi, 29-30 January 1996 and Seminar on Performance Indicators in Distance Education, at New Delhi on 3-4 July 1996. Introduction of the concept of performance indicators was helpful for institutions on pondering over what is happening in the institutions and how to improve the same to exploit their performance.
- Seminar on Student Support Systems in Distance Education, at New Delhi, 7-8 February 1996 was helpful for DE Institutions in knowing working conditions, issues involved in student support services and how to deal with them.
- Workshop on Training for Distance Educators in Dual Mode Universities in India, was organized by COL-DEC at Dr. BRAOU, Hyderabad, 21 November 1996.
- A number of times the DEC has assisted organization of IDEA conferences or given part funding for organizing the same, e.g.
  - (a) IV IDEA Conference-BRAOU, Hyderabad, in 1996.
  - (b) VIII IDEA Conference-YCMOU, Nashik, in 2001.
  - (c) IX IDEA Conference- Jammu University, in 2002.
  - (d) XII IDEA Conference- Mumbai University, in 2006.
- Seminar on Quality Assurance in Distance Higher Education, jointly organized by DEC-AIU and University of Delhi, at CPDHE, University of Delhi, 17-18 November 1998.
- IGNOU-DEC Conference on *Janotthan Hetu Doorasth Shiksha*, at Kota Open University (Presently Vardhaman Mahaveer Open University), Kota, Rajasthan, 8-9 March 2002. The State Government was also involved in the conference to seek its cooperation in development of DE system in Rajasthan.
- INQAAHE Conference/Workshop on Distance Teacher Education Networking & Collaboration in collaboration with NAAC at Bangalore, 2000-01.
- Meetings and Conference of Vice Chancellors of Open Universities have been taking place frequently. Directors of CCIs are also invited on occasions of National and International Conferences and Seminars. Such meetings are helpful to address issues on a common platform and arrive at solutions for the same.
- A national workshop was organized in Shillong for capacity building of personnel working at OUs and CCIs to address the issues confronting the system in the 21st century.

In addition to these, the DEC funded a number of round tables and workshops to train the faculty and staff of DE institutions for development of multi-media course-ware, learner support services, course design and development of self learning materials. Many a time the

DEC has arranged resource persons to conduct seminars/workshops at DE institutions in different parts of the country.

Memorandum of Understandings (MoU) with Apex Bodies

With a view to promoting excellence in distance education, DEC has forged strong relationships with national apex bodies like University Grants Commission (UGC), All India Council for Technical Education (AICTE), National Assessment and Accreditation Council (NAAC) and National Council for Teacher Education (NCTE). First MoU between DEC and NCTE was signed in 2001 for maintaining quality in teacher education programmes offered through distance mode. The MoU was thereafter signed in 2004 and subsequently in 2007 to have a continued effort in maintaining quality in teacher education in the country.

Through an MoU, DEC and NCTE have also jointly developed a National M.Ed. programme which was formally launched in August 2007. It is now kept in the DEC common pool of programmes that any university/institution can adopt and adapt from DEC/IGNOU and apply to the NCTE Regional Committee for approval of its implementation.

In May 2007, a MoU has jointly signed between UGC, AICTE and DEC agree to work in close cooperation, in pursuit of excellence in Technical and General Education through distance and mixed mode in the country. To ensure quality of technical and general education offered through distance and mixed mode, UGC and AICTE agreed to utilize the expertise and involvement of DEC in such functions as review of the programmes and courses, curricula, norms and standards and approval of new courses and institutions, periodic review of the institutions/programmes and coordination of inspection and approval activities. This MoU is aimed to avoid the duplication of efforts in streamlining the activities.

Quality of Programmes

Distance education is predominantly a learner-centered system that supports independent learning based on the packaged course. Quality of the packaged course depends largely upon the quality of the learning materials included in the packaged course. In fact, the learning material is the most important ingredient in the entire teaching-learning process. Quality materials can only usher in quality in education.

The DEC has been advocating that the institutions offer programmes through distance mode is that may follow the broad framework for model curriculum prescribed by the UGC Guidelines for design, development and delivery of programmes through distance mode in general were prepared and circulated to all. Programme specific norms for offering education through distance mode have also been prepared. So far norms and guidelines for offering programmes in computer education, library science, management programmes have been developed. For maintaining standards in offering teacher education through distance mode, the NCTE-DEC have jointly developed norms for Bachelor of Education and Master of Education programmes. Recently, the DEC has developed a handbook on how to develop Self Learning Materials that has been widely circulated to all DE institutions.

Therefore, in pursuance of the policy of promotion of quality and standards in the DE system, DEC had directed all DE institutions in the country to submit their learning materials to DEC for assessment and evaluation of their quality. It was, in fact, mandatory from 2004 onward for all institutions to seek prior approval of their programmes from DEC before starting any new programme. An advertisement was released in February 2004 in all national newspapers advising institutions to obtain programme approval and institutional recognition of DEC for offering programmes through distance mode.

The Gazette Notification No. 44 issued by the Government of India in 1995 further strengthens this. Accordingly,

> ...the qualifications awarded through Distance Education by the Universities established by an Act of Parliament or State Legislature, Institutions Deemed to be Universities under Section 3 of the UGC Act, 1956 and Institutions of National Importance declared under an Act of Parliament stand automatically recognized for the purpose of employment to posts and services under Central Government, provided it has been approved by Distance Education Council....

In pursuance of its mandate, the DEC took up the activity of approval/recognition of programmes/institutions. A *Handbook on Recognition* process was developed, published and posted on the DEC website. The handbook contained the formats in which institutions should send information. DEC minimum requirements were also stated in the same. Advertisements were published in national newspapers in 2003/2004 and through letters to all universities as per the AIU publication at the time, enclosing a copy of the handbook prepared notifying that institutions should get their programmes recognized by the DEC.

In the light of this responsibility assigned to DEC a three tier process for recognition of institutions and approval of their programmes was formulated as follows:

1. **Scanning institutional information**: The information provided by an DE institution on proforma I/II is verified at DEC for fulfillment of DEC minimum norms on infrastructure, faculty, delivery system, student support system, etc.

2. **Institutional visit**: The information provided by the institution is vetted by a team of experts to assess their preparedness for offering programmes through distance mode as per the information provided by them.

3. **Approval of programmes**: The institution submits a complete set of printed material of its programmes to DEC, which was then evaluated through Expert Committees for the content, quality and self-instructional nature of programmes.

Expert committees comprising experts from Higher Education and Distance Education would visit institutions to see their infrastructure and preparedness to offer programmes through distance mode.

Programme approval was done through a process of programme evaluation. The learning material submitted by institutions was evaluated through a committee comprising subject expert/s and distance education experts. The committees evaluated the various programmes for their content, quality and self learning format. The committee would either approve the programme if found suitable, or recommend modifications or reject it outright. The decision of the committee was conveyed to the institutions.

Out of the approximately 200 programmes received at DEC about 45 programmes of 23 universities were approved by DEC. About 140 of them were recommended for revision and the rest were rejected by the committees. This was a meager number compared to the total programmes over 3000 in number on offer by the DE institutions.

There were several reasons for the committee to reject so many programmes. The lacunae, other than incomplete set of the learning materials or only sample course materials sent. Many a time study material books purchased from the market; sometimes the syllabus did not match with the course materials submitted to DEC. Therefore, many programmes could not be evaluated by the committees.

Programmes were rejected for the following reasons:

- There were a number of grammatical mistakes in the course materials.
- Presentation of the material was bookish and not at all interactive.
- Links between sections were missing.
- Illustrations/graphics, visuals, etc. were of poor quality or were totally missing.
- Further readings/bibliography were not included.
- References were not given at the end of the materials.
- Materials were prepared by individuals.
- Course materials were sketchy and superficial and did not match the level of the programme.

Thereafter the process of approval of programmes were reviewed at DEC and deliberated in the meetings of the Council wherein a decision was taken that programmes offered through distance mode by universities/institutions should be approved by Statutory Bodies of the concerned university/institution, and DEC would hereafter give institutional recognition after evaluating their preparedness to offer programmes through distance mode.

Recognition of Institutions

In a recent decision of the Council, the programme approval process was repealed and institutional recognition was instituted by the DEC. As per the decision of the Council all programmes approved by the respective authorities of the institution will be considered as recognized by the DEC, and also the institutions need to take approval of the respective apex bodies for specific programmes wherever necessary. For recognition purposes, mainly the processes and infrastructural facilities of the institution will be considered which inter alia include the following:

(i) The study material should be prepared based on the Model Curriculum prescribed by the UGC/DEC or other Statutory Bodies as the case may be;

(ii) The study material should be in Self-Learning Format as per DEC Guidelines;

(iii) Core faculty should be in position as per DEC Guidelines;

(iv) In case of Professional/Specific Programmes norms/guidelines of the respective apex body are to be followed and approval/recognition sought, wherever necessary;

(v) Institution should follow criteria like eligibility for admission, duration of the programme, etc. as per the guidelines of the respective apex bodies;

(vi) Hands-on experiences/practicals should be arranged as per requirements of the programme/course.

The *Handbook for Recognition* (2007) developed by the DEC describes the entire process of recognition that has just made a beginning.

Development Grants

The DEC provides financial assistance to State Open Universities (SOUs), since the eighth plan period. Since the ninth plan, the UGC accorded the responsibility of funding to CCIs/ Directorates of Distance Education attached to DEC. The development grants are given for overall development and in order to induce quality in the system. It is given to institutions for development in various components like Development of Course Materials, Student Support Services, Staff Training and Development, Applications of New Technology, Computerization, Library, Research and Development, Quality Assurance Measures, Networking of DE System, etc.

The unassigned grants are meant for travel by heads of institutions and faculty members for attending seminars and conferences, for publications and for organizing seminars, with the idea of encouraging exchange of ideas and experiences. The detail of the grants provided to various Distance Education Institutions (DEIs) is given in Table 16.1.

Table 16.1: Distance Education Council Grants to DEIs

Year	SOUs (Rupees in million)		CCIs (Rupees in million)
	Development Grants	Unassigned Grants	Development Grants
1993-94	6.00	0.6	-
1994-95	5.70	0.6	-
1995-96	8.50	1	-
1996-97	9.82	0.95	-
1997-98	30.00	-	-
1998-99	37.80	-	10
1999-00	93.35	1.85	44.40
2000-01	118.80	0.55	69.00
2001-02	74.92	3.50	32.92
2002-03	nil	nil	nil
2003-04	51.70	5.50	27.00
2004-05	56.00	4.35	30.25
2005-06	120.91	4.40	23.83
2006-07	401.30	5.25	152.20

Source: Indira Gandhi National Open University, Annual Reports

Research and Development

Research and development forms the backbone of any system in order to bring in quality and standards. Being a dynamic system driven by societal, economic and technological changes, it has been changing rapidly and dramatically. The changing technological environment of distance education and paradigm shift affecting it needs to be periodically reviewed. Also the growing acceptance of DE system in our country and the innovations being an integral part of the DE system it has become imperative to evaluate the system. There is an ample proof of growth of distance education research which is evident from the increasing number of journals, seminars, workshops, symposia, etc. analyzing the evolution and growth of the system.

The DEC research project scheme was launched by DEC for encouraging systemic research among distance educators working at State Open Universities during 1996-97, to begin with. Subsequently, it was extended to faculty members working at Directorates of Distance Education/Correspondence Course Institutes of conventional universities and recently the scheme has been thrown open to any teacher/academic interested in doing research on the DE system.

DEC funds two types of projects—Major and Minor. Data presented in Table 16.2 reveals that DEC has so far funded 68 research projects, 49 major and 19 minor research projects. More than Rs. 5 million has been spent by DEC on systemic research. Further analysis reveals that most of the projects were funded to faculty members working at SOUs and the remaining to those at Directorates of Distance Education attached to conventional universities and recently to teachers working in the conventional system who are interested in pursuing research in the DE system. The research conducted so far has been in the following thrust areas: programme evaluation and impact studies, integrated use of ICT, curriculum development, communicating the subject through distance mode, professional development, management of distance education, innovative and effective learning strategies, etc.

Table 16.2: Analysis of DEC Research Projects Funded and Completed Including Refunded

Plan Period	Major	Minor	Amount Sanctioned
VIIIth Plan Period	13	7	2,36,000
IXth Plan Period	17	10	13,61,000
Xth Plan Period	19	2	34,64,700
Grand Total	49	19	50,88,700

Source: Distance Education Council unpublished records

The DEC has recently announced Research and Teaching Assistantships that would provide an opportunity to research scholars to undertake advanced study and research in the DE system. These assistantships would be tenable at any Open University/Directorate of Distance Education attached to a Dual Mode University. The research and teaching assistant will do whole time research work under an approved guide in a subject selected by him/her and approved by the Council. The duration of the research and teaching assistantship would be of three years, extendable up to a period of five years. This would also make the scholar to contribute in the work of the university where he/she is attached.

Strategies for Furthering Quality

1. In order to promote quality and standard in the DE system and encourage DE institutions to develop and offer quality programmes, DEC could invite all DE institutions to submit their best programmes. DEC would get these evaluated on priority and place all the approved programmes in the DEC "common pool of programmes", which any DE institution could adopt and offer in the area under its jurisdiction. This would not only bring in quality in the system but would also give fillip to the DE system and motivate all DE institutions to systematically develop

quality programmes and place them in the DEC common pool of programmes based on their specializations and availability of expertise.

2. The DEC could also identify nodal institutions for development of standard programmes based on the national need that could be placed in the common pool of programmes.
3. The DEC should liaise with State Councils of Higher Education/State Directorates of Higher Education to monitor and ensure minimum standards are maintained in the curriculum and minimum core faculty is sanctioned for the DE Institutions.
4. Further, the State Councils of Higher Education should ensure that universities from outside the state would not open their Student Learning Centres (Study Centres) within the state unless their Acts permits. This would also tackle the problem of mushrooming of franchisee centres by private providers. State Councils of Higher Education may also be asked to see to it that the posts prescribed by DEC, are sanctioned and are filled up.
5. Based on its experience in assessing the institutions and practices elsewhere in the world, the DEC can periodically review the mechanism to assess the institutions, accredit them and ascertain their standards. Rausaria and Lele (2002) have spelled out parameters for assessing quality in assessing programmes. Lele and Bhushan (2001) propose a different line of action to determine quality in distance education, wherein the parameters are an amalgamation of those used in the industry, service and education sector.
6. At present, the DEC Expert Committees are sent to various DEIs for institutional assessment. The terms of reference of this Committee should include evaluation of print material, which could oversee the quality of the course materials, which is indeed the mainstay of the DE system. The Committee should also review the entire process of course design and development which has been highlighted by Srivastava (2005a; 2005b).

Conclusion

With persistence from DEC to bring in quality in the system, most of the institutions are complying with guidelines and are coming forward to get their institutions evaluated and assessed. The institutions have understood the importance of study material in self-learning format. The DEC has been successful in creating awareness in the general public and stakeholders for quality in distance education by evaluating many DEIs for ascertaining their preparedness to offer programmes through distance mode. During the Tenth plan period (2002-07) there has been a greater response from institutions in the following areas:

- Transformation of print material into self-learning format.
- Study material is also being prepared in other media like audio, video, CD-ROMs, etc.
- Provision of face-to-face counselling is being made by all DEIs.
- Counselling is also being taken up by a few DEIs through radio broadcasting.
- Study centres are being set up without franchising with private providers.
- Vocational/technical programmes through DE mode are taking precedence over traditional programmes.

- More DEIs are organizing training for their course writers in the development of self-learning materials.

Thus, it is obvious that many institutions have realized the potential of DE and have adopted it to advance higher education to meet the growing demand for training, skill development and promotion of lifelong learning on a scale that was unknown before, without giving heed to the quality aspects. This is indeed having a negative impact on the total DE system in the country. There is utmost need to check the dilution of quality in the system which the DEC can do through its various initiatives with 'Carrot and Stick' approach. Implementation of credit transfer scheme would automatically impose necessity to imbibe quality, if an institution wants to seek a stamp of acceptance of its qualifications by other institutions.

Bibliography

Abbot, Robert A. and Leaman, David C. (1982) "Quality Control and Quality Assurance", in Heyel, Carl, ed., *The Encyclopedia of Management,* Third Edition, Van Nostrand Reinhold, New York, pp. 998-1009.

Abernathy, William J. and Corcoran, John E. (1983) "Relearning from the Old Masters: Lessons of the American System of Manufacturing", *Journal of Operations Management,* August, pp. 155-68.

Adam Jr. Ever H. (1984) "Quality Assurance Broadens the Concept of Quality Control, *The Pulse Report,* American Productivity Center, January, p. 4.

ADEC (2002) "Guiding Principles for Distance Teaching and Learning", *American Distance Education Consortium.* Accessed March 11, 2005 at: http://www.adec.edu/admin/papers/distance-teaching_principles.html

Aly, N. and Akpori, J. (2001) "Total Quality Management in California Public Higher Education", *Quality Assurance in Education,* 9(3).

American Federation of Teachers (2000) "Distance Education—Guidelines for Good Practice".

Anderson, G. (2006) "Assuring Quality/Resisting Quality Assurance: Academics' Responses to 'Quality' in Some Australian Universities", *Quality in Higher Education*, Vol. 12, No. 2, 161-73.

Anderson, John C., Rungtusaratham, M. and Schroeder, R.G. (1994) "Theoretical Model of Total Quality Management", *Academy of Management Review*, Vol. 19, No. 3, July, pp. 472-509.

Armour, Richard et al. (1994) "Developing a Quality Culture in an Institution of Higher Education: Some Experiences in Hong Kong", *Sixth International Conference on Assessing Quality in Higher Education.*

ASQC (1986) "ASQC: 40 Years of Growth and Change," *Quality Progress*, May, pp. 56-67.

Association of Indian Universities (2003) *University Institutions in India* (AIU members), New Delhi: Association of Indian Universities, November.

Australian Universities Quality Agency (2007) AUQA Audit Manual, Version 4.0., Australian Universities Quality Agency, Melbourne.

Avdjieva, M. and Wilson, M. (2002) "Exploring the Development of Quality in Higher Education", *Managing Service Quality*, Vol. 12, No. 6, 372-83.

Axland, S. (1991) "Looking for a Quality Education", *Quality Progress,* October.

Barnalee, C. (1995) *Introduction to Total Quality in Education*, Inter Universities Press, Montreal.

Barrow, R. (1991) "The Educated Intelligence", Paper presented at Conference of Philosophy of Education Society, Roehampton.

Bass, K., Dellana, S. and Herbert, F. (1996) "Assessing the Use of Total Quality Management in the Business School Classroom", *Journal of Education for Business,* 72(4).

Baugher, K.H. (1991) "LEARN: The Student Quality Team Process for Improving Teaching and Learning", in Hubbard, D.L. (ed.) *Continuous Quality Improvement: Making the Transition to Education,* Maryville, MO.

Beckles, H., Perry, A. and Whitely, P. (2002) *The Brain Train: Quality Higher Education and Caribbean Development*, BUS, Kingston, Jamaica.

Bicking, Charles A. (1958) "The Technical Aspects of Quality Control", *Industrial Quality Control,* March, p. 7.

Biles, P. (1995) "National Network on Line to Support Quality", Portwillis, March.

Billing, D. (1996) "Managing Quality Policy and Projects in a University", *Total Quality Management,* 7.

Billings, D.M., Conners, H.R. and Skiba, D.J. (2001) "Benchmarking Best Practices in Web-based Nursing Courses", *Advances in Nursing Science,* Vol. 23, No. 3.

Binns, F. and Otto, A. (2006) "Quality Assurance in Open Distance Education—Towards a Culture of Quality: A Case Study from the Kyambogo University", Uganda, in Koul, B.N. and Kanwar, A. (eds.), *Towards a Culture of Quality*, COL, Vancouver.

Bo, I. (1997) "The Development of a System for Quality Assurance in Distance Education: A Case Study from Norway" in Tait, A. (ed.), *Quality Assurance in Higher Education: Selected Case Studies*, COL, Vancouver.

Bonser, C.F. (1992) "Total Quality Education", *Public Administration Review*, 52(5).

Borahan, N.G. and Ziarati, R. (2002) "Developing Quality Criteria for Application in the Higher Educational Sector in Turkey", *Total Quality Management*, 13(7).

Bossert, J.L. (1991) *Quality Function Deployment: A Practitioner's Approach*, ASQC Quality Press, Milwaukee.

Bourds, G. et al. (1994) *Beyond Total Quality Management: Toward the Emerging Paradigm*, McGraw Hill, Singapore.

Bowen, D.E. and Lawler, E.E. III (1992) "Total Quality-oriented Human Resource Management", *Organisational Dynamics,* Spring, pp. 29-41.

Bresler, W. (1993) "Editor's Note", *Educational Record*, 74(2).

Brigham, S.E. (1993) "Lessons We Can Learn from Industry", *Change,* 25(3).

British Standards Institutions, 1991.

BS EN ISO 9000 (2000).

Bureau of Indian Standards (1991) *Quality Management and Quality System Elements—Guidelines*, New Delhi.

Burkhalter, B.B. (1996) "How can Institutions of Higher Education Achieve Quality within the New Economy?", *Total Quality Management,* 29.

Burlage, F. (1997) "Master the Art of Kaizen", *The European*, Vol. 20, February, p. 12.

Butcher, R. and Hope, A. (2006) "Embracing Change: Quality Assurance at the Open University of Hong Kong", *Perspectives on Distance Education*, Commonwealth of Learning.

Calvert, J. (2001) "Deakin University: Going Online at a Dual Mode University", *International Review of Research in Open and Distance Learning*, Vol. 1, No. 2, http://www.irrodl.org/index.php/irrodl/article/view/20/52

Calvert, J. (2005) "Distance Education at the Crossroads", *Distance Education*, Vol. 26, No. 2, 227-38.

Campbell, C. and Rozsnyai, C. (2002) *Quality Assurance and the Development of Course Programmes*, UNESCO-CEPES, Bucharest. Accessed March 11, 2005 at: http://www.cepes.ro/publications/pdf/Campbell &Rozsnyai. pdf

Cartin, Thomas J. (2000) *Principles and Practices of Organisational Performance Excellence*, Prentice Hall of India Pvt. Ltd., New Delhi.

Chaffee, E.E. and Tierncy, W.G. (1988) *Collegiate Culture and Leadership Strategies*, McMillan, New York.

Chakraborti, T. (1997) "TQM—A Hard Climb", *The Economic Times Supplement*, India, March 28-April 3.

Chalmers, D. and O'Brien, M. (2005) "Education Development Units and the Enhancement of University Teaching", in K. Fraser (ed.), *Educational Development and Leadership in Higher Education Developing an Effective Institutional Strategy*, Routledge Falmer, London.

Chandler Jr., Alfred D. (1977) *The Visible Hand,* Harvard University Press, Cambridge, pp. 50-64.

Chappel, R.T. (1994) "Can TQM in Public Education Survive with Co-production?", *Quality Progress*, July.

CHEA (2002) Specialized Accreditation and Assuring Quality in Distance Learning: CHEA Monograph Series Number 2. Washington, DC: Council for Higher Education Accreditation.

Cheng, Y.C. (1996) *The Pursuit of School Effectiveness: Theory, Policy and Research*, The Hong Kong Institute of Educational Research, The Chinese University of Hong Kong, Hong Kong.

Chinese University of Hong Kong (1995) "Mechanisms for Maintaining and Improving Teaching and Learning Quality", a document prepared for the Teaching and Learning Quality Process Audit conducted by the UGC in January 1996.

Chizmar, J.F. (1994) "Total Quality Management (TQM) of Teaching and Learning", *Journal of Economic Education*, Spring, 25(2).

Chorn, N.H. (1991) "Total Quality Management: Panacea or Pitfall?" *International Journal of Physical Distribution and Logistics Management,* 4(8).

Clayton, M. (1995) "Encouraging the Kaizen Approach to Quality in University", *Total Quality Management,* 6.

Cleary, B.A. (1999) "Understanding and Inspiring Learning in a Quality Classroom", *Proceedings of the 53rd Annual Quality Congress.*

Coate, L.E. (1990) "TQM at Oregon State University", *The Journal for Quality and Participation*, pp. 56-65.

Cohen, S.G. and Bailey, D.E. (1997) "What Makes Teams Work: Group Effectiveness Research from the Shop Floor to the Executive Suite", *Journal of Management*, Vol. 23, May, pp. 239-90.

COL (1997) *Planning and Management of Distance Education.*

Cole, B. (1995) "Applying Total Quality Management Principles to Faculty Selection", *Higher Education*, 29(1).

Corbitt, B., Holt, D. and Segrave, S. (2006) "Strategic Design for Web-based Teaching and Learning: Making Corporate Technology Systems Work for the Learning Organisation", *International Journal of Web-Based Learning and Teaching Technologies*, Vol. 1, No. 4, 15-35.

Council for Higher Education Accreditation (2002) "Accreditation and Assuring Quality in Distance Learning", *CHEA Monograph Series*, Number 1.

Covey, S.R. (1989) *The Seven Habits of Highly Effective People*, Simson and Schuster Ltd., London.

Cowles, D. and Gilbreath, G. (1992) "Total Quality Management at Virginia Commonwealth University: An Urban University Struggles with the Realities of TQM", Paper presented at the Centre for Higher Education Studies Seminar on Implementing Total Quality Management in Higher Education, Institute of Education, London.

Crawford, F.W. (1991) *Total Quality Management*, CVCP, Occasional Paper, London.

Crawford, K. (1990) *Total Quality Management: Implementation, Assessment and Evaluation,* Washington, DC.

Crawford, L.E.D. and Shutler, P. (1999) "Total Quality Management in Education: Problems and Issues for the Classroom Teacher", *The International Journal of Educational Management,* 13, pp. 67-72.

Creech, B. (1994) *The Five Pillars of TQM: How to Make TQM Work for You*, Trauman Tally Books, New York.

Crosby, P.B. (1995) *Quality is Still Free: Making Quality Certain in Uncertain Times*, McGraw-Hill, New York.

——. (1984) *Quality Without Tears*, McGraw Hill, New York.

——. (1979) *Quality is Free*, McGraw-Hill, New York.

Crumrine, B. and Runnels, T. (1991) *Total Quality Management in Vocational—Technical Education,* Moore – Norman Vo-Tech Center, Norman.

Dahlgard, J.J., Kristensen, K. and Kanji, G.K. (1995) "TQM and Education", *Total Quality Management*, 6(5/6).

Dale, B.G. (2004) *Managing Quality*, Blackwell, First Indian Reprint.

Dale, B.G. and Plunkett, J.J. (1980) *Managing Quality*, Philip Allan, Hertfordshire.

Daniel, J. (1996) *Mega-universities and Knowledge Media Technology Strategies for Higher Education,* Kogan Page, London.

Daniel, J. (1999) "Open Learning and/or Distance Education: Which One for What Purpose?", in Harry K. (ed.), *Higher Education Through Open and Distance Learning*, pp. 292-98, Routledge and Commonwealth of Learning, London.

David, E. (1991) "Total Quality Management in Higher Education", *Management Services*, 35(12).

Day, R.G. (1993) *Quality Function Deployment: Linking a Company with its Customer*, ASQC Quality Press, and Milwaukee.

De Cosmo, R.D., Parker, J.S and Heveshy, M.A. (1991) "Total Quality Management goes to Community College", in Sherr, L.A. and Tester, D.K. (eds.), *Total Quality Management in Higher Education: New Directions for Institutional Research.*

De Jager, H.J and Nieuwenhuis, F.J. (2005) "Linkages between Total Quality Management and the Outcomes—Based Approach in an Education Environment", *Quality in Higher Education.*

De Shields, O.W. Jr., Kora, A. and Kaynak, E. (2005) "Determinants of Business Student Satisfaction and Retention in Higher Education: Applying Herzberg's Two Factor Theory", *The International Journal of Educational Management*, 19(2).

Deakin University (2004a) "Deakin Online", *Management Plan 2003-2007.* Deakin University. Retrieved 14 March, 2007, from the World Wide Web: http://theguide.deakin.edu.au/TheDeakinGuide.nsf/7264c32fe71924374a2566f3000a65de/db963375aa298c9fca256ea60083a6c0/$FILE/Deakin%20Online%20Management%20Plan%202003-2007.pdf

——. (2004b) Taking Deakin University Forward 2004. Deakin University. Retrieved 9 March, 2007, from the World Wide Web: http://theguide.deakin.edu.au/TheDeakinGuide.nsf/7264c32fe71924374a2566f3000a65de/806a621f49a62f52ca256e90001a1f2a/$FILE/TDUF04.pdf

Dean Jr., J.W. and Bowen, D.E. (1994) *Management Theory and Total Quality.*

DEC (1996) *Performance Indicators in Distance Education*, National Seminar Report, New Delhi: DEC.

Deming, W. Edwards (1993) *The New Economics for Industry, Government, Education*, MIT Centre for Advanced Engineering, Cambridge, MA.

Deming, W.E. (1986) *Out of Crisis*, MIT Centre for Advance Engineering, Cambridge.

Deshmukh, A. (2006) "Quality Assurance and Best Practices at Yashwant Rao Chavan Maharastra Open University", in Koul, B.N. and Kanwar, A. (eds.), *Towards a Culture of Quality*, COL, Vancouver.

Deshpande, P.M. and Mugridge, I. (eds.) (1994) "Quality Assurance in Higher Education", Papers presented to a Symposium on Quality Assurance, New Delhi, COL, Vancouver.

Dobyns, L. and Crawford-Mason (1991) *Quality or Else*, Houghton-Miffin, Boston, M.A.

Dorsky, Lawrence R. (1984) "Management Commitment to Japanese Apple Pie", *Quality Progress*, February, pp. 14-18.

Dougherty (1996) "Organising for Innovation", *Handbook of Organisation Studies*, Sage Publications, London.

Dowlatshahi, S. (1996) "Total Quality Mangement in Higher Education", *Total Quality Management*, 7.

Downey, C.J., Frase, L.E. and Peters, J.J. (1994) *The Quality Education Challenge*, Corwin Press. Thousand Oaks, California.

Eastmond, D.V. (1998) "Adult Learners and Internet-based Distance Education", in Cahoon, B. (ed.), *Adult Learning and the Internet*, Jossey-Bass Publishers, San Francisco.

Eaton, Judith S. (2001) "Maintaining the Delicate Balance: Distance Learning, Higher Education Accreditation, and the Politics of Self-regulation", *American Council on Education.*

Edwards-Henry, A. (2006) *Evaluation Report — CD Presentations – UWI Distance Education Centre (UWIDEC)*, IDU, St Augustine.

EFA Global Monitoring Report (2005) UNICEF.

Elmuti, D., Kathawala, Y. and Manipallili, M. (1996) "Are Total Quality Management Programmes in Higher Education Worth the Effort?", *International Journal of Quality and Reliability Management*, 13(6).

England, E. and Finney, A. (1999) *Managing Multi-media: Project Management for Interactive Media*, 2nd edition, Addison-Wesley, England.

Ewell, P.T. (1993) "Total Quality and Academic Practice: The Idea We have been Waiting For?", *Change*, 25, May/June.

Fairhurst, John (2002) "Quality Assuring an Electronically Delivered Distance Learning Programme", 17th BILETA Annual Conference, April 5-6, 2002.

Feigenbaum, A.V. (1961) *Total Quality Control: Engineering and Management*, McGraw-Hill, New York.

——. (1983) *Total Quality Control*, 3rd ed., McGraw-Hill, New York.

Ferrell, O.C. and Fraedrich, J. (1991) *Business Ethics: Ethical Decision Making and Cases*, Houghton Mifflin, Boston.

Fishbein, M. and Ajzen, I. (1975) *Belief, Attitude, Intention and Behaviour: An Introduction to Theory and Research*, Addison-Wesley Publisher.

Floistad, G. (1995) "Community Culture, Ethics, Professionalism and Human Values: A View from Norway", *Journal of Human Values.*

Flood, R.L. (1993) *Beyond TQM*, John Wiley, UK.

Franz, R.S. (1998) "Whatever You Do, Don't Treat Your Students Like Customers", *Journal of Management Education,* 22(1).

Frazier, A. (1997) *Roadmap for Quality Transformation in Education,* St. Lucie Press, Florida.

Freeman, R. (2004) *Planning and Implementing Open and Distance Learning Systems: A Handbook for Decision Makers*, The Commonwealth of Learning, Vancouver.

Freeston, K.R. (1992) "Getting Started with TQM", *Educational Leadership*, November, 50(3).

Frydenberg, J. (2002) "Quality Standards in e-Learning: A Matrix of Analysis", *International Review of Open and Distance Learning,* October. Accessed March 11, 2005 at: http://www.irrodl.org/content/v3.2/frydenberg.html

Fuller, Timothy F. (1985) "Eliminating Complexity from Work: Improving Productivity by Enhancing Quality", *National Productivity Review*, Autumn, pp. 327-44.

Garbutt, S. (1996) "The Transfer of TQM from Industry to Education", *Education and Training,* 38(7).

Garvin, A.D. (1984) "What Does Product Quality Really Mean?", *Sloan Management Review*, Fall.

——. (1987) "Competing on the Eight Dimensions of Quality", *Harvard Business Review.*

Gift, S. Leo-Rhynie, E. and Moniquette, J. (2006) "Quality Assurance of Transnational Education in the English-speaking Caribbean", in *The UWI Quality Education Forum.* Number 12, January, Office of the Board of Undergraduate Studies (OBUS), Mona.

Goetsch, D.L. and Davis, S.B. (1997) *Introduction to Total Quality*, 2nd ed., Prentice Hall, NJ.

Gordon, G. (2002) "The Roles of Leadership and Ownership in Building an Effective Quality Culture", *Quality in Higher Education*, Vol. 8, No. 1, 97-106.

Government of India (1995) *Gazette Notification No. 44* (dated 1st March), New Delhi: MHRD, Government of India.

Govinda, R. and Varghese, N.V. (1992) "Quality of Primary Education: An Empirical Study", *Journal of Education Planning and Administration*, 6(1), January.

Graduate Careers Australia (2006) Graduate Course Experience 2005—The Report of the Course Experience Questionnaire, Graduate Careers Australia and Australian Council for Academic Research, Melbourne.

Grant, R.M. (1995) *Contemporary Strategy Analysis: Concepts, Techniques, Applications*, Blackwell Publishers, Oxford.

Green, D. (1994) "What is Quality in Higher Education? Concepts, Policies and Practice", in Green, D. (ed.), *What is Quality in Higher Education?*, SRHE and Open University Press, Buckingham.

Green, D. and Harvey, L. (1993) "Defining Quality", *Assessment and Evaluation in Higher Education: An International Journal*, 18(1).

Gundri, L.K., Kickul, J.R. and Prather, C.W. (1994) "Building the Creative Organisation", *Organisational Dynamics*, Spring.

Guri-Rosenblit, S. (1997) "Quality Assurance Procedures at the Open University of Israel", in Tait, A. (ed.) *Quality Assurance in Higher Education: Selected Case Studies*, COL, Vancouver.

Hagan, J. (1997) *Management of Quality: Strategies to Improve Quality and Bottom Line,* Oxford University Press, New Delhi.

Hammer, M. and Champy, J. (1992) *Reengineering the Corporation: A Manifesto for Business Revaluation*, Harper Business, New York.

Hansen, W.L. and Jackson, M. (1996) "Total Quality Improvement in the Classroom", *Quality in Higher Education*, 2(3).

Harman, G. (2000) *Quality Assurance in Higher Education,* Ministry of University Affairs & UNESCO PROAP, Bangkok.

Harris, R.W. (1994) "Allien or Ally? TQM, Academic Quality and New Public Management", *Quality Assurance in Education*, 2(3), pp. 33-39.

Harvey, L. (1994) "Continuous Quality Improvement: A System-wide View of Quality in Higher Education", *System Wide Curriculum Change.*

Harvey, L. (1995) "Editorial: The Quality Agenda", *Quality in Higher Education*, 1(1).

——. (2000) Student Satisfaction Manual, Open University Press, Buckingham.

——. (2002) "The End of Quality?", *Quality in Higher Education*, 8(1).

Harvey, L. and Knight, P.T. (1996) *Transforming Higher Education*, SRHE and Open University Press, Buckingham.

Harvey, L. and Green, D. (1993) "Defining Quality", *Assessment and Evaluation in Higher Education,* Vol. 18, No. 1.

Hawkridge, D. (2003) "Globalisation, Education and Distance Education", in *Models of Open and Distance Learning*, International Research Foundation for Open Learning, COL.

Hay, R. et al. (2002) Breaking the Mould: Deakin University, the First Twenty-Five Years, Geelong, Victoria, Deakin University Australia.

Hayward, F.M. (2006) "Accreditation and Quality Assurance in University Education in Developing Countries: Insights and Lessons from Experience", *Presentation for the 1st International Conference on Assessing Quality in Higher Education,* December 11-13, University of the Punjab, Lahore, Pakistan.

Hazel, S. (1993) "Total Quality in Higher Education", *Management Services,* 37(10).

HEFCE (2006) *Review of Quality Assurance Framework—Phase Two Outcomes,* HEFCE, 2006/45.

Herrington, A. et al. (2001) *Quality Guidelines for Online Courses: The Development of an Instrument to Audit Online Units*, in G. Kennedy, M. Keppell, C.

Hillkirk, J. (1993) "World-Famous Quality Expert Died at 92", *USA Today*, December 21, pp. 13-23.

Hills, J.M. and Stewart-David, D. (2001) "A Tool for Total Quality Management of Educational Provision Illustrated using Advanced Coastal Management Courses", *The TQM Magazine,* 13(6).

HO, S.K. and Wearn, K. (1996) "A TQM Model for Enabling Student Learning", *Innovations in Training and Education International,* 33.

Hodgettes, R.M. (1996) "A Conversation with Steve Kerr", *Organisational Dynamics*, Spring.

Holmberg, B. (1981) *Status and Trends of Distance Education*, Kogan Page, London.

Holmes, G. and McElwee, G. (1995) "Total Quality Management in Higher Education: How to Approach Human Resource Management", *The TQM Magazine*, 7(6).

Hong Kong Council for Academic Accreditation (1992) "Higher Education and its Quality Assurance in the People's Republic of China".

Hounshel, David A. (1984) *From the American System to Mass Production,* 1800-1932, John Hopkins Press, Baltimore, pp. 15-17.

Howell, S.C. et al. (2007) "Distance Education and the Six Regional Accrediting Commission: A Comparative Analysis", *Submitted to ERIC Digest*, March 5.

Hubbard, D. (1994) "Can Higher Education Learn from Factories?", *Quality Progress,* 27(5).

Hunt, V.D. (1993) *Managing Quality: Integrating Quality and Business Strategy*, Homewood, Irwin.

IADB (1999) *Facing Up to Inequality in Latin America: Economic and Social Progress in Latin America, 1998-1999 Report*, Distributed by the Johns Hopkins University Press for the Inter-American Development Bank (IADB), Washington, DC.

IGNOU (1985) Indira Gandhi National Open University Act (1985) and The Statutes of the University, New Delhi.

——. (1994-2007) IGNOU Annual Reports, New Delhi: IGNOU.

IHEP (2000) *Quality on the Line: Benchmarks for Success in Internet-based Distance Education*, Institute for Higher Education Policy, Washington, DC.: Accessed April 23, 2005 at: http://www.ihep.com/Pubs/PDF/Quality.pdf

Imai, M. (1986) *Kaizen: The Key to Japan's Competitive Success*, Random House, New York.

Inglis, A. (2005) "Quality Improvement, Quality Assurance, and Benchmarking: Comparing Two Frameworks for Managing Quality Processes in Open and Distance Learning", *International Review of Research in Open and Distance Learning*, Vol. 6, No. 1, http://www.irrodl.org/index.php/irrodl/article/view/221/304

Inglis, A. (2005) "Quality Improvement, Quality Assurance, and Benchmarking: Comparing Two Frameworks for Managing Quality Processes in Open and Distance Learning", *International Review of Research in Open and Distance Learning*. [Online] Vol. 6, Issue I. Accessed April 24, 2005 at: http://www.irrodl.org/content/v6.1/inglis.html

Inglis, A., Ling, P. and Joosten, V. (1999) *Delivering Digitally: Managing the Transition to the Knowledge Media*, Kogan Page, London.

Ishikawa, K. (1985) *What is Total Quality Control?* Prentice Hall, New Jersey.

ITU (2004) "Internet Indicators: Hosts, Users and Number of PCs", *International Telecommunication Union*, Website accessed December 14, 2004 at: http://www.itu.int/ITU-D/ict/statistics/

Jevons, F.R. (1982) "How Different is the Distance Student?" in Daniel J.S. and Stroud M.A. (eds.), *Learning at a Distance: A World Perspective*, Athabasca University, Edmonton.

Jones, F. and Fletcher, B.C. (1996) "Taking Work Home: A Study of Daily Functions in Work Stressors, Effects on Moods and Impacts on Mental Partners", *Journal of Occupational and Organisational Psychology*, March.

Juma, M.N. (2003) "Ensuring Quality of Distance Education for Higher Education: The Case Study of African Virtual University (AVU)", Association for the Development of Education in Africa (ADEA) Biennial Meeting, Mauritius.

Jung, I. (2005) *Innovative and Good Practices of Open and Distance Learning in Asia and Pacific*, UNESCO, Bangkok.

Jung, I.S. (2001) "Korea", in Jegede, O. and Shive, G. (eds.), *Open and Distance Education in the Asia and Pacific Region*, Open University of Hong Kong Press, Hong Kong.

——. (2004) *Quality Assurance and Accreditation Mechanisms of Distance Education for Higher Education in the Asia—Pacific Region: Five Selected Cases*, UNESCO Workshop on Exporters and Importers of Cross-Border Higher Education, Beijing, China.

Juran, J.M. (1976) "Consumerism and Product Quality," *Quality Progress*, July, p. 20.

——. (1986) "The Quality Triology: A Universal Approach to Managing for Quality", *Quality Progress*, 19.

——. (1988) "The Quality Function", in Juran, J.M. and Gryna, F.M. (eds.), *Juran's Quality Control Handbook*, 4th ed., McGraw-Hill, New York.

——. (1988) *Juran on Planning for Quality*, Free Press, New York, pp. 5-7.

Kambon, A. and Busby, L. (2000) *Education and Its Impact on Povert Equity or Exclusion*, EFA in the Caribbean: Assessment 2000, Monograph Series No. 16, UNESCO, Kingston, Jamaica.

Kandula, S. (1997) "Critical Appraisal of TQM as an OD Intervention", *Indian Journal of Training and Development*, January-March.

Kanji, G.K. (1998) "Measurement of Business Excellence", *Total Quality Management*, 9.

Kanji, G.K. and Tambi, M.B.A. (1999) "Total Quality Management in UK Higher Education Institutions", *Total Quality Management*, 10(1).

Kanji, G.K., Tambi, A.M.A. and Wallace, W. (1999) "A Comparative Study of Quality Practice in Higher Education Institutions in the US and Malaysia, *Total Quality Management*, 10(3).

Kanji, Gopal K. and Asher, Mike (1996) *100 Methods for TQM*, Response Books, New Delhi.

Kano, N. (1989) "Quality Sweating Theory: Crisis Consciousness, Vision and Leadership", *Quality (Journal of the Japanese Society for Quality Control)*, Vol. 19, pp. 32-42.

Kano, N. (1997) "A Perspective on Quality Activities in American Firms", in Tushman, Michael L. and Anderson, Philip (eds.), *Managing Strategic Innovation and Change (A Collection of Readings)*, Oxford University Press, pp. 402-16.

Kaplan, R.S. and Norton, D.P. (1992) "The Balanced Scorecard—Measures that Drive Performance", *Harvard Businees Review,* Vol. 70, January-February.

——. (1996) "Using the Balanced Scorecard as a Strategic Management System", *Harvard Business Review,* Vol. 74, January-February.

Keegan, D. (1986) *The Foundation of Distance Education*, Croom Helm, London.

Kelda, Joseph N. (1996) *Integrating Reengineering with Total Quality*, ASQC Press, USA.

Kelemean, M. (2003) *Managing Quality*, Sage Publications, London.

Kells, H.R. (1995) "Creating a Culture of Evaluation and Self-regulation in Higher Education", *Total Quality Management,* 6.

Kelly, J.M. (2000) *Total Quality Management: A How to Programme for the High-performance Business*, Alexander Hamilton Institute, Inc., USA.

Kilfoil, W.R. (2007) *Acquiring Accreditation in Distance Learning*, COL Knowledge Series.

Kirkpatrick, D. (2005) *Quality Assurance in Open and Distance Learning*, COL Knowledge Series.

Knight, P. (2006) "Quality Enhancement and Educational Professional Development", *Quality in Higher Education*, Vol. 12, No. 1, 29-40.

Knowledge Media Division Deakin University (2006) The 10 Core Quality Principles. Deakin University. Retrieved 2 February 2007, from the World Wide Web: http://www.deakin.edu.au/quality/10-principles.php

Konidari, V. and Abernot, Y. (2006) "From TQM to Learning Organization", *The International Journal of Quality and Reliability Management,* 23(1).

Kotler, P. (2005) *Marketing Management*, Eleventh edition, Pearson Education, LPE, India.

Koul, B. (2003) "New UWIDEC Pedagogy", Paper presented to the first meeting of the *UWIDEC Academic Programme Committee*, March 24, UWI, Cave Hill Campus, Barbados.

Koul, B.N. and Kanwar, A. (2006) *Towards a Culture of Quality*, COL, Vancouver.

Kreitner, R. and Kinicki, A. (1998) *Organisational Behaviour*, Irwin McGraw Hill, North America.

Kuboni, O., Thurab-Nkhosi, D. and Chen, T. (2002a) "The Expanded Use of ICTs in UWIDEC: An Analysis of Readiness for On-line Course Delivery", Paper presented at Prospects and Possibilities in Education, University of the West Indies, Cave Hill, Barbados, March 24-28.

——. (2002b) "Incorporating Web-based Learning into a Mixed–mode Distance Education Delivery Format: Challenges and Possibilities", Paper presented at the Second Pan Commonwealth Forum on Open Learning in Durban South Africa, July 29-August 02.

Kwan, Y.K.P. (1996) "Application of Total Quality Management in Education: Retrospect and Prospect", *International Journal of Educational Management,* 10(5).

Landquist, R. (1997) "Quality in Higher Education—Approaches to its Management and Improvement", Lecentiate Thesis, Division of Quality Technology and Statistics, University of Technology.

Larsen, K., Martin, J.P. and Morris, R. (2002) "Trade in Educational Services: Trends and Emerging Issues", Working Paper, OECD, Paris.

Lawrence, J.J. and McCollugh, M.A. (2001) "A Conceptual Framework for Guaranteeing Higher Education", *Quality Assurance in Education,* 9(3).

Lee, J. and Dziuban, C. (2002) "Using Quality Assurance Strategies for Online Programs", *Educational Technology Review* [Online serial], Vol 10, Issue 2, pp. 69-78. Accessed April 26, 2005 at: http://www.aace.org/pubs/etr/issue3/lee.cfm

Lee, M., Thurab-Nkhosi, D. and Giannini-Gachago, D. (2005) "Using Informal Collaboration to Develop Quality Assurance Processes for e-Learning in Developing Countries: The Case of the University of Botswana and The University of the West Indies Distance Education Centre", *International Journal of Education and*

Development using Information and Communication Technology (IJEDICT) [Online], Vol. 1, Issue I, pp. 108-27. Accessed March 26, 2005 at: http://ijedict.dec.uwi.edu//viewarticle.php?id=31&layout=html

Legon, Ronald (2006) "Comparison of the Quality Matters Rubric to Accreditation Standards for Distance Learning", *Quality Matters Program*, University of Baltimore.

Lele, Nalini, A. and Bhushan, Bharat (2001) "Model for Assessment and Accreditation of Distance Education Institutions", Special Number on Assessment and Accreditation in Higher Education, *University News*, 39 (36), pp. 74-79.

Leo-Rhynie, E. (2006) "A Concern for Quality, a Need for Accountability" in *The UWI Quality Education Forum,* Number 12, January, Office of the Board of Undergraduate Studies (OBUS), Mona.

Leventhal, M. (2005) "The Quality—Trade Nexus: How Globalisation of Quality Standards and Educational Marketing Interact", Presented at AIEC.

Lewis, R. (2005) *External Examiner System in the United Kingdom: Fresh Challenges to an Old System,* Public Policy for Academic Quality (PPAQ), website : http://www.unc.edu/ppaq/docs/ExExaminers.html

Lewis, R.G. and Smith, H.D. (1994) *Total Quality in Higher Education*, St Lucie Press, Delray Beach, FL.

——. (2004) *Total Quality in Higher Education*, St. Lucie Press, Florida.

Lindop, N. (1985) "Academic Validation in the Public Sector of Higher Education (Report of the Committee of Enquiry)", HMSO, London.

Liston, C. (1999) *Managing Quality and Standards*, Open University Press, USA.

Lockwood, F. (1998) *The Design and Production of Self-instructional Material*, Kogan Page, London.

Lockwood, F. and Gooley, A. (eds.) (2000) *Innovation in Open and Distance Learning*, Kogan Page, London.

Lomas, L. (2004) "Embedding Quality: The Challenges for Higher Education", *Quality Assurance in Education,* 12(4).

London, Julie (2004) "OLA Student and Portal Members: Online Survey Result", Internal report.

Long, M. and Hayden, M. (2001) Paying Their Way: A Survey of Australian Undergraduate University Student Finances, 2000, Australian Vice-Chancellors' Committee, Canberra.

Longford, D.P. and Clearly, B.A. (1995) *Orchestrating Learning with Quality*, pp. 39-43.

Lovelock, C.H. (1983) "Classifying Services to Gain Strategic Marketing Insights", *Journal of Marketing*, 47, pp. 9-20.

Lozier, G.G. and Teeter, D.J. (1996) "Quality Improvements Pursuits in American Higher Education", *Total Quality Management,* 7.

Luthans, Fred (1993) "Meeting the New Paradigm Challenges through Total Quality Management", *Management Quarterly*, Spring, pp. 2-13.

——. (1995) *Organisational Behaviour*, McGraw-Hill International Editions, Seventh Edition, Singapore.

Macy, G., Neal, J. and Waner, K.K. (1998) "Harder than I Thought: A Qualitative Study of the Implementation of a Total Quality Management Approach in Business Education", *Innovative Higher Education*, 23(1).

Madu, C.N., Kuli, C.H. and Winokur, D. (1994) "TQM in the University: A Quality Code of Honor", *Total Quality Management*, 5(5/6).

Management Extra (2005) *Quality and Operations Management,* Elsevier, UK.

Marchese, J. (1991) "TQM Reaches the Academy", *American Association for Higher Education Bulletin,* pp. 433-46.

Marshall, L. (2006) *Quick Skills Modules: Project Managing Your Stud,* Carrick Institute for Higher Education Award Submission.

Marshall, S. and Gregor, S. (2002). "Distance Education in the Online World: Implications for Higher Education" in Discenza, R., Howard, C. and Schenk, K.D. (eds.), *The Design and Management of Effective Distance Learning Programs,* Hershey, PA, USA: Idea Group Publishing, 21-36.

Marshall, Stewart (2004) "Blended Learning/Asynchronous Delivery: A UWIDEC Project for 2004/2005", Paper prepared for the meeting of the Academic Programmes Committee, October , UWIDEC, Cave Hill, Barbados.

Martin, A.L. (2003) 2002 Institutional Audit Reports Analysis and Comment, Australian Universities Quality Agency. Retrieved 22 March, 2007, from the World Wide Web: http://www.auqa.edu.au/qualityenhancement/publications/occasional/publications/index.shtml

Mathews, W.E. (1993) "TQM: A Time for Change", *Journal for Quality and Participation*, 2(1).

McGettrick, A., Dunnett, A. and Harvey, B. (1997) "Continuous Quality Improvement in Higher Education", *Quality in Higher Education,* 3(3).

McInnis, C. and Hartley, R. (2002) Managing Study and Work: The Impact of Full-time Study and Paid Work on the Undergraduate Experience in Australian Universities (02/6), Department of Education Science and Training, Canberra.

McKinnon, K.R., Walker, S.H. and Davis, D. (2000) *Benchmarking: A Manual for Australian Universities*, ACT: Higher Education Division, Department of Employment, Education, and Youth Affairs, Canberra.

McNaught and Petrovic, T. (eds.) (2001) *Meeting at the Crossroads: Proceedings of ASCILITE*, The University of Melbourne, Melbourne.

McShane, Steven L. and Glinow, M.A.V. (2001) *Organisational Behaviour*, Tata McGraw-Hill Publishing Co. Ltd., New Delhi.

Meade, P. (1995) "Utilizing the University as a Learning Organization to Facilitate Quality Improvement", *Quality in Higher Education,* 1(2).

Mehra, M. (1999) "Competing through Innovation", *Quality for Business Transformation*, Institute of Directors, New Delhi.

Michigan Virtual University (2002) *Standards for Quality Online Courses*, Accessed March 11, 2005 at: http://standards.mivu.org/

Milakovich, M.E. (1993) *Improving Service Quality*, St. Lucie Press, Delray Beach, FL.

Miller, R.I. (1991) *Applying the Deming Method to Higher Education for More Effective Human Resource Management*, The College and Personnel Association, Washington, DC.

Montano, C. and Utter, G. (1999) "Total Quality Management in Higher Education", *Quality Progress,* 32(8).

Moore, M.G. (1973) "Toward a Theory of Independent Learning and Teaching", *Journal of Higher Education*, 44.

Morgan, G. (1986) *Images of Organisation*, Sage Publications, London.

Morgatroyd, S. and Morgan, J. (1993) *Total Quality Management and the School,* Open University Press, Madison, W.I.

Morris, D.S. and Haigh, R.H. (1996) "Introducing Total Quality Management into the Student Service Department of a College of Further Education in the UK", *Total Quality Management,* 7.

Mortimore, P. and Stone, C. (1990) "Measuring Educational Quality", *British Journal of Educational Studies*, 39(1).

Motwani, J., Kumar, A. and Mohamed, Z. (1996) "Implementing QFD for Improving Quality in Education: An Example", *Journal of Professional Services Marketing,* 14(2).

Mukherjee, S.P. (1995) "Quality Assurance in an Education System", *Total Quality Management,* pp. 571-87.

Mukhopadhyay, M. (2001) *Total Quality Management in Education*, Sage Publications, New Delhi.

Mukhopadhyay, M. and Philips, S. (eds.) (1994) *Open Schooling: Selected Experiences*, COL, Vancouver.

Murgatroyd, S. and Morgan, C. (1993) *Total Quality Management and the School*, Open University Press, Buckingham.

Navaratnam, K.K. (1997) "Quality Management in Education must be a Never-Ending Journey" in Watson, K., Modgil, C. and Modgil, S. (eds.), *Educational Dilemmas: Debate and Diversity,* Vol. VI: *Quality in Education,* Cassel, London.

Niepce, W. and Molleman, E. (1998) "Work Design Issues in Lean Production from a Sociotechnical Systems Perspective: Neo-Taylorsism or the Next Step in Sociotechnical Design?", *Human Relations*, Vol. 51, March, pp. 259-87.

Nilakant, V. and Ram Narayan S. (1998) *Managing Organisational Change*, Response Books, New Delhi.

Norman, R. (1984) *Service Management: Strategy and Leadership in Service Business*, John Wiley & Sons, UK.

Oakland, J.S. (1989) *Total Quality Management*, Heinemann Publishing Co., Oxford.

Oblinger, D. and Rush, S. (1997) *The Learning Revolution: The Challenge of Information Technology in the Academy*, Anker Publishing, Prolton, M.A.

OBUS (2000) *The UWI Quality Strategy: The Quality Assurance System at the University of the West Indies*, Office of the Board of Undergraduate Studies (OBUS), Mona.

——. (1997) *Quality Assurance at the University of the West Indies: The Self-Assessment*, Office of the Board of Undergraduate Studies (OBUS), Mona.

Olian, J.D. and Rynes, S.L. (1991) "Making Total Quality Work: Aligning Organisations' Performance Measures and Stakeholders", *Human Resource Management*, 30.

Oliver, R. (2003) Exploring Benchmarks and Standards for Assuring Quality Online Teaching and Learning in Higher Education. 16th Open and Distance Learning Association of Australia Biennial Forum. Retrieved 10 February 2007, from the World Wide Web: http://www.odlaa.org/publications/2003Proceedings/pdfs/oliver.pdf

Owen, J.V. (1992) "Concurrent Engineering", *Manufacturing Engineering*, Vol. 109, November, pp. 69-73.

Owens, Debra A. (Undated) "QA/QC and ASQC History", Unpublished paper, American Society for Quality Control.

Owlia, M.S. and Aspinwall, E.M. (1996) "Quality in Higher Education—A Survey", *Total Quality Management*, 7.

Padhi, Nayantara (2007) "Impact of Globalisation on Accreditation and Quality Management of Open and Distance Learning Institutions: A Study", *Malaysian Journal of Distance Education*, 9(1).

Paine, Lynne S. (1996) "Managing for Organisational Integrity", *Harvard Business Review*, March-April.

Palo, S., Panigrahi, S. and Padhi, N. (2002) "Managing Organisational Change in the Aftermath of Total Quality Management", *Management Insight*, Vol. 3, No. 1, September, pp. 15-23.

Perraton, H. (1997) *International Research in Open and Distance Learning: Report of a Feasibility Study*, International Research Foundation for Open Learning.

Perry, A. (2002) Quality Assurance at UWI, www.una.an/nl/activiteiten/unica/docs/12_Nov_GS_5_Anthony_Perry.ppt

Peters, O. (1967) "Distance Education and Industrial Production: A Comparative Interpretation in Outline" in Sewart, D. Keegan D. and Holmberg, D. (eds.) (1983), *Distance Education: International Perspectives*, Croom Helm Routledge, London and New York.

——. (1973) *Die didaktische Structure des Fernunterrichts. Unterschungen Zu einer industrialisierten,* Form des Lehrens and Lerness, Beltz, Weinheim.

Petersen, J. (1999) "Internationalising Quality Assurance in Higher Education", *CHEA*, Washington, DC.

Petersen, John C. (1995) "Higher Education Quality Assurance in the United States—Recent Developments", Accrediting Commission for Community and Junior Colleges, Western Association of Schools and Colleges.

Peterson, S.L., Kovel-Jarboe, P. and Schwartz, S.A. (1997) "Quality Improvement in Higher Education: Implications for Student Retentions", *Quality in Higher Education*, 3(2).

Petrick, Joseph A. and Quinn, John F. (1996) *Management Ethics and Organisation Integrity*, Sage Publications, Newbury Park, CA.

Pfeffer, N. and Coote, A. (1991) "Is Quality Good for You?", Social Policy Paper No. 5, Institute for Public Policy Research, London.

Phipps et al. (1998) "Assuring Quality in Distance Learning—A Preliminary Review", a report prepared for Council for Higher Education Accreditation by The Institute for Higher Education Policy, Washington, DC.

Pitman, G. et al. (1995) "QFD Application in an Educational Setting: A Pilot Field Study", *International Journal of Quality and Reliability Management*, 12(6).

Plato (1955) *The Republic*, Translated by Lee, D., Penguin U.K.

Porter, E. (1979) "How Competitive Forces Shape Strategy", *Harvard Business Review*, Vol. 57, March-April.

——. (1985) *Competitive Advantage: Creating and Sustaining Superior Performance,* The Free Press, New York.

Price, F. (1989) "Out of Bedlam: Management by Quality Leadership", *Management Decision*, 27.

Procter and Gamble (1992) "Report to the Total Quality Leadership Steering Committee and Working Commits", Cincinnati, Ohio.

Puffer, S.M. (1994) "Understanding the Bear: A Portrait of Russian Business Leaders", *Academy of Management Executive*, February.

QAA (2007) "Distance Learning Guidelines", *Quality Assurance Agency for Higher Education*. Accessed March 30, 2007 at: http://www.qaa.ac.uk/academicinfrastructure/codeofpractice/distancelearning/default.asp#4

Radford, G.S. (1922) *The Control of Quality in Manufacturing*, Ronal Press, New York.

Rahdolph, W.A. (1995) "Navigating the Journey to Empowerment", *Organisational Dynamics*, Spring.

Ramage, T. (2005) "The No Significant Difference", *Phenomena: A Literature Review*. Accessed May 27, 2005 at http://www.usq.edu.au/electpub/e-jist/docs/html2002/ramage.html

Rampey, J. and Roberts, H. (1992) "Perspectives in Total Quality", *Proceedings of Total quality Forum IV*, Procter and Gamble, Cincinnati, Ohio.

Ramsden, P. (1991) "A Performance Indicator of Teaching Quality in Higher Education: The Course Experience Questionnaire", *Studies in Higher Education*, Vol. 16, No. 2, 129-50.

Rausaria, R.R. and Lele, Nalini A. (2002) "Self Assessment of Distance Education Institutions: Identification of Parameters for Programme Assessment", *Indian Journal of Open Learning*, 11(1), pp 147-57.

Reddy, G.R. (1987) "Planning, Management and Monitoring of Distance Education", *Distance Education in Asia and the Pacific*, Vol. I, ADB, Manila.

Reddy, Jack (1980) "Incorporating Quality in Competitive Strategies", *Sloan Management Review*, Spring.

Reid, C.N. and Robertshaw, M. (1991) "The Quest for Quality, East and West", *Quality in Education: ASPESA Forum*, 91.

Reid, I.C. (2005) "Quality Assurance, Open and Distance Learning, and Australian Universities", *International Review of Research in Open and Distance Learning*, Vol. 6, No. 1, http://www.irrodl.org/index.php/irrodl/article/view/222/305

Rhodes, L.A. (1992) "On the Road to Quality", *Educational Leadership*, 50, pp. 76-80.

Robinson, A.G. and Stern, S. (1997) *Corporate Creativity: How Innovation and Improvement Actually Happen*, Beret-Koehler Publishers, San Francisco.

Robinson, E.T. (2004) "Accreditation of Distance Education Programmes: A Primer", *American Journal of Pharmaceutical Education*, Vol. 68, No. 4.

Sahney, S., Banwet, D.K. and Karunes, S. (2004) "Customer Requirement Construct: The Premise for TQM in Education", *International Journal of Productivity and Performance Management*, 53(5/6).

Sahney, S., Karunes, S. and Banwet, D.K. (2002) *Total Quality Management in Higher Education in India—A Diagnostic Study of Select Engineering and Management Institutions*, Unpublished Thesis Dept. of Management Studies, IIT, Delhi.

SAI Global (2002) "Management System Self-evaluation Guidance ISO 9001:2000", Unpublished document.

——. (2005) "Certification Audit report", Unpublished report.

Sakthivel, P.B., Rajendran, G. and Raju, R. (2005) "TQM Implementation and Students Satisfaction of Academic Performance", *The TQM Magazine*, 17(16).

Sallis, E. (1993) *Total Quality Management in Education*, Kogan Page, London.

——. (1996) *Total Quality Management in Education*, Prentice Hall, New Jersey.

Schmidt, Warren H. and Finnegan, Jerome P. (1992) *The Race without a Finish Line*, Jossey-Bass, San Francisco.

Schmoker, M. and Wilson, R.B. (1993) "Adapting Total Quality does not Mean Turning Learning into Business", *Educational Leadership*, 51(1).

Schragel, F. (1993) "Total Quality in Education", *Quality Progress*, October.

Schrock, E.M. and Lefevre, H.L. (eds.) (1988) *The Good and Bad News about Quality*, Quality Management Division, ASQC, Milwaukee, WI.

Scott, G. (2006) Accessing the Student Voice—Using CEQuery to Identify What Retains Students and Promotes Engagement in Productive Learning in Australian Higher Education, Department of Education, Science and Training, Barton, Australian Capital Territory.

Scrabec Jr., Q. (2000) "A Quality Education is not Customer Driven", *Journal of Education for Business*, 75(5).

Segrave, S., Holt, D. and Farmer, J. (2005). "The Power of the Three Model for Enhancing Capacities for Effective Online Teaching and Learning: Benefits, Initiatives and Future Directions", *Australasian Journal of Educational Technology*, Vol. 21, No. 1, 118-35.

Sensicle, Allan (1995) "Quality Assurance in Tertiary Education", Hong Kong Institute of Education Seminar.

Shah, Aman et al. (2002) "QAC Project—The Influence of Bias Factors on Student Ratings of Teaching", City University of Hong Kong.

Sharma, D.D. (2002) *Total Quality Management: Principles, Practice and Cases*, Sultan Chand & Sons, New Delhi.

Sherr, L.A. and Lozier, G.G. (1991) "Total Quality Management in Higher Education", in Terenzini, P.T. and Chaffee, E.E. (eds.), *Total Quality Management in Higher Education*, Jossy-Buss, San Franciso.

Siegel, P. and Byrne, S. (1994) *Using Quality to Redesign School Systems*, New York, pp. 20-23.

Silver, H. (1994) *External Examining in the UK: How Did it Start?*, HEQC "External Examining in Focus", November 2004, London.

Silver, H., Stennant, A. and Williams, R. (1995) *The External Examiner System: Possible Futures*, QSC, London.

Singh, A. (1991) "TQM: Concept and Practice in India", *Productivity*, 32(3).

Sirvanci, M.B. (2004) "Critical Issues for TQM Implementation in Higher Education", *The TQM Magazine*, 16(6).

Sitkin, S.B. (1994) "Distinguishing Control from Learning in Total Quality Management: A Contingency Perspective", *Academy of Management Review*, 19.

Smith, A. (2004) "Öff-Campus Support in Distance Learning—How do Your Students Define Quality?", *Quality Assurance in Education*, 12(1).

Smith, Merritt Roe (1977) *Harpers Ferry Armoury and the New Technology*, Cornell University Press, New York.

Sohal, A.S., Tay, G.S. and Wirth, A. (1989) "Total Quality Control in an Asian Division of a Multinational Corporation", *International Journal of Quality and Reliability Management*, Vol. 6, No. 6, pp. 60-74.

Spanbauer, S.J. (1989) *Measuring and Costing Quality in Education*, Fox Valley Technical College Foundation, Appleton, W.I.

—— (1995) "Reactivating Higher Education with Total Quality Management: Using Quality and Productivity Concepts, Techniques and Tools to Improve Higher Education", *Total Quality Management*, 6(5&6).

Spencer, B.A. (1994) "Models of Organisation and Total Quality Management: A Comparison and Critical Valuation", *The Academy of Management Review*, 19(3), pp. 446-71.

Srivastava, Manjulika (2005a) "Quality Interaction and Independence: Review of the Course Development Practices of IGNOU", *University News*, 43(43), pp. 36-42.

——. (2005b) "Benchmarks of Quality Assurance in the Development of Learning Materials: A Study of IGNOU's Practices", *ICDE Conference Proceedings*, New Delhi: IGNOU, November.

Stamatis, D.H. (1996) *Total Quality Service: Principle, Practice and Implementation*, St. Lucie Press, Florida.

Stella, A. (2004) "Quality Assurance in Distance Education: The Challenges to be Addressed", *Higher Education*, Vol. 47.

Stern, B. and Tsend, D. (1993) "US Business Schools' Reaction to the Total Quality Movement", *Journal of Education for Business*, September/October.

Sternberg, R.J. and Lubart, T.I. (1996) "Investing in Creativity", *American Psychologist*, July.

STRIDE, IGNOU (2002) *Open and Distance Education*, Handbook 1, New Delhi.

Summers, Donna C.S. (1997) *Quality*, Prentice Hall, USA, pp. 7-13.

Sursock, A. (2001) *Towards Accreditation Schemes for Higher Education in Europe*, CHERI, The Open University, London.

Swink, M.L., Scandvig, J.C. and Mabert, V.A. (1996) "Customising Concurrent Engineering Processes: Five Case Studies", *Journal of Product Innovation Management*, Vol. 13, pp. 229-44.

Tait, A. (1997) *Quality Assurance in Higher Education: Selected Case Studies*, COL, Vancouver.

Tau, D.R. (2006) "Quality Assurance in Distance Education: Towards a Culture of Quality in Botswana College of Distance and Open Learning (BOCODOL)", in Koul, B.N. and Kanwar, A. (eds.), *Towards a Culture of Quality*, COL, Vancouver.

Taylor, J.C. (1995) "Distance Educational Technologies: The Fourth Generation", *Australian Journal of Educational Technology*, 11(2).

——. (1999) "Distance Education: The Fifth Generation", Paper presented at the 19th ICDE World Conference on Open Learning and Distance Education, Vienna.

——. (2001) "5th Generation Distance Education", *DETYA's Higher Education Series*, Report No. 40, June.

Tenner, A. and Detoro, I.J. (1992) *Total Quality Management: Three Steps of Continuous Improvement*, Addison-Willey, M.A.

Thakkar, J., Desmukh, S.G. and Shastree, A. (2006) "Total Quality Management in Self-financed Technical Institutions", *Quality Assurance in Education*, 14(1).

The Quality Assurance Agency for Higher Education (1999) "Distance Learning Guidelines".

Thiagarajan, T. and Zairi, M. (1997) "Understanding the Fundamentals of TQM", *Productivity*, No. 3.

Thurab-Nkhosi, D. and Seecharan, S.L. (2005) "Moving from Print-based Distance Education to Blended Learning: Initial Challenges of an Evolving Process. [The Case of UWIDEC, St. Augustine]" Presented at CATE-2005 Int. Conf. on Technology-based Education, Aug. 29-31, Aruba.

Trumbull, M. (1993) "What's Total Quality Management?", *The Christian Science Monitor*, May 3, p. 12.

Tuttle, T. (1994) "Is Total Quality Worth the Effort? How Do We Know?", *New Directions for Higher Education*, 21(32).

Twigg, Carol A. (2001) "Quality Assurance for Whom?", Center for Academic Transformation, Rensselaer Polytechnic Institute, New York, USA.

Umar, A. (2006) "Quality Assurance Procedures in Teacher Education: The Case of the National Teachers' Institute, Kaduna, Nigeria", in Koul, B.N. and Kanwar, A. (eds.), *Towards a Culture of Quality*, COL, Vancouver.

UNDP (2006) *Human Development Report 2006,* United Nations Development Program, New York.

UNICEF, 2000.

University of Hong Kong (1996) "Teaching and Learning Quality Process Audit (TLQPA)", submission to the University Grants Committee in preparation for its 1996 Teaching and Learning Quality Process Audit.

UT (2001) *Rencana operasional Universitas Terbuka Tahun 2001-2005 (Operational Plan of Universitas Terbuka 2001-2005)*, Universitas Terbuka Jakarta.

——. (2002) *Quality assurance system of Universitas Terbuka (Sistem jaminan kualitas Universitas Terbuka)*, Universitas Terbuka Jakarta.

——. (2004) *Rencana strategis Universitas Terbuka 2005-2020 (Strategic Plan of Universitas Terbuka 2005-2020)*, Universitas Terbuka Jakarta.

——. (2004a) *Rencana operasional Universitas Terbuka 2005-2010 (Operational Plan of Universitas Terbuka 2005-2010)*, Universitas Terbuka Jakarta.

——. (2006) *Annual Report of Rector of Universitas Terbuka 2005*. Unpublished document.

van Damme, D. (2001) "Higher Education in the Age of Globalisation: The Need for a New Regulatory Framework for Recognition, Quality Assurance and Accreditation", Paper for UNESCO Expert Committee Meeting, Paris.

Varnavas, A.P. and Soteriou, A.C. (2002) "Towards Customer Driven Management in Hospitality Education: A Case Study of the Higher Hotel Institute, Cyprus", *The International Journal of Educational Management*, 16(2/3).

Vaughan, T. (1998) *Muli-media Making it Work: A Comprehensive Guide to Creating Stunning Multi-media from Start to Finish*. 4th edition, McGraw Hill, NY.

Vazzana, G., Elfrink, J. and Bachmann, D.P. (2000) "A Longitudinal Study of Total Quality Management Processes in Business Colleges", *Journal of Education for Business*, 76(2).

Vazzana, G.S., Winter, J.K. and Waner, K.K. (1997) "Can TQM Fill a Gap in Higher Education?", *Journal of Education for Business*, 72(5).

Wakhlu, B. (1994) *Total Quality Excellence Through Organisation-wide Transformation*, Wheeler Publication, New Delhi.

Waller, M.A. and Ahire, S. (1996) "Management Perception of the Link Between Product Quality and Customers View of Product Quality", *International Journal of Operations and Production Management*, 16(9).

Walsh, A., Hughes, H. and Maddox, D.P. (2002) "Total Quality Management Continuous Improvement: Is the Philosophy a Reality?", *Journal, of European Industrial Training*, 26(6).

Welch, T. (2003) *Criteria for Quality Distance Education in South Africa—2003*, Background paper 4a, National Association of Distance Education Organisations of South Africa (NADEOSA).

Weller, L.D. and Hatley, S.A. (1994) "Why are Educators Stonewalling TQM?", *The TQM Magazine*, 6(3).

Wellman, J. (2000) "Point of View: Accreditor Have to See", *The Chronicle of Higher Education*.

Westgaard, J. (1991) "Scholarship, Research and Teaching: A View from the Social Sciences", *Studies in Higher Education*, 16.

Whitely, P. (2000) "Assessing the Quality of Distance Education: The Case of the University of the West Indies", *Proceedings of the Conference Distance Education in Small Island States*, UWIDEC, Mona.

Wiers-Jenssen, J., Stensaker, B. and Groguard, J.B. (2002) "Student Satisfaction: Towards an Empirical Demonstration of the Concept," *Quality in Higher Education*, 8(2).

Wiklund, H. and Sandvik Wiklund, P. (1996) "Application of Quality Tools for Course Design—Improvement of Student Learning and Satisfaction"*,* *Improving Student Learning*, 6.

——. (1999) "A Student Focused Design and Improvement of University Courses", *Managing Service Quality*, 9(6).

——. (2000) *Student-driven Improvement Work, Towards Best Practice—Quality Improvement Initiatives in Nordic Higher Education Institutions*, Nordic Council of Ministers, Copenhagen.

——. (2001) "A Swedish Perspective on Total Quality Management in Higher Education", *Proceedings of the 4th International Quality Management and Organizational Development Conference*.

Wiklund, H., Wiklund, B.K.P.S. and Edvardsson, B. (2003) "Innovation and TQM in Swedish Higher Education Institutions—Possibilities and Pitfalls", *The TQM Magazine*, 15(12).

Wilkinson, T. (2006) "The Holistic Quality Thread in Distance Education", *22nd Annual Conference on Distance Teaching and Learning*, University of Wisconsin.

Williams, G. (1993) "Total Quality Management in Higher Education: Panacea or Placebo?", *Higher Education*, 25.

Williams, J. (2002) "The Student Satisfaction Approach: Student Feedback and its Potential Role in Quality Assessment and Enhancement", Paper presented at the 24th EAIR Forum, Prague, 8-11 September.

Wilson, K.L., Lissio, A. and Ramsden, P. (1997) "The Development, Validation and Application of the Course Experience Questionnaire", *Studies in Higher Education*, Vol. 22, No. 1, 33-53.

Wilson, R.M. and Gilligan, C. (1997) *Strategic Marketing Management: Planning, Implementation and Control*, Butterwort-Heinemann, Oxford.

Woodbury, Robert S. (1960) "The Legend of Eli Whitney and Interchangeable Parts", *Technology and Culture*, Summer, pp. 235-53.

Woodman, R.W., Sawyer, J.E. and Griffin, R.W. (1993) "Toward a Theory of Organisational Creativity", *Academy of Management Review*, April.

World Bank (2002) *Constructing Knowledge Societies: New Challenges for Tertiary Education*, The Bank, Washington, DC.

www.chea.org

www.distancelearningnet.org/reports

www.enqa.eu

www.iso.org

www.oecd.org/education

www.unesco.org

www.3.selu.edu

Wylie, V. (2002) "Policy for Distance Learning", UQC.

Yeung, Davey (2002) "Towards an Effective Quality Assurance Model of Web-based Learning: The Perspective of Academic Staff", *Online Journal of Distance Learning Administration*, Volume V, Number II, Summer.

Yudof, M.G. and Busch-Vishniac, I.J. (1996) "Total Quality: Myth or Management in Universities", *Change*, 28(6).

Zairi, M. (1991) *Total Quality Management for Engineers*, Woodland Publishing Ltd., UK.

——. (1995) "Total Quality Education for Superior Performance", *Training for Quality*, 3(1).

Zangwill, W.I. (1993) *Lighting Strategies for Innovation: How the World's Best Firms Create New Products*, Lexington, New York.

Contributors

Agung Sastrawan Putra is Head of Learning Materials Distribution Centre and Lecturer in Faculty of Mathematics and Natural Science in Indonesia's Universitas Terbuka (UT).

Aminudin Zuhairi, PhD is Head of Quality Assurance Centre and Senior Lecturer in Distance Education and Educational Management in Indonesia's Universitas Terbuka (UT).

Ann Deden is General Manager, Academic Products and Services for Open Universities Australia (OUA). In that capacity, she has expanded the curriculum into professional areas including teaching and nursing, implemented quality assurance measures, produced significant increases in student enrolments and retention, and worked closely with member universities to make effective use of the Web and Web-based services for effective online student support.

Axel Laurs is Dean of the School of Information & Social Sciences, one of three specialised schools within a single faculty at The Open Polytechnic of New Zealand. As Dean he sits on Executive, Chairs the Research Committee and contributes to the strategic direction setting and policy-making processes at institutional and faculty level.

Bharat Bhushan is also a Deputy Director at Distance Education Council, IGNOU. He has been associated in designing, developing the various DEC publications on norms and guidelines on distance education system.

Caryl-Louise Robinson is Director of the LifeWorks Unit of The Open Polytechnic of New Zealand. This unit provides foundation blended-learning (distance and face to face) programmes for a target market of those who have few or no formal qualifications and limited experience in tertiary education.

Dale Holt is Head, Educational Design, Professional Development and Research, Institute of Teaching and Learning, Deakin University. Holt has been involved in a broad range of course and unit developments, most notably, in recent times the development of units offered wholly online across Deakin. He has also coordinated major academic professional development programs at the University, including Deakin's highly successful Online Teaching and Learning Fellowship Program.

Danny Wong is currently the Vice President (Academic) of the Open University of Hong Kong. He joined the University in 1994, as the Dean of its School of Business and Administration. He is a Fellow of the Association of International Accountants, and is recognized as a Certified Practitioner of the American Production and Inventory Control Society.

Dewi Padmo is a Senior Lecturer at the Faculty of Teacher Training and Educational Science and Head of the Institute of Course Material Development, Examination, and Information System at Universitas Terbuka.

Dianne Thurab-Nkhosi is a distance education editor at The University of the West Indies, Distance Education Centre (UWIDEC), St. Augustine. Her experience in education, training, information and communication spans more than 20 years.

Kristanti A. Puspitasari is Head of Examination Centre and Lecturer in the Faculty of Mathematics and Natural Science at Universitas Terbuka.

Manjulika Srivastava, Professor of Distance Education, Indira Gandhi National Open University (IGNOU) is amongst the few Indians to have done doctorate in "Distance Education". She has been working with IGNOU since 1989 and is presently working as a Professor of Distance Education at Distance Education Council, IGNOU, which is the apex body for Distance Education in India. She is currently Director incharge in Vice Chancellor office, IGNOU.

Nalini A. Lele is Deputy Director in Distance Education Council, IGNOU. She has been associated with DEC since 1994 and has been involved in the role of determination of quality from the inception of the activity and has been a major contributor in the development of a number of instruments for assessment and determination of quality in the ODL system. She is currently Deputy Director in Vice Chancellor office, IGNOU.

Richard Lewis has recently completed a four year period as President of the International Network of Quality Assurance Agencies in Higher Education (INQAAHE), an organisation with which he has been involved since its foundation in 1991. He has recently retired from the post of Co Director of the Centre for Higher Education Research and Information (CHERI) at the Open University of the United Kingdom and is now an associate of the Centre.

Rowan Anderson is the Academic Adviser to the School of Business at The Open Polytechnic of New Zealand. She assists the Dean of the School to provide academic leadership of the school, through activities such as course and/or qualification development, quality assurance, moderation and evaluation.

Sally Rawnsley manages the Design and Development Centre (DDC) at the Open Polytechnic of New Zealand. DDC's role is to plan, design, develop and publish learning materials in a range of media.

Stewart Marshall is the Director of The University of the West Indies Distance Education Centre (UWIDEC). UWIDEC currently operates in 16 countries and 30 sites throughout the Caribbean. Marshall is also Project Director of the Caribbean Universities Project for Integrated Distance Education (CUPIDE).

Stuart Palmer is Senior Lecturer, Educational Design, Professional Development and Research, Institute of Teaching and Learning, Deakin University. Palmer is an awarded engineering educator, including the Australasian Association for Engineering Education McGraw-Hill New Engineering Educator Award in 1999.

Todd Chun Ying Ng is the Planning Coordinator for the Open University of Hong Kong, responsible for institutional planning, quality assurance coordination, course evaluation, student statistics, market surveys and various institutional projects. His areas of expertise include institutional planning, management information, quality assurance, accounting and marketing.